GHOSTS IN MY HEART

Memories of an extraordinary childhood in South Africa

DELYSE ALORAH ARLIOTIS

GHOSTS IN MY HEART
Memories of an extraordinary
childhood in South Africa

Copyright © 2020 by Tara Delyse Collingwood
Contact: author.mymemoir@gmail.com

First Edition—2020

Cover design by DC Cover Creations
Editing by Karla Joy McMechan
Typesetting by DTP Impressions

ISBN: 9 781999 739263

All rights reserved: No part of this book may be reproduced, stored in a retrieval system or transmitted in any form or by any means: electronic, mechanical, photocopying, recording, scanning or otherwise without prior written permission from the copyright holder.

Attributions: Due to the difficulties in obtaining permission to use short quotations for epigraphs, I am providing full credit to the authors in appreciation for their work, along with notes explaining what may not be common knowledge. If there are any errors or omissions the author will be pleased to insert the appropriate acknowledgements in subsequent printings.

Disclaimer: I have done my utmost to trace people mentioned in this book. I have taken care to ask for permission to use people's names. I have otherwise provided pseudonyms to protect their privacy. The stories told within this book have given form to my life and are not about finger-pointing, blame, shame or ridiculing friends, family or people I met or associated with during my childhood. It is important that my story remain true to my own memory. If there are any errors or omissions the author will be pleased to insert the appropriate acknowledgements in subsequent printings

Quotations, Photographs and Illustrations: I have endeavoured to credit all sources and photographers. I extend my apologies to anyone who is not properly credited and invite you to contact me. Omissions can be corrected in future editions.

Dedicated to my parents
George and Gwendoline Arliotis

May love find you and bind you together forever more.

CONTENTS

PREFACE 1
PROLOGUE 7

PART I

Chapter 1	Johannesburg, 1962	14
Chapter 2	Early Memories, 1950s	16
Chapter 3	Nannies	31
Chapter 4	Strange Happenings	35
Chapter 5	Social Events	45
Chapter 6	Tennis and Sundowners	51
Chapter 7	A Gentleman Goes Farming	53
Chapter 8	Parkview via Port Elizabeth	58
Chapter 9	Parents—Out and About	72
Chapter 10	Interesting Friends	77

PART II

Chapter 11	The Penthouse	98
Chapter 12	Parktown via Roosevelt Park, 1956	109
Chapter 13	Doris and Nicholas—San Francisco	116
Chapter 14	Russian Royalty	124
Chapter 15	Father Comes to Visit	131

PART III

Chapter 16	Edith Vermeulen	136
Chapter 17	Hillbrow	151
Chapter 18	Tea for Two	158
Chapter 19	Carney and John	161
Chapter 20	My Brother	167
Chapter 21	Laeticia and China	171
Chapter 22	Weekends	177
Chapter 23	The Ugly Side of Life	184
Chapter 24	Jimmy Spills the Beans	189

Chapter 25	Life Goes On	194
Chapter 26	Arma Court, 1958–60	196
Chapter 27	Father, What Will Become of Us?	207

PART IV

Chapter 28	Del Monico Mansions, 1960–62	228
Chapter 29	A School Friendship	240
Chapter 30	Longford Hotel	246
Chapter 31	Renee and Gay	250
Chapter 32	Louis Blanché	255
Chapter 33	'Lana Turner'—Party Time	258
Chapter 34	Mornings after the Nights Before	263
Chapter 35	Daryl Returns	268
Chapter 36	Survival—My Health	272
Chapter 37	Two Angels Appear	274
Chapter 38	First Love	280
Chapter 39	College	283

PART V

Chapter 40	Mother—Cancer	296
Chapter 41	My Father	303
Chapter 42	My Greek Grandparents	308
Chapter 43	Au Revoir	314
Chapter 44	The Final Curtain	319

EPILOGUE	326
NOTES	331
ACKNOWLEDGEMENTS	340
ABOUT THE AUTHOR	340

PREFACE

This memoir, for reasons I will attempt to explain, is not your usual memoir. The chapters I have written are vignettes of my young life. My 'memory boxes' contained individual episodes which each held a trauma, a shock, or difficulties beyond a child's capabilities or understanding. The boxes were kept closed, sealed and separated.

The boxes closed and separated in my head even as I wrote, because in my young life nothing *did* blend or flow. Each episode of life was kept safely in a box with different memories in each.

When I began writing this book, I opened one box at a time and wrote it down, never allowing the vignettes to merge. Nothing encouraged me to bleed the episodes into one another or combine the boxes.

The first draft was a huge challenge to write. It was distressing and emotional one day, then amusing, insightful and funny the next. An emotional rollercoaster.

As I opened each box more hidden memories came flooding in, often a movie would run before me that took my breath away. After each writing day, I set time aside to mull over what I had written. At times I needed days or weeks to relive and reconcile an event or episode.

The second draft was a truly cathartic journey. Slowly I was beginning to heal, to understand, to find clarity. Missing pieces were found. Many issues continued to shock or upset me, but I began a long process: to forgive myself and others, unconditionally.

The third draft was written a year later and that was me, the writer, objectively and creatively weaving the story together in the best way I knew how. But the memory boxes remained.

Once the editing process began, my editor often suggested we merge one chapter with another. The child within resisted. Yet the sensible adult understood exactly what she was attempting to do. Each suggestion became a jolt, my mind struggling with deep-seated emotions versus logic.

It was, at times, difficult for my editor and myself until we reached an understanding of how my writing sequence worked. We finally grasped that each chapter written had been from a sealed memory. I had never opened any of those 'memory boxes' until I began writing.

I have mellowed since that first draft: towards the people, places and events about which I have written, and how they shaped my life; yet there are still certain vignettes of my life which bring tears to my eyes.

Throughout my childhood I'd been haunted by the secret conversations amongst my father and his family and the vagueness about my mother's past: secrets, always secrets, with no answers. Until I began opening these boxes.

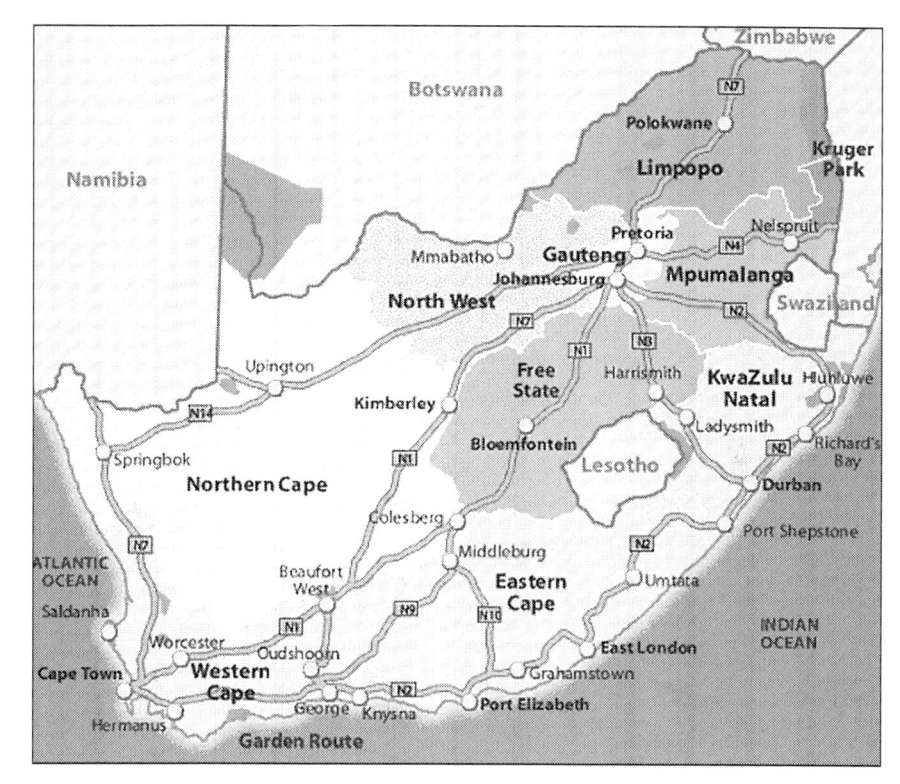

South Africa

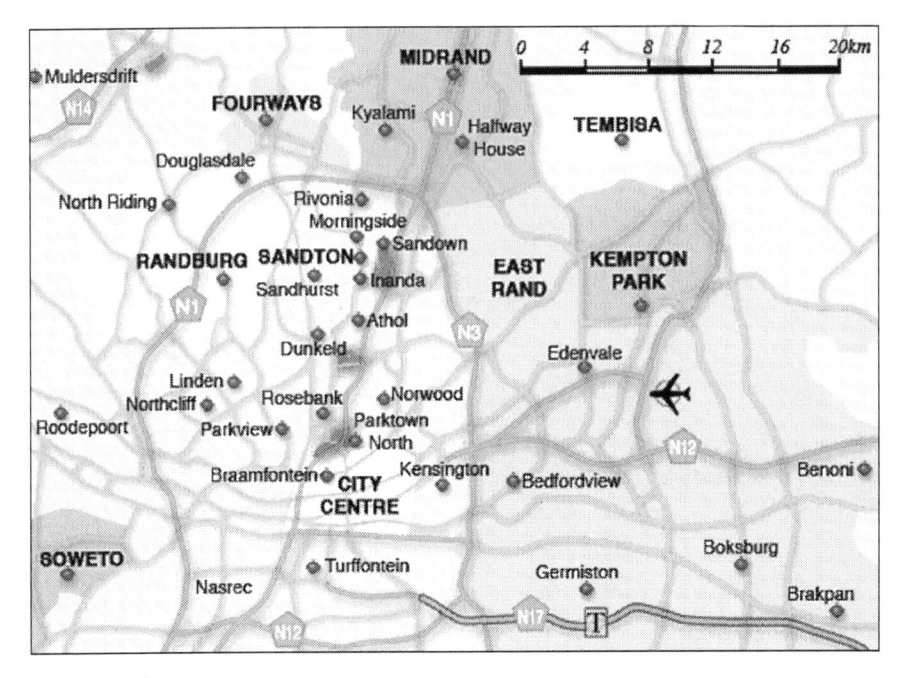

Johannesburg

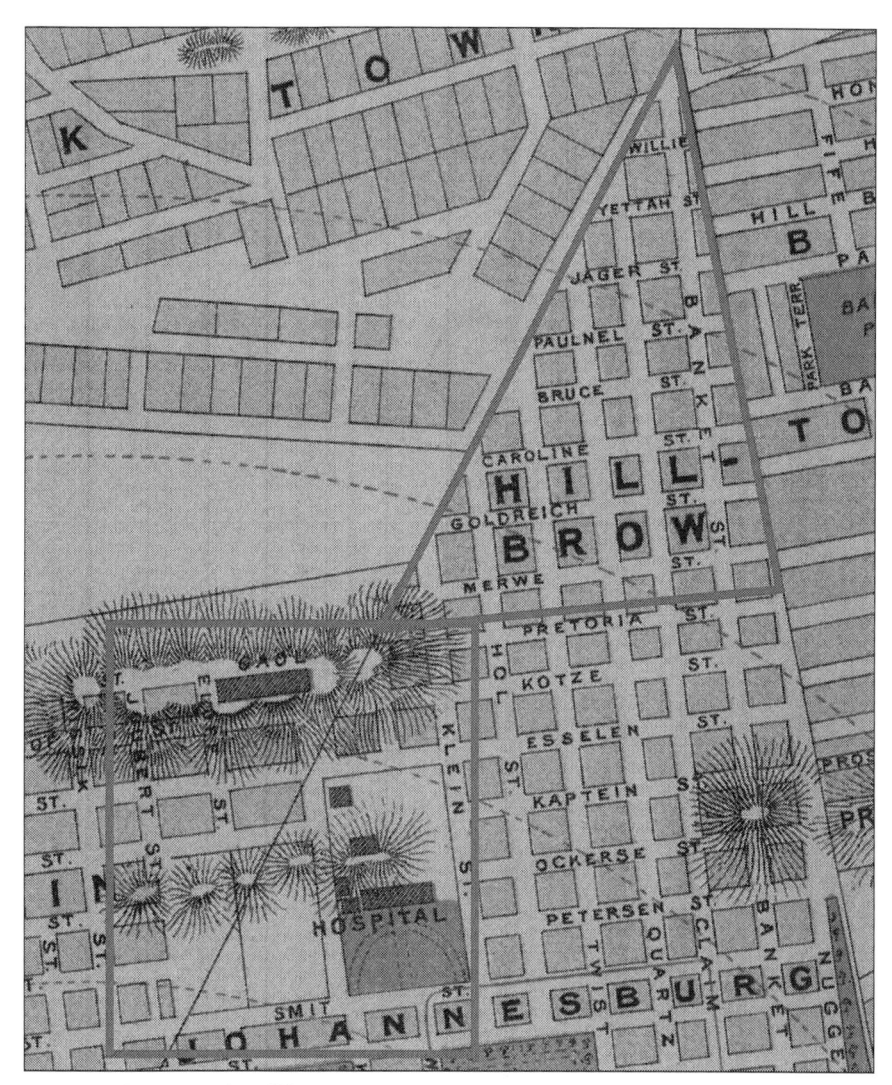

Original Map of Hillbrow

PROLOGUE

*We are Africans not because we were born in Africa,
but because Africa was born in us.
My friend Jan* [1]

On Thursday the 29th of November 1945 my Grandmother, Dorothy Campbell-Gilchrist, was brutally murdered by three young black men at her home in Johannesburg, South Africa. One of the men, Samuel Sikepe, had been employed days before by my grandmother's second husband, Herbert Campbell-Gilchrist.

On that fateful day, Samuel Sikepe, the new houseboy, allowed two accomplices to enter my grandparents' home in the affluent suburb of Forest Town. Their intention was to rob and take whatever they were able to carry. Unfortunately, my grandmother arrived home unexpectedly. The men overpowered her in the main passage and bound her hands and feet. My grandmother began to struggle and scream.

As my grandmother lay on the floor, one of the men attempted to gag her. He held her by the throat and covered her mouth to stifle her screams. According to the trial notes, this extreme force smashed her Adam's apple and badly bruised her face. Her mouth and cheeks were covered in blood with cuts and scratches to the mouth. They then tied a pillow around her face. In the process of their trying to silence her, she had been brutally murdered.

The three men continued ransacking every room in the house, including slashing open the mattresses looking for valuables. Every cupboard and drawer was thrown open and emptied. They took valuables, money and mainly men's clothing including six suits. They found an automatic pistol and a revolver hidden in the house. As a parting gesture, Sikepe shot my grandmother, leaving her lying face downwards, dead in the passageway. He had also draped my grandmother's limp, bleeding body with a clean white sheet, perhaps unable to face what they had done.

At the time my mother, born Gwendoline Constance Victoria Collingwood, and my father, George Arliotis, were living in Port Elizabeth in the Cape Province of South Africa. They had decided to settle there because my mother was being ostracised by her parents for marrying a Greek, and the emotional distress my mother had been under when they were living in Johannesburg affected the newly married couple. However, the moment my parents received the telegram revealing the shocking news of the murder, they immediately made the 12-hour trip to Johannesburg, arriving in time for my grandmother's funeral. They went directly there and sat alone, having been estranged from family for so long.

All the people who attended the funeral service expressed shock, disbelief and rage that a white woman had been murdered by her black servant. The thought of a black man touching her white skin sent shivers down their spines. Filled with anger, the men standing at her graveside whispered hateful comments about the killers.

Once the funeral service and burial at West Park Cemetery was over, my parents were followed closely by reporters and curious members of the public who were hounding them for comments. My stepgrandfather, Campbell-Gilchrist, silently drove them back to the house in Forest Town. My father must have felt uncomfortable but remained firmly at my mother's side. Campbell-Gilchrist had never met my father, 'George the Greek', until that day.

My parents expected the evening to be one of quiet reflection and mourning, but it soon became a night of terror. That night was never forgotten by either of my parents, according to my father, who shared this story with me when he was in his seventies. It had never been mentioned before.

The tragic day of the funeral brought up intense emotions for my mother and her stepfather. That evening, without thinking, they had returned to the very place where the murder happened. This ill-thought-out arrangement exposed raw emotions as the evening progressed.

At the house my step-grandfather drank a few shots of brandy in quick succession. It was a hot balmy night and, even though my father drank only a few sips of brandy, he soon felt his head reeling and his temper flaring at the attitude of the soft-faced, pompous Englishman, Campbell-Gilchrist. My mother became emotional and overwhelmed. The grim circumstances hit them, and her stepfather's mood changed suddenly.

Campbell-Gilchrist became loud and aggressive towards my father. He was a gentleman and usually very proper, but he had never cared for my mother's choice of husband. Campbell-Gilchrist made scathing remarks about my parents and irrational statements about South Africa.

"What can you expect in this bloody country?" he asked.

His torment continued late into the night. "*You* and this no-good bloody Greek!" he yelled at my mother who was shaking and tearful. He stumbled out of the room into the passageway. There he saw remnants of a blood stain on the carpet, exactly where he had found Dorothy lying dead. My grandfather weaved his way back to the living room, his legs unsteady. He took a revolver out of his desk drawer, fired a few random shots into the ceiling and then attempted to shoot my father.

Fortunately for my parents, his aim was exceptionally bad that night. They ran frantically from the house into Torwood Road, passing inquisitive reporters and shocked neighbours, and escaped to the safety of their car, driving off at high speed. This intensified my mother's distress. The shock of it all remained forever imprinted on her memory.

That night my parents escaped from the Torwood Road house and the waiting photographers unharmed. They vowed never to see Herbert Campbell-Gilchrist again. His hysterical, drunken behaviour was too much to deal with after the violent death of her mother. It affected my parents for many months. They returned to Port Elizabeth, depleted and suffering from shock.

My mother had been well provided for by her stepfather during her young life. He had raised her after her father died during World War I, and she had always respected him. But, after the disturbing events that unfolded following my grandmother's funeral, my mother cut all ties with him. Five months after my grandmother's murder Herbert Campbell-Gilchrist's reputation was further tarnished when he married a woman twenty years younger than himself, which left many speculating on the truth behind my grandmother's murder.

My grandmother's violent murder scarred my mother mentally and emotionally for the rest of her life. She was never able to come to terms with it. It shocked her to the core. She remained deeply traumatised for many years as the frightful story lived on. It appeared in national newspapers, and there were always inquisitive neighbours, as well as complete strangers, watching and gossiping carelessly around her. People who came in contact with my parents socially would remark sheepishly, "Yes, a shocking business...."

According to my mother, "an intensive manhunt was led by the Prime Minister of South Africa, Jan Smuts,"[2] who was known to my grandparents. In December 1945 three men were discovered more than a hundred miles from the scene of the crime wearing my grandfather's clothes and carrying his guns. After a dramatic gun battle in the veld (grassland) with police, they were taken into custody.

In June of 1946 my mother attended the murder trial in Pretoria. She sat through the gruesome details of what her mother had endured on that fateful day in November 1945. It was harrowing. Judge Ramsbottom, 'a greatly revered judge', meticulously considered the evidence, then gave his verdict. His decision was that Samuel Sikepe alone would receive the death penalty. That verdict was later overruled by the Minister of Justice, Harry Lawrence.[3]

In August 1946 an appeal was rigorously argued for the other two accused, Joseph Ndwakulu and Jack Sheshonga, as there was insufficient evidence to prove that all three men were guilty of the murder. The sentence stood firm as laid down by the Minister of Justice, and all three of the men were sentenced to death and duly hanged at Pretoria Central Prison.[4]

The outcome weighed heavily on my mother's conscience, which added to her fragile state.

After her mother's brutal murder, and after enduring the trial, my mother developed a deep fear of black men, known then in South Africa as 'natives', especially if they were close by. Her fear was extreme. Her mind would conjure up pictures of her mother's murder or of herself being killed violently. She carried such thoughts in her mind throughout her life.

To my knowledge, my mother had no verbal contact with any black person unless in a 'madam-servant' scenario. Otherwise, she would not address them. Firstly, out of fear and, secondly, from a superior disregard for the 'native' people.

After what took place, from that day forward, my parents were certainly not ready for parenthood two years later. During my early childhood our home contained an atmosphere of tragedy and emptiness. My mother was fragile, withdrawn, often lost in her own world of terror and turmoil. She relied on my father's absolute fearlessness to carry her through life.

In November 1947, exactly two years after my grandmother was murdered, I was born. My mother endured forty-eight hours of painful labour that ended with me being a forceps delivery.

May 1945: The end of WW2 is declared.

March 1946: Gold discovery in Odendaalsrust.
Vast sums of money made by shareholders.

In 1947: South Africa hosts the British Royal Family.
A train was especially built for their use.

1948: A Policy of apartheid[5] is adopted in South Africa.
The National Party takes power.

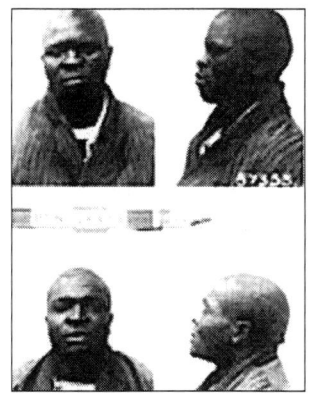

Two of the men charged with murder

Pretoria Central Prison Museum

Excerpt from The Star, 1945

With a bullet-scarred car as a background, three captured native convicts were paraded yesterday in front of two men, the husband of Mrs. Campbell-Gilchrist, murdered in her Forest Town Home, Johannesburg, 11 days ago, and the Rev. S. Henrice, who, with his wife was assaulted at Fountains on Wednesday, his assailants making their getaway in his car at 70 miles an hour.

In the early dawn of Thursday morning a car answering to the description of the Rev. S. Henrice's car seen going at high speed through Potgietersrust. The police opened fire, but without apparent result.

"We raced after them and a three-mile chase at 85 miles an hour took place. A shot however struck one of the tyres of the car, and the natives abandoned it and ran into the veld. The police pick-up van made after one of the natives and I made after the other. We eventually captured the three natives, who did not put up a fight."

Jan Christiaan Smuts

Royal Visit 1947

12   Prologue

PART I

Your holy heart, when you begin to feel it fully,
will invite you into pain you have long ago locked away.

First, your own personal unresolved anguish.
Then, the collective pain of all you have forgotten:
A history remembered by the stardust in your cells,
the rust in your bones.

Alison Nappi[6]

PART 1

Chapter 1

Johannesburg, 1962

...for truth is always strange; stranger than fiction...

Lord Byron, Don Juan[7]

It was 5 p.m. when I finally climbed onto a red double-decker 'whites only' bus. The double decker buses brought in from England were clearly marked '*Whites Only*'.

It had taken approximately an hour to sort through the cupboards and pack all my belongings into the only suitcase we had. Without a word or a backward glance at my mother, who sat in silence throughout, I stormed out of 5 Del Monico Mansions and out of my mother's life forever. I was fifteen. I walked away from the drab old building that had been my 'home' for three years, knowing that I would never return.

I walked quickly, mechanically, placing one sure foot in front of the other, away from a mother who had never loved me. I walked the two miles with determination in every step. The suitcase, filled to the brim with my life, became awkward and heavy. My strides were long and purposeful as I headed into central Johannesburg in the direction of Marshalltown and the Bus Depot. I found myself running part of the way, the suitcase thumping the back of my legs as I ran. From there I would get a bus to the suburbs.

I stood there waiting, feeling numb, robotic yet resolute. Then I stepped onto the bus just as it began to move. Staring blindly out of the window with the outside world a blur, I was aware of nothing and no one except my racing heart. The motion of the bus calmed me as it weaved its way along the main road travelling east out of the city.

Slowly the past twenty-four hours began to hit me. I was in shock at what had occurred the night before. My mother had crossed a line.

I had slept at friends' overnight, returning home at first light to pack. Somewhere in my mind I knew I was leaving for good. I had no plan, yet I felt driven to leave. I wanted a life, my own life. I needed a chance to be 'me'. The hour-long bus journey felt like an eternity.

Finally, I stepped off the bus and began a slow, deliberate, walk through the leafy green suburb of Kensington, passing familiar houses and people but looking straight ahead. As I got nearer to my aunt's house, I could feel my rigid body, my jaw locked, my facial muscles tight.

When I arrived at the door of Aunt Alexandra's cottage, I stopped dead, unable to breathe or lift an arm to knock. I realised that my decision had been impulsive, unplanned, mechanical. I had packed, walked out, got on a bus and here I was. I stood very still, unaware of time. Suddenly I wanted to throw up, but I sucked in air and held my breath tightly. I don't remember breathing. I was completely frozen, my heart pounding loudly. Eventually I plucked up the courage to knock. My aunt answered the door with a wide, surprised, smile. "I have come to live with you," I heard myself saying.

"Well, you had better come in," she replied, gazing deeply into my eyes. She took the suitcase from me and led me gently by the hand to the kitchen. She guided me to a chair at the kitchen table and immediately put the kettle on. We sat down, and she reached over to hold my hand. We sat in complete silence. Neither of us uttered a word as we quietly sipped our hot tea. My aunt never asked, and I never offered a reason or a story.

Over the next weeks or months, my life settled into a pleasant daily rhythm. I was alive, but *what* was yet to come—I would never have envisaged!

1961: British South Africa leaves the Commonwealth and becomes a Republic

… PART 1

Chapter 2

Early Memories, 1950s

It was not curiosity that killed the goose who laid the golden egg, but an insatiable greed that devoured common sense.

E.A. Bucchianeri, Brushstrokes of a Gadfly[8]

I remember clearly sitting on the vast manicured lawn under the majestic Oak tree in the front garden, watching sparkling, tiny, fairy beings dancing around the Snowdrops. Northcliff holds deeply cherished childhood memories for me, inspired by pretty butterflies, talking to fairies under the Oak tree and playing under warm summer skies. It was a solitary but carefree time. Long, sunny afternoons in a vast colourful garden filled with glorious flowers and shady green trees.

I would often lie under a large shady tree looking upwards at the vast African sky. Wispy white clouds, birds and butterflies would float by. The fine butterfly wings would echo the gentle mood of these idyllic days. Those peaceful afternoons were surely heaven. I was three years old.

I was left to spend most of my time alone. I was lonely; yet I exuded joy and happiness. I lived in my own world and was happy there. I spent the days wandering around the perfectly kept gardens, the manicured lawns and neat flower beds. I knew every nook and cranny. Occasionally I would have a tea party with my dolls under the Wisteria.

Abraham, the black houseboy, with his perfect white teeth and wide smile, had been a victim of polio as a child. His right leg was disfigured and thin, his limp, pronounced. I remember him clearly. Abraham would run towards me, hobbling onto the lower lawn where I would be lazing, daydreaming, or running and skipping about. Those afternoons were idyllic, the days dreamy, the summers filled with golden sunshine. I loved nature, trees, flowers—especially Wisteria. Then there were the bees, butterflies and at night glow worms and fireflies.

I would run towards Abraham, giggling happily. He would catch me, throw me up in the air and swing me around. We would laugh and laugh. We kept up this game until he was too tired to continue. Abraham was kind and gentle to me, and I became very attached to him. Had my parents seen us together, a *servant* touching my lily-white skin and holding my white little body, they would not have approved. Nor the neighbours! Not back in the 1950s in South Africa. Abraham would probably have been dismissed, but we were both innocent and naive.

The big-hearted black man was the only adult at home who had my interests at heart. Perhaps he missed his own children who lived many miles away in a rural village. He cared. The variety of nannies that my brother and I had over the years took their break in the mid-afternoon, leaving us unsupervised until bath time. Daryl was eighteen months older and would run off to play on his own.

To an outsider, my mother would have appeared preoccupied, uncaring, almost negligent, but in those days women in South Africa relied on skilled or unskilled nannies and staff to bring up their children. Mothers would shop, get beautified, meet friends for tea or long lunch parties and then take afternoon naps. Mother's attitude towards parenting may also have been associated with her own childhood experiences, having had formal, detached, parents. This was not unusual in families and parents from the upper echelons of society.

Where was my mother while I was wandering about alone? How did she fill her time and what caused her to be completely removed from her children? Mentally and emotionally, she was unavailable to us. As I grew up, I was unable to ask or confide in her about anything. I had learned that it was futile to try. The umbilical bond between us had been severed long before.

My mother's interests lay solely in being the perfect wife to a husband she adored. Her only aim was to be the very best hostess to his friends and associates. I do believe my parents had social and financial status in those days, and she saw herself as one of the 'social elite'.

My bright, sociable, mother was rarely at home by day or night. Neither of my parents ever attended any of my school events: Sports Day, concerts, Prize Giving, or Parents' Day. I recall feeling that it was so unfair. I would always be the only girl with no mother at events, unlike all the others at school. Nor do I recall my mother reading our school reports or asking how a school day went. There were occasions when she was around, usually to give instructions to Nanny.

I soon accepted that I had to find my own way in life. I did the best I could with what I understood from a child's perspective and developed a mind of my own from an early age. There were times when I felt utterly lonely, loneliness so deep that it overwhelmed me, but with various distractions those feelings would pass.

In later years I pondered: Had my mother, perhaps, also experienced a childhood void of love, affection and kindness? Or, had the murder of her mother held her heart captive and her mind in silent torment? Her heart seemed completely closed to any feelings of love, except towards my father. To this day I am unable to answer that question.

I would like to have known more about my parents to gain a better understanding of their initial years together after their unannounced registry-office marriage in November 1936. My father left the safety and comfort of his close-knit family, his brother Robert who was his best friend, their ballroom dancing life (they were dance champions) and an exciting social life in a bustling city where both of them had grown up.

Why did they choose to live in Port Elizabeth of all cities? Was it my mother's distinguished parents who forced my parents to begin a life together elsewhere? I do believe that her mother completely disowned her. My mother never spoke of their wedding day or of the consequences of her actions, *not ever*. What she did share was that her parents were appalled at the idea of their precious Gwendoline Constance Victoria marrying 'a common Greek'. The two families were never to meet.

When I was in my teens, quite out of the blue, my mother mentioned that, months before she met my father, it had been pre-arranged for her to marry a British Baronet. She met my father at a dance and fell deeply, intoxicatingly, in love. He waltzed into her life one evening, and she was instantly seduced by his charm and his devil-may-care attitude.

Yet, my mother *was* quintessentially British in manner and outlook. Her life appeared to be so very civilised on the surface. Once married, Greek was not allowed to be spoken in their home and food was traditional British fare, served and eaten at a formal table.

How could their marriage work? They were from very different cultures with centuries of ancestral history behind them. Their beliefs differed. They had contradictory ideas, not to mention arguments over religion.

Had my mother's mother and her second husband Campbell-Gilchrist agreed to meet the Arliotis family, they would have discovered, to their surprise, that my father's parents were from a distinguished Corfiot family. My father's mother, Contessa Ekaterina Theodosius-Arliotis, and his father, Constantine Arliotis, were educated, refined, people with an interesting aristocratic lineage. My Grandfather Constantine was an established man of the world who spoke many languages fluently, including Chinese.

To this day, there is an elegantly furnished Arliotis Villa on the island of Corfu[9], but because of bureaucracy, lost documents, church fires and inadequate legal evidence, we were unable to lay claim to it. The villa remains locked. Close to that villa, high in the hills of central Corfu, stands a small church, old but proud. It was built for the private use of the Arliotis family, eons ago. The Arliotis family also owned a productive farming estate in Lancashire, England, with extensive land dating back to the 1800s. It is possible that my Greek grandparents spent some years living in London. My grandfather Constantine received 'The Freedom of the City of London' award in the mid-1980s. Sadly the original scroll, which was in my care, was stolen in London along with other family documents some twenty years ago.

My Grandmother Ekaterina's ancient ancestors were from Venice, Italy, which afforded her the grand title of Contessa. The origin of the title dates back to the 1500s. This my grandmother never spoke of, nor did she use the title whilst living in South Africa. Her gracious demeanour conveyed her lineage perfectly. My grandfather was from a prominent aristocratic Corfiot family who were active in the Church, politics, culture and known of throughout Greece, if not the world, during the 1800s and 1900s.

After the death of Grandmother Dorothy, my parents left Port Elizabeth where they had lived for ten years and returned to live in Johannesburg. They were soon back in the social swing of things, living the 'high life', partly on my mother's generous inheritance. My father was a member at both the Country Club and the Wanderers Club, and he was a keen golfer. He attended Turffontein horse race meetings every Saturday afternoon.

My pretty, smiling, socialite mother had a life filled with luncheon and tea appointments. Once back in the big city she enjoyed being chauffeur-driven to the hairdresser, beautician, or her favourite dress designer, where designs and fabrics were carefully selected for her haute couture evening gowns. My monogrammed dressing gowns and winter coats were couturier-designed according to my mother's wishes. Henry Shields took good care of mother's seasonal wardrobe.

> *Back in the 1950s, Commissioner Street was the city's fashion promenade. Johannesburg's most fashionable women would parade in the latest European couture collections and watch fashion shows at John Orr's Tea Room.*

There was John Orr's, Ansteys or Stuttafords for shopping and taking tea with friends. The well-heeled white South African women, like my mother, met for morning tea in one of the department stores. The starched tablecloths, silver cutlery, fine crockery and smart waiters attended to their every need. All stores had lifts driven by uniformed operators who took customers to various levels. Upon arrival at each floor the operator would announce which departments were situated there.

These self-indulgent socialites, whose lives were filled with endless days of shopping, grooming and lunches, would arrive dressed to kill, complete with matching hats, gloves, seamed stockings and hair freshly washed and set. The 'social-set' would enjoy mornings away from home, whilst maids, cooks, gardeners and nannies kept their homes, gardens and offspring, safe and in spotlessly clean, pristine, condition.

The glamorous ladies, perhaps minor aristocrats or wives of busy CEO's, would partake in an elegant English morning or afternoon tea. A three-tiered solid silver cake stand would be placed proudly in the centre of each table, offering a fine selection of dainty finger sandwiches, little cakes and freshly baked scones. The background sound was soft tinkling piano music.

The main interest of those mornings was the fashion parade. Tall, elegant, models would walk through the plush tea room, showing off the latest collection available in-store. These mannequins paraded around, weaving their way effortlessly between tables, selecting those with the best customers to stop and show off the fabric, cut, style and designer. Price was never mentioned.

When mother wished to leave, the restaurant manager would telephone my father's office to arrange for the car to come. This was not something most families could afford, even in those days of plenty in South Africa. The car would arrive soon after to collect her. The chauffeur would drive her wherever she wished to go; then, seeing her safely home, would drive back to the city centre to wait for my father.

Mother never said 'hello' or 'goodbye' to us before leaving for any of her outings. She always left the house swiftly. When she arrived back, she would go directly to her bedroom to undress and rest. I never saw her mornings or bedtime either, for a hug or kiss. Oh, yes! I had Nanny and there was a housemaid, an ironing girl, Chef William, the chauffeur and Abraham, our houseboy who worked around the house and helped the gardener. The chauffeur kept the cars washed, polished and immaculate.

My mother struggled to teach new servants their daily duties, which included setting a table with correct silverware and rules of service. She preferred to employ staff who had already been trained. My parents required perfect service from their black servants to enable them to live a life of unflustered leisure and luxury.

The servants were keen to learn and paid close attention to the commands and constant instructions, to the best of their ability. Although kind, my mother was crisp and formal with staff and remained aloof but determined to have her household at its best. She expected her uneducated black servants, from rural communities, to meet her high standards and personal needs. She presumed they understood; yet many of them had never seen the items used on the table nor at mealtimes. Her attitude soon taught them to remain subservient and about white privilege.

In the afternoons I would pass my mother's bedroom door regularly. I would stand peering inside wistfully, hoping to catch a glimpse of her. She would be lying on her bed, elegantly paging through a glossy magazine, eating her favourite chocolates from a beautiful glossy black box kept well out of my reach. Then she would nap before preparing herself for the evening.

The main focus of *her* day was my father's arrival home from work in the evening. She woke from her nap with plenty of time to dress carefully, selecting a beautiful dress and jewellery to compliment the outfit. Everything was carefully considered. She knew that my father would notice and comment. She was his prize possession, and he expected her to look perfect. In later years my father's comments were occasionally uncomplimentary, casually delivered but implying that her taste or posture were 'not as it once was' or comparing her to other women. This must have hurt her deeply. He was her world, and his criticism cut deep.

My father was a natural charmer. I am certain that he was known as a philanderer amongst his male friends. His roving eye never missed a beautiful woman. He was strikingly handsome, suave, sophisticated, charismatic, a 'ladies' man' through and through. Women of all ages found his charm captivating. It must have been easy for him to become a philanderer. He was considered by his male friends to be the 'Playboy' of his social circle.

Father would arrive home most evenings at 6.30 p.m., on time for 'sundowners'. Before his arrival drinks were set out on a silver trolley in readiness for the 'master'. The servants were always ready in fresh white uniforms, standing to attention in the entrance hall of the house nervously awaiting his arrival. His entrance was well choreographed: after greeting the staff and having a brief conversation with them, my father immediately went to the lounge where my mother stood in the middle of the room like a mannequin in a shop window display.

My father would glide across the threshold of the room without a word, walking purposefully towards my mother as she stood in anticipation. He would hold her tenderly by the shoulders while admiring her. She would twirl around like a fashion model, smiling. They would kiss gently.

"You look beautiful tonight, Darling…"

She would smile lovingly, as she reached elegantly to get her drink, her arm adorned with a platinum and diamond bracelet. She would sip from the tall crystal glass filled with fine Scotch whisky topped up with chilled soda water. Her shining bleached blonde hair, beautifully set, had not a hair out of place. The magnificent diamonds around her neck glistened as the dappled afternoon sunlight streamed through the window and fell across her throat.

I would peep into the lounge to watch them, even though I had been told many times when I skipped into the room spontaneously that children were to be 'seen and not heard', and I would be sent on my way. My brother and I were not permitted to put our toes over the threshold of the lounge. It was a place for 'grown-ups'.

Our evening meals were served early in the vast kitchen or, on rare occasions, a small table was set in our playroom, an extension of Daryl's bedroom. In the kitchen, a table was set formally for two: myself and my brother.

The resident chef, William, would serve our dinner, then stand proudly to attention in starched white jacket and trousers. Abraham, the houseboy, always stood beside him with a broad smile on his face, his white jacket draped with a bright red sash and a clean linen cloth over his arm. Nanny hovered, encouraging us to 'eat-up'. It was a silent, lifeless event with little or no talking. My brother rarely spoke, not even to me. He was shy and insecure, an unhappy boy.

After our meal, the two male servants quickly cleared away and then prepared the main dining room for my parents' dinner service at 8 p.m. Their dinner would usually consist of four or five small courses. Our untrained nanny took us to our bedrooms: Daryl to his with a huge dark oak four-poster bed and me next door to a vast double room in the southeast corner of the house. I was very aware that I was all alone in that corner of a very large and daunting house.

Next to my bedroom was the small linen room. When powerful electrical storms occurred, I would find my mother hiding in there, terrified. As a small child I thought it was a game, but soon realised that my mother was crying quietly and shaking in fear. I would stand in the dark with her whilst the storm raged. I understood, even then, how fragile she was.

Nanny would tuck me into bed so tightly that I was unable to wiggle or move. "Goodnight, Miss," she would smile warmly and put out the light, closing the door as she stepped into the well-lit passage. Slivers of light would shine into my room from under the door. I would lie there, motionless, feeling trapped, staring at the dark shapes and shadows around the dimly lit room. The heavy red curtains with abstract dark figures seemed sinister at night. I lay on my back, rigid and stiff, long into the night. Our toys were packed away neatly in places we were unable to reach. Neither of us had a teddy, doll, or fluffy toy for comfort. It was lonely and the dark nights were long.

Each morning, after I had been served breakfast, I always ran off to sit cross-legged on the wide grassy verge outside the house, directly opposite the main school entrance and offices of the principal and secretary of Northcliff Junior. The principal would greet me cheerfully with a wave.

"Can I come today?" I would ask.

"Not yet, next year!"

Once I did begin my schooling, a year early, I was moved into Class 2 within six months. I was always the youngest girl in class, yet more serious and mature.

Several times during the year, usually before the change of seasons, my mother would decide it was time to replenish my wardrobe. She would call her personal dressmaker to discuss new additions. Then I would be placed on the back seat of the shiny black Cadillac, alone with the chauffeur, to be driven to the dressmaker for a fitting.

On other occasions, I was sent by car, often to the local hairdresser, Joan, for a haircut. My mother never accompanied me anywhere, except to the dentist. Only three or four years old, I felt small and insecure sitting in the middle of the long bench seat of the huge car, my legs dangling midair.

Very occasionally when my father was home all weekend, he would put my brother and me into the car and drive himself down to the Northcliff Shopping Centre. One Saturday he had a craving for ham and good cheddar cheese for brunch, so off we went. Looking dashing as ever, he stepped out of his long, sleek Cadillac parked directly in front of the local café and strolled inside nonchalantly with the two of us wandering in behind him.

Daryl and I stood behind my father, fidgeting and looking at all the sweets and slabs of chocolate with big eyes. After browsing around and inspecting what was on offer in the glass-fronted display fridge, he decided and announced to the dark-haired, gold-toothed, Greek man behind the counter what he wished to buy.

The man, with slicked-back greasy hair, called to his friend at the other end of the long marble counter, "Ελάτε εδώ και κοιτάξτε αυτόν τον αλαζονικό ανόητο που στέκεται εδώ." [Come and look at this arrogant fool standing here.]

My father stared blankly at the man who smiled at him widely across the counter as they continued.

"Πάω να του πουλήσω το παλιό κρέας και το τυρί." [I am going to sell him the old meat and cheese.]

"Γιατί όχι?" [Why not?] "Ποτέ δεν θα ξέρει!" [He will never know!]

The older man began to chuckle, twirling the ends of his thick moustache. "Βρίσκεται στο πίσω μέρος του ψυγείου." [It is all at the back of the fridge.]

My father smiled back at the two men, posing and posturing for their pleasure. He was enjoying himself!

"Κοιτάξτε τον! ποιος πιστεύει ότι είναι?" [Look at him! Who does he think he is?]

The men continued talking about my father whilst the gold-toothed man wrapped the sliced ham and wedge of cheese carefully: First in greaseproof paper, then white wrapping paper and finally into a paper bag, all the while smiling broadly.

My father stood, watching closely, smiling back in a supercilious manner. When the man handed him the paper bag, my father looked inside, wrinkled up his nose, glared at the greasy-haired Greek shop owner and asked in perfect Greek: "τι είναι αυτό?" [What is this?]

The man was noticeably startled. He staggered backwards clumsily, grabbing the countertop to balance himself. Beads of sweat quickly appeared on his top lip. His friend at the end of the counter went pale, the perspiration giving his face a wax-like appearance. My father continued to address the man in perfect Greek:

"Παρακαλώ, πάρτε αυτό το παλιό ζαμπόν και τυρί και απολαύστε τον εαυτό σας." [Please, take this old ham and cheese and enjoy it yourself.] "Επιμένω!" [I insist!]

The men had been caught out by someone who did not look remotely like other Greeks they knew. They were both pale, embarrassed and suddenly anxious to please.

My father smiled wryly at them both and continued: "Τώρα, μπορείτε να μου κόψετε λεπτές φέτες από τα φρέσκα κρέατα ή πρέπει να έρθω και να το κάνω μόνος μου;" [Now, cut me thin slices of fresh meat. Or should I come and do it myself?]

The shop owner stumbled forward, his eyes wide with surprise. He could not believe what was happening to him. He tried to smile as he began to perspire profusely. He looked bewildered.

Talking quietly to himself, we could hear faint, emotional, whispers of "Πο! Πο! Πο!" [Oh! Oh! Oh!]

He reached down into the display fridge for a huge, glazed ham. Then, shaking slightly, he picked up a long-bladed carving knife.

My father watched him curiously, his dark brown eyes smiling with amusement, and observed, "Φαίνεται νευρικός, μην κόβεις τον εαυτό σου με αυτό το κοφτερό μαχαίρι" [You look nervous. Don't cut yourself with that sharp knife!] "Έλα, επιτρέψτε μου να το κάνω αυτό για σένα!" [Come, let me do that for you!]

By then both men looked as if they were about to shed crocodile tears. Their nasty prank had backfired! The shop owner began to beg and plead with my father, grovelling and bowing repeatedly.

"Συγνώμη, λυπάμαι πολύ, δεν ήξερα ότι ήσασταν Έλληνας" [Excuse me, I am so sorry, I did not know you were Greek.] "Παρακαλώ πάρτε ό, τι θέλετε από το κατάστημά μου" [Please take anything you want from my shop.] "Ήταν ένα μεγάλο λάθος" [It was a big mistake!]

Making the sign of the cross on his chest several times, he looked up towards the sky, hoping for divine intervention, mumbling, "Πο! Πο! Πο!" The shame he felt was palpable.

"Μάνα Μου! Μάνα Μου!" [My mother! My mother!], he repeated over and over.

The older, waxy man ran around the counter to my brother and me. He was taken aback by my father's ability to speak perfect Greek and that he was a Greek! He bent down, nervously smiling falsely,

"What you like, pretty tsildren?" he asked in hesitant English. "Please, take what you like."

My brother was quick to reply: "I'd like a coke."

The waxy man, his face gleaming, ran hastily to the back of the shop and in minutes returned with a wooden crate of two dozen Coca-Colas.

Whilst the greasy haired, gold-toothed, Greek was agonising over what he had done to a fellow Greek, he cried to himself, "Πο, πο, πο! Είμαστε σε τόσο μεγάλο πρόβλημα."[Oh, oh, oh! We are in so much trouble.], his hand waving in the air. "ΠΑΡΑΚΑΛΩ!Θα η γυναίκα σου σαν κουτί με σοκολάτες." [PLEASE! Would your wife like a box of chocolates?] "Τι γίνεται με τα υπέροχα παιδιά σας? Τι θα ήθελαν?" [What about your lovely tsildren? What do they like?] "Παρακαλώ, πάρτε αυτό που σας αρέσει!" [Please, take what you like!]

This went on for some time. By then my father had grown bored of the fiasco. When it was over, the Greek men bowed and scraped over and over as we attempted to leave the shop. We had created quite a stir. The men were busily packing the boot of my father's car with the crate of Coca-Colas, boxes of chocolates for my mother covered in lilac ribbons (her favourite colour), several smaller boxes for me and the whole leg of glazed ham. There were dozens of fresh rolls and an enormous wedge of cheddar cheese.

I got in and sat on the bench seat next to my father. In his haste for us to depart, the shop-owner slammed the car door too soon, onto my tiny precious little fingers. I felt blinding pain as I let out a terrifying scream. Hastily, he reopened the door, his eyes filled with tears, his face a mask of sheer terror. Could his day get any worse? The gold-toothed man was utterly depleted. My father shouted out to him, quickly put the car into reverse, spun it around and raced towards home at high speed, with me screaming my head off.

At the commencement of my first school year my parents were notified of ballet classes that would be held at the school. I was thrilled when I was enrolled for the classes. As per usual, I was sent to the first ballet class unaccompanied. Before I left, mummy dearest lifted her golden head from her pillow as she lay draped on the bed in a soft floral silk frock, the full skirt flowing gently across the bed. She looked up with glazed disinterest in her soft blue eyes and handed me an envelope with the fee for the class.

My mother explained slowly (I was four years old) where I needed to go for the class: "Cross the road carefully, go into the school and look for the ballet classroom."

With my dark eyes wide, I glared at her lying there. In my reluctance to go alone, I hesitated.

"Off you go...quickly," she said lazily.

Clutching the white envelope tightly in one hand, my pink ballet shoes in the other, I trotted off obediently. It was late afternoon; the school grounds were almost empty; the red brick buildings, silent. I was scared. I took a deep breath and raced along the paved driveway to find the classroom.

Soon I was standing poised at the wall-mounted ballet barre, ready. The joy that day gave me was instantaneous and memorable. I was instantly in love with dance. At the very first position taught to us, I was excited and aglow with happiness, in a way I had never experienced before. I knew from that day forward: doing what you love is everything! The classes remain amongst my most cherished moments. Ballet was a romantic escape from my lonely life, yet somewhere deep in my heart I knew that classical ballet would become a big part of my life. I had never been happier. I blossomed.

There was a downside to being a family who was considered to be affluent, 'hoity toity' and upper class. To the outside world we must have appeared so; but I had no idea what it meant to be different in that way. Walking home through the Northcliff School grounds from a dance class one day, I was grabbed by two older girls. They must have been ten or eleven years of age.

I was dragged to the side of the buildings where I was assaulted physically and abused verbally for being the 'rich little girl'. I was spat at, slapped, pushed, pinched, shaken and kicked.

"Big baby, big baby! Cry, go on, cry!"

"Cry, baby bunting!" they teased as they continued the onslaught.

"You think you are so smart. Smarty pants! Smarty pants!" they sang together over and over as they lashed out, hitting me across the head and face and pulling my hair. I was terrified! The torment went on for what seemed like hours...

At some point I felt unable to endure any more punishment for being a 'rich girl'. I began pleading for my life, offering to fetch 'lots of money' and all my toys.

"You can have all my toys, I have lots of special ones."

"I can bring you lots of money too."

I never understood why, but they fell for it. Perhaps they knew that they had gone too far. I had no idea. The bullies let go of me while they considered my tearful pleas. As they let go of my arms, I pulled away and ran for my life! My chest tight and aching, my throat on fire, my body hurting as I ran at full speed, my knees constantly buckling under me, but I kept running and running...

Finally reaching home, I was devastated to find myself alone in a silent house. On that dreadful day I needed comfort; but, as usual, my mother was out. Nanny was having an afternoon rest. There was no one to reassure me, to soothe my broken heart, attend to the shock or to clean my wounds. I needed to be held, to feel safe. I sobbed long and hard in the silent house void of any love. A deep emptiness filled my heart and permeated deep into my bones. I felt sad and alone in an unpredictable world, and I still had no idea what 'being rich' meant.

My sobs went unheard and, with that, my vulnerability grew. Mistrust of the world around me began. It had been a very frightening and harrowing experience. During the following week I felt physically ill, my small body battered and bruised. I was unable to walk properly and developed a hobbling gait. I was in pain and discomfort; yet my mother and Nanny paid no attention to it. My difficulty in walking fully upright continued for about a fortnight, without comment.

From that day I became fearful of being away from home or alone amongst strangers. I never saw the girls who bullied and assaulted me ever again, but I was traumatised by the incident for years to come.

In my adult years I had a 'light bulb moment'. I realised how deeply that assault had affected my ability to believe in myself and to achieve financial success. I was hesitant regarding success or of showing any outward signs of wealth. I realised when in my forties that I had regularly sabotaged myself to curtail financial success. The implications scared me.

After less than two years at ballet school we suddenly moved from the elegant Cape Dutch house in Northcliff to another suburb of

PART 1

Johannesburg. We left behind my happy days, my school, a wonderful ballet teacher and Abraham, my precious friend and self-appointed guardian. It was a swift removal from all that was familiar. Before I knew it, we were living in a new area, in a very different type of home and in a new school, living another chapter of our lives. Nothing was ever the same for me. I was no longer a happy child.

I was never sent back to ballet classes. My constant requests fell on deaf ears. My leotard, pink tights, tutu, ballet shoes and little vanity case disappeared. For many years thereafter I knew my vocation would have been, and probably should have been, that of a professional ballet dancer. It was in my heart.

As life unfolded our wealthy lifestyle was to change dramatically.

1950: Population classified by race. Group Areas Act passed to officially segregate blacks and whites.

PART 1

Chapter 3

Nannies

*White women in South Africa
would rather be murdered in their beds
than have to make them.*

Nannies came and went. I don't recall any one in particular from my pre-school years. Until I was eight, we had a succession of untrained nannies about which my parents knew little or nothing, yet they gave them full responsibility for their children. Mother had nothing to do with day-to-day childcare. The nannies did everything my mother was unable or unwilling to do for her children. Having ever-changing nannies meant that our routine also changed frequently, but it always lacked stimulation, had little structure and was often restrictive.

The nanny-of-the-moment did not accompany me when I went places with the chauffeur. I remember being sent alone, and Nanny was given other chores to do in the house until I returned. I went alone to dance classes, the dressmaker and for a monthly hair trim. I have no idea why I was unaccompanied; but, as a very young child, those outings were daunting.

The reasons for the frequent dismissal or disappearance of a nanny were never explained. My parents quickly replaced them, never considering how unsettling and disruptive it was for my brother and me. The nannies never appeared to be happy working for my mother. They were given a lot of responsibility and required to 'stay in' three nights a week while my parents went gallivanting until late. Then Nanny was expected to start work at 7 a.m. the following morning.

There was a lack of communication between mother, our nanny and the maids. She would offer vague instructions and expected the black women to follow them. Many of the nannies in service were disinterested in the job and could be harsh and unpleasant. It puzzled me and made me unhappy. Nannies were usually uneducated, offering little mental stimulation or structure. There was no creative playtime. They were simply there to make sure I was safe and looking like a Walkie-Talkie doll. I was washed, kept clean, dressed smartly, fed and put to bed.

As I grew older, I began to wonder why my mother decided to have a child after waiting ten years. Was it family pressure? It must have been obvious by then that being a mother was not a responsibility she wanted. She was detached from my brother and me and emotionally unavailable. We were never hugged, held, kissed nor comforted. Today her actions would be considered emotional neglect. We were never a priority, never a pleasure.

I became aware that my mother displayed conflicting personas. I began to watch closely. I have no idea why I did that, but I soon got to know her two personalities. There was the refined, elegant social butterfly, perfect hostess, ballroom dancer and sporty gal. The other persona appeared preoccupied, unhappy and distant. She was an unwilling home maker, disinterested in mothering her children and often a withdrawn, unaffectionate wife. Yet, whoever met my mother socially took to her immediately. With her well-bred manners, finesse and a ready dimpled smile, she was liked and admired. She made friends with everyone. People found her charming and a good listener with a warm sense of humour. Her gentle laughter and 'anything goes' attitude made her very popular indeed.

These qualities were displayed when on a social stage; yet, once the parties or social gatherings were over, she changed. She stepped back into her other self. She became quiet, highly strung, uncommunicative and self-absorbed. She thrived on attention. For those reasons we never got to know or enjoy that social butterfly who was unable to love us. She was seen by others as a confident, delightful woman. I understood by then that with us she would revert to her inner world, far away and out of reach.

My mother made little effort to speak with me or Daryl when she was alone with us. Even in our early years, she rarely spent time with us. It only happened when circumstances forced us upon her. She would be distant and vague. "Ask Nanny..." was her response to any questions or requests.

I believe it came from her own Edwardian upbringing with children sent off with nannies and governesses and parents spending perhaps an hour or two per day with their children. Like those before her, she felt no guilt at going off on holidays and leaving children in the care of untrained staff for weeks or months.

When I was a young child, her actions left me feeling rejected and unloved. My mother who drifted about in a preoccupied haze was never tactile or affectionate. My huge heart was open and longing to be held and loved. It was my grandmother who taught me about loving kindness and affection. She genuinely loved and cared for me. I held onto those feelings of not belonging throughout my young life. Yet, there was a strong, inquisitive, determined, spirit within me.

My parents were exceptional personalities socially, but rarely showed us demonstrative affection or gestures of kindness, support, or encouragement. Yet, when I was alone with my father, he made me feel that I was the apple of my father's eye, his little princess.

My soft-hearted brother was totally ignored and disregarded by both parents. When I was about nine years of age, I learnt that he was 'adopted'. I did not know what that meant until several years later. I kept it to myself until in my teens when I plucked up enough courage to ask my Aunt Alex. She said he arrived soon after my mother fell pregnant with me. She never held him or picked him up as a baby, claiming he was too big and heavy for her.

Neither of us were ever comforted by our mother, even when ill or in pain. Even before I started school, she left it to Nanny and the other staff to get me up, wash me, lay out my clothes and dress me before sitting down to breakfast with my brother. Once I was at school, Nanny would walk me to the school gate until I was familiar with directions. Then I was expected to go alone. My brother usually left home early, often before breakfast.

In the afternoons we were alone and unsupervised. If either my brother or I did something 'naughty', Mother would stare at us with her piercing blue eyes and say, "Wait until *your father* gets home!" Then she would spin around dramatically and walk away.

We had no books, toys, games or playthings close at hand to amuse ourselves with. Everything had to be pristinely tidy. It was very much a 'show house' and we were part of the display. Outward appearances were everything. Toys were packed away from view. The huge garden, with all my secret hiding places, the colourful flowers and large shrubs, along with my vivid imagination became a special playground. Abraham would be in the garden to watch over me. It was where my world opened up in glorious African sunshine.

Occasionally I would wander far up towards the back boundary of the house where the servants lived. They would be sitting on the vast lawn around a large traditional cast iron 'potjie' pot filled with steaming phutu, taking turns to grab a handful of food from the pot.[10] Nanny would shoo me away, annoyed that I was intruding.

Yet, Abraham spent most of his free hours with me in the garden. He made sure I was safe roaming around the property alone. He did this out of loyalty to his 'master', my father.

My brother disappeared every afternoon and was never missed. Once he began swimming at school, he went back each afternoon to use the pool and swam throughout the summer. He was a real water baby! Occasionally I would cross the road alone and walk through the vast school grounds to the pool. I would spend the sunny afternoon watching the swimmers and dipping my toes into the cool water at the shallow end. I had developed a traumatic fear of water.

My mother communicated with Nanny or kitchen staff on rare occasions. Otherwise it was left to my father. She appeared to be removed from what took place in the home and incapable of managing staff, the house, or her children without my father there to take the lead and supervise everything. He had a lot on his shoulders.

PART 1

Chapter 4

Strange Happenings

To children, the world and everything in it is new, something that gives rise to astonishment.

Jostein Gaarder, Sophie's World[11]

I was bright, gregarious, intense, shrewd and pretty. I observed everything, absorbed conversations, learnt words, phrases, languages and gestures. I paid attention to detail. I remembered people—their appearance, characters, mannerisms, every intricate detail. I retained it. I was incredibly curious. Whether or not I inherited this from my English grandmother, Dorothy—said to have been a powerful Medium—I am not certain; but, from a very young age, I knew things about people. I understood what a child usually does not.

My mother was oblivious to my sharp mind, keenness to learn and creative senses. She was preoccupied with the tragic loss of her mother. The murder haunted her during her waking hours, and she dreamt of violent murders at night. She was terrified in a large house alone with the black servants while my father was at work. She was a prisoner to her past.

I spent those days in my own self-created world. A keen observer with a curious desire to know and see everything. My desire to explore the world around me often had serious consequences.

PART 1

Experience of Drowning—NDE

I remember the afternoon clearly. It changed me. I was three or four years old. After that day I was different. For a long while, I was removed from life, never fully present, living in my own little bubble. I seemed to view my parents through older, wiser eyes. I became quiet and withdrawn.

I don't recall how I came to be at our neighbour's house unaccompanied; but there I was standing close to the edge of a swimming pool with three older children. The pool was in the process of being drained, with little water remaining, or so it seemed to us children. Lying in the shallow water was a shiny object. The three of us were staring down at it. The sun caught it, which made the gold shimmer brightly. We could see what looked like a gold bangle. How did it get there? Who could it belong to? We wondered. We talked amongst ourselves asking questions about the shining gold object in the shallow water. We stood staring with the sun's glare in our eyes, our young minds curious.

The older children encouraged me to go down the rungs of the steps. They were not brave enough to take the risk themselves. They began taunting me, urging me to go down the metal steps and retrieve the shiny object.

"I bet you wouldn't dare," a boy said tauntingly.

"Yes, I would!" I replied defiantly. I stood firm at the poolside.

The three older children continued to tease me, coaxing me to get the bangle.

"Fetch the gold bracelet! Go on, I dare you!" two boys shouted.

I felt uncomfortable and hot. They were unrelenting. They teased and jeered. I began to weaken, feeling tearful at their taunts. My tummy was in a tight knot. Something inside me was screaming a very definite, "No!" It did not feel right to climb down the pool stairs. The others were ganging up on me, prodding and pushing me towards the edge.

Slowly I began to climb down, holding on tight, facing the wall, looking over my shoulder at the water shining in the sunlight. I was blinded by the glare but went down one more rung towards the shimmering surface of the water. The sun hurt my eyes. I went down another rung, holding on tightly. I was nervous and feeling pressured. They were shouting at me to reach down and retrieve the shimmering gold bangle.

I finally got to the last rung. I let go of my grip on the rail with one of my hands and my body seemed to swing round to face the water as I let go. I stumbled as I put my right foot down on the slanted surface of the pool, but the water level was higher than I expected. I twisted my swinging body away from the metal ladder. I leant over towards the golden item, completely letting go of my grip. As I took the first unsteady step towards the golden object, I felt searing pain shoot through my foot. I gasped and screamed. I took another step, trying to steady myself. I felt another sharp pain under my foot as shards of glass sliced through the sole of my foot. I screamed in agonising pain. I gasped for air, lost my balance and fell face down into the water.

I was struggling, my arms flailing about, water splashing into my eyes, pain shooting through my little feet. I opened my mouth to scream. As I did, I swallowed mouthfuls of water; my nose filled, my chest was burning; I could see the water around me turning red and with that I went under. I struggled to get up, my arms flailing, but under I went again. Up I got, gasping for breath, feeling panic, fear, pain…, then going under deeper. I could no longer breathe.

It happened so fast. Soon I was drifting away, lightheaded, as my body surrendered, floating towards the deep end. I was lifeless, drifting. It was deep and dark. I lost consciousness. Then, instant light—I saw ahead of me a bright golden light and seemed to be floating with my eyes open, as if in a dream. I was under water, moving gently into a vast ocean of nothingness. I was at peace. I saw bright light leading to a tunnel that beckoned to me. My heart was happy. A feeling of deep serenity washed over me. It was not unfamiliar.

I continued drifting into the depths towards this luminous light. There was a calmness as I drifted endlessly towards forever…in what seemed like eternity…. I was weightless; time was no more…. The azure water was forming a soft, protective energy around me. I heard dolphins. I knew I was safe. All around me water, deep water. I was close to Paradise; yet, on some higher plane of understanding, my wandering soul understood that I needed to go back to my earthly habitat.

In a nano-second of enlightenment,
I knew that the human spirit survives the death of the physical body.
I understood it all.

Suddenly there was a powerful surge in the water. It became turbulent. A thrashing sound echoed in my ears. In an instant I was lifted high up towards the sky, out of the blue water. A young black man held me high above his head as he struggled to sustain the weight of both of us against the weight of the water. He waded through the water fully clothed. Then, taking one giant step with super-human effort, he lifted us both from the pool. Our two bodies were as one, a heavy trail of water pouring behind us as he moved. The young man cradled me in his arms. I sagged against him. He ran swiftly, carrying me in his arms down the road to our property. I could feel vibrations, sounds, rapid movement, his breath, his heartbeat. I was limp, weak, unconscious.

The local maids and my nanny, sitting together on the grassy verge saw him coming. They began screaming. My nanny ran to him, shouting in their African tongue. My mother, hearing their screams, ran out of the house and began to scream uncontrollably. Nanny, with the housemaid and a few others, ran towards the young man and, as a group, carried me safely into the house. I heard sounds of chaos echoing in my eardrums, raised voices, weeping, wailing. I sensed panic. Was I dead? I did not know. At that precise moment, neither did they. I was not back in my body. I don't recall what occurred next, nor do I recall the days that followed.

What happened during those 'lost days' was never spoken about; but I remember waking in a cosy bedroom with my father and Dr. Solomon sitting beside me. I was weak like a rag doll and dreamy.

"Is she going to be alright?" I vaguely heard my father's voice. I felt him lightly stroking my forehead.

"Will she fully recover, Doctor?" my father asked nervously.

"She needs time," Dr. Solomon replied kindly.

I drifted back and forth between consciousness and unconsciousness: sleep, wake…sleep, wake…. Days passed. Finally, one bright sunny morning I awoke from what seemed to me to have been a dream, fully conscious and aware that I was being carried—this time in my nanny's arms. She was carrying me towards the bathroom. It had been carefully planned between my mother and Nanny.

My mother had run a small amount of water in the bathtub while Nanny gently undressed me. She carefully wrapped me in a towel and slowly began to lower me feet first into the bathtub. A voice rose up from deep in my belly. It was the sound of a frightened animal. I began to scream with all my might. It was a wild sound; something I had never heard before. I fainted. I was gone…far…far away. Gone.

Nanny carried me back to bed. My mother, shocked and tearful, returned with a cold cloth for my forehead and a small bowl of warm water to give me a bed-bath. Once more at the sight of water came screams, animal like, wild feral sounds that terrified us all. Those sounds came from a time long, long ago, in my ancient memory.

I was not placed in water or near water for many more months. I remained in a sick-bed for a month or more. Finally, when my feet and hands had healed (the cuts I sustained from a broken bottle on the floor of the pool had been deep), I allowed Nanny to wash my face and hands with a warm cloth. Months later I would stand upright in a small basin of water that covered my feet and Nanny would gently sponge me down. The children who had coaxed me into the pool were never seen again.

This experience left me with a traumatic fear of water. I could not sit in a bathtub for almost two years and did not overcome this fear until I was about ten years of age. In my adult years I developed a deep respect for the power of water, with an unexplainable connection in my heart to oceans, rivers and vast bodies of water.

Dancing with the Lamp

On one occasion, when I was four years of age, my parents acquired a beautiful Dresden porcelain table lamp. It had been placed safely on top of a cabinet, waiting for a plug to be fitted. I was captivated by the beautiful dancing girls on it and their delicate figures. I reached up on tiptoes, got the lamp down carefully, placed it on the floor next to me and began to examine the figures more closely. I watched the dancers as they came alive, dancing around the lamp—especially for me! Oh, how I wished to see them light up. *How did it work?* I wondered. I was determined to find a way to light up the pretty lamp.

I saw the cord with two exposed wires. I noticed the empty plug socket at the wall with two holes. I stood there wondering. I gripped the exposed wires in my plump little fingers and held them carefully in my hand. I placed my tiny fingers into the plug socket holding the wires in place and turned the switch on.

I remember a shrill scream coming out of me as the unearthed current surrounded me in a blue haze, my body doing a frenzied dance. My mother ran into the room and grabbed me around the waist to pull me away. In that instant we came together as one, doing an electrifying dance. The delicate lamp tipped over onto the parquet floor, shattering into dozens of pieces. Only then did the blue haze retreat and our frantic, gyrating dance came to an abrupt end, leaving us in a dazed heap on the floor.

Needless to say, Dr. Solomon was called, my mother was sedated and I was kept in bed for several days. My right arm turned an alarmingly deep blue. The lamp 'episode' was never mentioned.

The Plastic Theatre—Northcliff Hill

One Saturday afternoon when I was five years old, my mother and I were invited by a group of mothers from my ballet class to a Talent Contest held at the Plastic Theatre on Northcliff Hill.

The Plastic Theatre in Northcliff was managed by Hugo Koletti, father of the famous 50's pop-star, Eve Boswell. On the plateau of the hill they had opened a tearoom, dancehall and roadhouse, in addition to the theatre. It was a popular weekend venue. It is recorded that in 1955 the tearoom caught fire due to curtains blowing onto burning candles. The complex burnt down, and smart Townhouses now mark the spot.

This outing was the first and only time that I was taken out socially with my mother for years afterwards. On this occasion she could not refuse the invitation. The theatre seated about a thousand people and was packed to capacity. For reasons unknown to me, we had front row seats.

It was a popular children's Talent Contest with entrants aged from nine to sixteen years of age. They were children who could sing, dance, play a musical instrument or showcase their talent to a high standard. This contest was taken seriously with many of the entrants coming from well-known dance schools, drama clubs, musical groups and choirs. They had often performed at the theatre before.

During one of the dance performances a sudden urge directed me to get onto the stage. This surge of energy projected me onto my feet. I raced towards the steps at the side of the stage and, as I did so, it instantly stopped the dance performance. The audience gasped loudly. I ran to the middle of the stage, stood in front of the stand-mounted microphone, curtsied graciously and began to recite. With my arms high up in the air, standing on tip-toes, I gestured with my hands and fingers to express my eloquently presented prayer. I spoke clearly, looking directly towards the audience:

Thank you, God, for the food we eat.
Thank you, God, for the world so sweet.
Thank you, God, for the birds that sing.
Thank you, God, for everything.

I could see my mother crying gently, perhaps embarrassed or mystified. Nothing and no one interrupted me as I spoke until I was finished. The huge crowd clapped and cheered. They were on their feet! My mother remained seated and continued to weep softly into her embroidered handkerchief. As I presented my prayer, I was unaware of the audience. I believed that I was talking directly to God.

Eve Boswell walked across the vast stage, the tight bodice of her top giving her an unusually tiny waistline; her full, knee-length skirt bounced as she walked. She came towards me and knelt down, her skirt ballooning around both of us. She spoke gently, her eyes gleaming in the spotlights. She took me by the hand and led me off the main stage to the side until the final curtain call. It was then announced that I was the winner, much to the annoyance and chagrin of the genuine contestants. I took it in my stride, unperturbed by the fuss. My mother, on the other hand, wept all the way home.

A week later, much to my parents' surprise, the Koletti's arrived at the house on a Saturday afternoon. They had come to personally present me with my prizes, including a cash sum. I received three long-playing vinyl records with songs I remember to this day, including 'Lavender Blue' (Dilly-Dilly) by the popular Danny Kaye and 'Hi-Lili, Hi-Lo' sung by Leslie Caron. I sang those songs out loud so often that my Aunt Alexandra began calling me 'Dilly'.

PART 1

My father was very amused, and immediately put the record on to play. I sat on the floor at the radiogram, listening while he chatted cordially with the Kolettis. My mother remained out of sight. Hugo Koletti suggested to my father that I be sent to drama classes and to enter me into the next Talent Show. That never happened. I was never taken to the Plastic Theatre again.

Early Morning Bicycle Ride

On my sixth birthday my father surprised me with a special gift. My first bicycle! It was a bright red two-wheeler, obtained through one of his business interests, Raleigh Cycles. My father stood in the lounge with a beaming smile on his handsome face as he handed me the gleaming bike. There were no instructions, only the pleasure of giving and the surprise of receiving, with no time taken to teach me how to ride.

Very early the following morning, before a new day had fully emerged, the world around me was silent. I remember the morning dew hanging like diamond beads from the trees, the school buildings across the street lost in soft mist and the sunrise gradually beginning to arouse colours in a big, wide, African sky. The house was silent, everyone, sound asleep. Soon the veil would lift, giving way to cars, trucks, sirens, lawnmowers and the open-window chatter of servants.

Carefully, I took my bike out of the side door, wheeling it to the west side of the house. The bike shone in the early morning light as I wheeled it up towards the driveway, which was the start of a long, paved path that meandered gently down to the front lawn.

Halfway down the path there were four stone steps with a low retainer wall on either side, bedecked with large rocks and river stones and planted with rare cacti and tall succulent plants. Beyond the stone walls the garden began to roll out in colourful splendour with a profusion of flowering plants bordering the perfect green lawn that often enticed me to throw off my shoes and dance.

My morning ride was planned to stop well before the steps. After all, it was a practice run. I sat on the new leather saddle for a few moments, my skin cold, my eyes closed, my mind filled with heady dreams. In my imagination my new bicycle was about to take me on an adventure to the end of the world!

I set off with a push from my feet. Before I knew it, I was speeding down the steep pathway. I felt exhilarated, gleeful and happy. I was whizzing down the path at full speed, everything a crazy, hazy blur, travelling at an alarming speed. Suddenly I hit a rock, the bike took to the skies and I was flying! I was high above the ground, deliriously happy, laughing loudly and shouting up to the sky, "Yippee! Yippee!"

I flew through the air, clearing the rockery before crashing to the ground on the other side with a heavy thud. I let out an almighty scream at the shock of my sudden, hard landing. This woke my parents with a start, and both came running out of the house in their night attire, alarmed and flustered.

Abraham and Chef William saved the day. They came running around from the back of the house, scooped up the bicycle and carried me inside. My parents, chattering excitedly, followed close behind. I was placed on one of the long leather sofas and covered with a soft cashmere blanket.

Nanny rushed in with a tray of sweet tea, as well as a bottle of my father's finest brandy. After a generous sip of brandy my parents smiled at one another and began to relax. Nanny sat me up and gave me hot tea with spoonsful of honey.

My father telephoned Dr. Solomon to come at once. He did, and I was examined thoroughly. I had a few deep gashes, grazes, with several large bruises appearing on my hips and legs. He dressed my wounds, saying, "Nothing too serious."

But my beautiful bike, I thought, *it's completely buckled and bent.*

What a morning that was. All before the day had begun. It was not quite six o'clock. That same morning, my shiny, twisted bike was placed in the boot of the sleek black Cadillac by Father's smartly dressed chauffeur and off it went, never to return.

A few months later I saw my bicycle again. I was taken by surprise, and it left me sad and upset. My father had given my bike to Eric Towse for his son, Alan, who was a nasty brat. He was riding around in circles on their lawn where we were having Saturday brunch. My precious bicycle was all straightened out with a crossbar added to make it a 'boy's bike'. I watched and listened to my father and Eric amusedly chatting about it as if I did not exist. I knew it was my bike!

PART 1

I was annoyed that it had been given to Alan and devastated that it had been taken away from me.

*Northcliff Hill is 1807 metres high.
The Ridge is one metre lower than Observatory Ridge,
the highest point in Johannesburg.*

Chapter 5

Social Events

Colonial South Africa—confident white men with their exclusive clubs, boozy lunches, fancy parties and glamorous wives

On most Saturday evenings a 'Braaivleis'[12] was held at the house in Northcliff. This was no casual affair. There could be as many as three hundred guests attending, rarely fewer than a hundred. On other occasions intimate dinner parties were held for twenty close friends, from their exclusive social circle. Saturday parties were legendary, and anyone invited never missed a chance to attend!

Abraham, the houseboy, with the help of several other servants, started two or three large fires in specially made 'braai-barrels' during the afternoon. My father would oversee the fires, getting the flames to burn down to the right heat for cooking different cuts of meat perfectly. My father and Abraham watched attentively, ordering the younger staff members to keep adding coal and logs. This gave the meat a traditional wood-smoked flavour.

As the afternoon wore on, the fires reached a constant heat with coal and wood being added continually. Abraham's pitch-black skin would glisten; his crisp white shirt remained spotless. It was blazing hot standing at the fires under the African sun, yet he never complained. As he stood guard over the 'braai-barrels', Abraham always had a smile on his face. He loved Saturday evenings. His 'master' allowed him to stand amongst smart white people, which made him feel proud to be part of an important white family. On those nights he did not feel like a lowly servant.

As the sun sank lower and began to set, the sky became red. Golden sparks jumping high out of the fires created a magical glow to the early evening. The billowing smoke looked red against the sky. The golden red sky hung like a glowing canopy over the magnificent garden. Oh, Africa! What a magnificent land! It was surely heaven on earth.

Dozens of chairs and bamboo couches with comfortable cushions were placed around the patio area. A drinks bar was set up against the wall in one corner, with a men-only bar in the billiard room, where men collected later in the evening. In the centre of the patio area was a sweeping stone staircase, which led to the vast garden and manicured lawn.

The cooking area was set up down there, where the hot fires smouldered. They were positioned close to the giant Oak tree where beautifully set tables were placed. The white flowing tablecloths covered long tables laden with food. A colourful self-service cold table was laid out with an array of salads and side dishes of every kind. Arrangements of fruit dripping out of wicker baskets, watermelons hollowed and filled with chilled fruit punch, freshly baked breads, home-made sauces, a selection of green and black olives and more. The tables were laden with various side salads to accompany the meat cuts on display: thick steaks, chops, ribs, sausages and the specialty lamb 'sosaties'[13] marinated in a Cape Malay mix.

The cooking meat gave off mouthwatering aromas that wafted around. The braai would be packed with sizzling meat almost ready to be served. To one side another large table stood with a magnificent silver engraved bowl filled to the brim with chunks of ice to cool a vast selection of fine wines. The beautiful glassware sparkled in the fairy lights under the tree.

My parents certainly knew how to squander money on others! On those laid-back evenings I was allowed to sit at the open window on a daybed in the coatroom, but not allowed to run around freely. The room overlooked the paved patio where Wisteria, hanging like giant bunches of purple grapes, surrounded the seating area. A heady aroma wafted into the room where I sat, longingly watching the stream of adults arriving.

Many of the guests would see me sitting at the window when they came in to leave a bag, purse or coat. They often stopped to say "Hello" and sat for a while.

I watched my parents and their friends through the window, but they had no time to acknowledge me during the busy evening. Neither my brother nor I were ever offered a morsel from the tables laden with this delicious food. We were always fed early by Chef William and Nanny, and that was that.

From that early age I began to feel invisible. I was placed at the window of the coatroom, otherwise used as a small study for my mother to do her correspondence. I was simply another pretty prop, showing off 'the perfect family' in a dramatic Hollywood movie in which I played a minor role. It was an unfolding production that continued through much of my childhood.

Attending these Saturday soiree's were prominent society people: Aristocrats, British elite, financiers, well-known representatives of the British-Africa mining companies, mining magnates from Rhodesia (now Zimbabwe), human rights lawyers, impresarios, jockeys and trainers who worked for my father and rode his horses. Champion golfers and tennis professionals like Eric Sturgess and Kuculjevic, musicians, occasionally a politician or retired diplomat.

Added to that mix were the nouveau riche of that era, sitting side by side with aristocratic old money. There were often British dignitaries alongside South African history makers, with one or two 'real' billionaires of South Africa's white high society. There were the famous, the infamous, the hangers-on, the social climbers, the ostentatious, the beautiful, the elegant, the ordinary, the hungry and, on occasion, the vulgar, along with dozens of overly confident suave males, blinded by hubris, escorting glamorous women hanging from their arms, adorned with gold, diamonds and furs draped over sun-kissed shoulders.

I still remember many of them by name because they were frequent guests or mentioned so often. Beauty queens, models, wives, girlfriends, often lovers in place of a wife would arrive with wealthy business associates of my father's. Last to arrive were my father's family. My gracious grandmother was one of the vintage props in the Hollywood-like production.

My mother oozed natural charm. She was vivacious in company with a gift for making every occasion special for her guests. She would weave her way between the guests, creating a flutter and a stir as she passed, sharing pleasantries with each group. She was seen as the most attractive of the ladies, beautifully dressed on one occasion in a midnight blue taffeta gown with tight strapless bodice and floating skirt. She was a sensation!

William, dressed in white including gloves, would follow her, carrying a silver tray with canapés, usually shellfish or smoked salmon and an iced silver bowl filled with imported caviar. Over superficial chatter, smatterings of gossip, outwardly polite gestures and laughter, the huge crowd sipped fine wine, dining in a somewhat rustic manner for most, until at bursting point.

My handsome father would glide amongst the crowd making sure that the food was to their liking and that everyone had eaten well. He would stop to charm and tease in English, Afrikaans, Dutch, Greek, Italian, Spanish or Portuguese and instruct staff in their native tongue.

"Don't you just *love* that man?" I would hear ladies whisper, but a few eyed him with suspicious envy. One such person was Jimmy Medley. My parents were a much-admired couple. They had the looks, glamour and exotic family backgrounds; and, for them, it had been love at first sight.

When all traces of food were cleared away by a multitude of servants in crisp white uniforms and wearing white gloves, plates were smashed and dancing began! The guests danced wildly and clumsily to Greek music until late. Towards the end of the crazy dancing my parents would slide onto the floor in an elegant display of ballroom dancing to applause and cheers. By then the sky was dark plum and the night was singing a midnight song and I had fallen into a deep sleep at the window.

Those evenings were impressive, and guests always left the party with happy memories. The family members: my aunts, uncle and grandmother never stayed until late, but left soon after they had eaten. My father always served his mother first. My aunts talked amongst themselves. They were socially reserved and preferred sitting away from the main crowd. They sat with straight backs and wide eyes and gossiped quietly with hands held elegantly over their mouths.

Granny looked as if she had stepped out of a bygone era: elegant, composed, graceful, always dressed in an exquisite hand-stitched black mourning frock (even though my grandfather had passed away many years before), diamonds sparkling at her throat. She was naturally regal, and guests found her manner worldly, exotic and intriguing.

Many placed her on a pedestal in the role of the Grande Dame, yet she was humble and kind without airs and grace. She was an enigma and of a class that had never existed in a country like South Africa.

Her daughters did not approve of the attention my grandmother was receiving at these parties. In later years, I noticed that Aunt Helen did her utmost to undermine her mother in company or when Granny had visitors.

Granny mingled with guests and briefly became the main focus. She would stop to meet and greet, elegantly extending her hand for it to be kissed, which left guests captivated. She did this social round for the sake of her favourite son. The family left early; then my father relaxed, and the party began in earnest.

Dearest grandmother would come to the coatroom where I sat propped up on the daybed. She would put a reassuring arm around me as she sang softly in her mother tongue, "κλείστε τα όμορφα μάτια σας όμορφο παιδί μου" [Close your eyes my beautiful child, close your eyes] as I drifted away into a beautiful dream filled with ancient memories.

I remember one Saturday night in particular. What an uproar there was that night! Carney and Johnny Steyn had decided to bring along their niece, Hettie, daughter of the prominent Police Commissioner. Unknown to my parents, Hettie was an habitual kleptomaniac! My parents discovered later that evening that stealing was her addiction and an obsession.

Johnny, one of my father's best friends and his only Afrikaans-speaking friend, came from Pretoria. He had retired in his thirties after inheriting his father's business empire. He and his gregarious wife, Carney, were regular guests. Carney and John were extroverts. They were mischievous and loved pranks. Their party antics were considered to be slightly vulgar, especially by my mother, even though she thoroughly enjoyed their company.

On more than one occasion, as my mother sat in the car ready to leave a crazy party in Pretoria, Johnny would lean in as if to kiss my mother goodnight and squash a bunch of grapes into her face. The juice would drip down onto her silver fox fur or couturier outfit, leaving her in a sticky mess for the hour-long drive home. My mother would be furious when they arrived home in the wee hours, my father, quietly amused. Similar antics continued during Pretoria visits, much to my mother's annoyance.

During that evening my mother walked into her bedroom to repair her lipstick. She sat at her dressing table, picked up her gold Helena Rubenstein lipstick case in her favourite shade, Red Velvet.

Hettie sauntered into the bedroom and stood against the far wall silently watching my mother apply Red Velvet lipstick to her cupid-bow lips. In her thick Dutch/Afrikaans accent Hettie exclaimed, "Oh Gwennie, that's a *'beau-ra-fill'* colour on you, hey! Please I try it. Maybe it suits me too."

Later, when my mother returned to the bedroom, her gold lipstick case was gone. Coats, jackets and evening bags were in a dishevelled heap on the bed. To the embarrassment of Carney and Johnny, Hettie had stolen several lipstick cases and expensive powder compacts from the evening bags in my parents' bedroom.

"Magtig, Gwennie! We are rea-ully very sorry, *hey*," Carney said sheepishly, before dragging Hettie out of the room with a firm grip on her arm. After an urgent call to Hettie's father in Pretoria, who spoke with her, the stolen items were retrieved, after which they made a hasty getaway via the back door.

My parents settled the unhappy ladies by popping bottles of pink champagne. Staff continued to pop more and more corks, pouring glass after glass of bubbles. Soon the unique sound of the Ink Spots wafted outside, loudly singing my mother's favourite tune, 'Always'. Within seconds, my parents were up dancing, swirling across the vast outdoor dance floor. The guests giggled, heady from several glasses of champagne swigged in quick succession. Everyone got up and began to dance to the Ink Spots' rendition of 'The Java Jive', which I learnt off by heart. I heard it that often.

The life that I observed resembled in many ways a fairy story, a complete work of fiction. My foundation was set by an early education in social correctness and morality. Yet, it held special magic with beautiful people in magnificent, surreal, settings.

PART 1

Chapter 6

Tennis and Sundowners

*The Afrikaner politicians looked 'sub-normal'
while their wives were 'mostly big, fat, red, hard women…
bursting out of their party clothes and tight gloves.*

Dame Margery Perham[14]

My mother was a good-looking woman. Her sea-blue eyes and golden blonde hair were set off by her perfect nose, dimples, cupids' bow lips and smooth fair skin. She was always well groomed, dressed impeccably, with never a hair out of place. Her regular Saturday morning hair and nail appointments were booked a year in advance. She had a dancer's shapely figure with legs that got many a discreet glance. She expected a lot of me from an early age. I was always 'on show', never permitted to be untidy or dirty.

For years after they met, my parents went dancing twice a week at their favourite fashionable nightclub, come what may. My mother kept trim and shapely with dancing and by playing tennis two afternoons a week, on the all-weather tennis court at the bottom of the garden.

Wednesday afternoons became known as 'Ladies Day'. It was a fun day for her and her best friends, but the tennis match between Molly, Edith, Margo, Doris, Anne and perhaps a few others was taken very seriously. They were all very competitive. My mother's tennis coach, Franjo Kukuljević, would give her a private lesson before the ladies arrived.

When the tennis was over, the ladies stayed on. The afternoon play was followed by 'drinkies' brought down to the court by the maids and young houseboys dressed in starched white uniforms. They carried trays of elegantly plated snacks and bottles of champagne to be served in the thatched pavilion next to the court.

PART 1

Sunday afternoons was mixed doubles with sundowners for all who remained after tennis. This often led to an impromptu dinner that Chef William was expected to prepare and serve at short notice. We would be fed by Nanny and put to bed.

Daryl and I were never taught to play tennis by our parents or a coach. Nor did we have rackets, even though there was a tennis court on the property. It never entered their minds to teach us to play. It was all about *their* enjoyment and *their* pleasure. Nothing else mattered!

Friday evenings were the nights my mother dreaded. She had taken an instant dislike to jockeys my father knew, but even greater was her dislike and mistrust of the trainers. She made that known to my father. My mother knew that my father would be unavailable from Friday evening until the final horse race on Saturday afternoon. On those evenings William stocked the bar before the men arrived. At the time, my father owned five thoroughbred racehorses, and Friday evenings were for discussion, planning and strategy.

Once the jockeys left, serious drinking began and went on long into the night. *My father adored gambling,* especially on the horses. On a 'good Saturday' he would arrive home smiling and smelling of alcohol, occasionally with a strong smell of stale perfume wafting around him. It was blatant. He would throw handfuls of paper money up into the air at my mother. On one such occasion he filled the tub with ten-pound notes while she sat in the bath. There were wet notes floating in the bath and strewn all over her bathroom floor. On other Saturdays he arrived home in a less exuberant mood, his face pale and drawn, his mood sombre. The prized horses had lost.

Wednesday evening was card night. My father's Jewish business associates and their wives had become good friends. They would arrive promptly at 7 p.m. every Wednesday evening for a serious game of rummy or canasta. They played for high stakes. During the evening Chef William served a light supper, having made dishes that would be to their taste, starting with blinis and sour cream with pickled cucumber slices, gefilte fish or baked salmon. This was followed by perfectly braised brisket and vegetables. To end the meal, William excelled with his secret recipe for Rugelach, which the guests loved. William would wrap a small parcel for each guest to take home.

PART 1

Chapter 7

A Gentleman Goes Farming

*Wild honey smells of freedom
Dust—like a ray of sun.
Like Violets—a young girl's mouth
And gold—like nothing.*

Anna Akhmatova[15]

During the period when my father owned five thoroughbred racehorses, he acquired extensive acreage of farmland on the border of the Crocodile River, north of Johannesburg. My father's plan was to build a grand house and cultivate the land. He loved being on the land, though I doubt if he ever got his hands dirty.

My father had a deep love of nature, animals and walking the land, wherever he was. That part of himself was well hidden behind the formal façade of his city life. He longed to be close to nature, even though his shrewdness in business—with all the 'wheeling and dealing'—kept his life in the city.

It was beautiful land, sloping gently down to the banks of the river. Plans were immediately put in place to grow quality feed for the horses and build a magnificent country estate. By the time we were taken to the farm, named 'Del-Dar,' three large, thatched bungalows and a stable block had already been built. My father employed a 'headboy' who hired the labourers and general farm workers. A large group of young black men were living rough on that land, getting ready for planting and for the arrival of the horses.

The cracks in my mother's composure began to show as soon as my father bought the land. Her deep fears of being surrounded by rural black workers in an isolated setting were ignored. The memory of her mother's murder continued to play over and over in her head with different scenarios. It never stopped. She was adamant that she would not live there and protested loudly, which was unusual. She voiced her concerns to my father and his family and swore that she would *never* live on a farm. However, my father was 'the boss' and decision maker. Had he actually intended for us to live on a farm—away from the city, from friends and their usual social set and safety? We were never sure. At times my mother became overwrought at the very mention of living on a farm. It was obvious that she felt trepidation about Father's plans. During those months there were ongoing discussions between the new farm manager, horse trainers, architects and my father.

Once the bungalows were complete and furnished, the family would take a leisurely drive out on a Sunday for picnics and walks. Chef William would be taken along to prepare lunch and teas. He would bake and cook for days before; and, when ready to leave, staff would pack the back of the jeep with baskets of food and drink from one of the well-stocked pantries. Once at the farmland, William would unpack and set up a service area. The food was beautifully prepared and served. It was all very civilised. The women sat around chatting and drinking tea. William served a traditional Victoria sponge and fresh scones with strawberry jam and cream. By then strawberries were growing in abundance on the farm.

The menfolk would walk for hours on the hard, dry earth and through tall, blonde grass, talking as they went and carrying architectural plans under their arms. My father's friends were amused by the idea of us living out 'in the sticks' and began calling him 'The Gentleman Farmer'. When they returned from their hike across the land, ending down at the Crocodile River, they were usually hot, tired and thirsty. Iced Castle beers would be waiting for them with biltong[16] and boerewors[17] to snack on. Hearty roast lamb sandwiches on freshly baked soft white bread came next.

After fruit juice and my favourite pink fairy cakes, my brother and I were left to roam and explore. We loved going down to the river. The large, smooth river stones made it fun to crisscross over to the other side. The farm side of the riverbank was covered by giant green Bamboo trees, while on the opposite side Weeping Willow trees adorned the bank. These graceful trees were easy to climb. I would sit in one of the trees and dream, imagining fairies living in the gnarled tree trunks.

One weekend my cousin, Antoinette, daughter of my father's brother, Robert, was visiting from Cape Town. She was spending her school break with my father's older sister, Aunt Helen, and her husband, Uncle Mac. My parents and family drove out to Del-Dar in convoy to view the next stage of the farm's progress. I loved Antoinette and was excited to spend time with her. I spent so much of my little life ignored and alone that Antoinette was like a breath of fresh air. I thought of her as a fun-loving older sister. She was approximately five or six years older.

It was almost too hot to be outdoors, but we wandered hand in hand away from the coolness of the bungalows, leaving the adults talking. We sauntered lazily, passing all of the parked cars. I got into the front seat of our Willy's station wagon; Cousin Antoinette jumped into the back. I began to role play at being her chauffeur, standing behind the steering wheel, steering it crazily, making all the relevant car-driving noises.

In his rush to get out, my father had forgotten the handbrake. I was bouncing up and down on the seat, playing with all the dials, the wheel, pedals and whatever I could reach. I was having the time of my life, whilst at the back Antoinette was happily singing the Monkey and Chimp song:

> 'Abba dabba dabba dabba dabba dabba dabba',
> said the monkey to the chimp.
> 'Abba dabba dabba dabba dabba dabba dabba',
> said the chimp to the monkey.
> All night long they chattered away.
> All day long they were happy and gay,
> swinging and swaying in a honky, tonky way.
> 'Abba dabba dabba dabba dabba dabba dabba',
> said the chimp, 'I love but you.'
> 'Abba dabba dabba' in monkey talk means
> 'Chimp, I love you too.'
> Then the ol' baboon, one night in June,
> married them, and very soon
> they sailed away on an abba dabba honeymoon.'

Suddenly the vehicle lurched forward and began moving, very slowly. We were heading gently towards the riverbank and the fast-flowing river. The sloping land allowed the car to begin moving a little faster, and the faster we moved the quicker Antoinette sang her song. Her words came out faster and faster, louder and louder, as she sat unperturbed, pinned to the back seat. We were picking up speed! I began screaming, I stuck my head out of the window while Antoinette continued her happy song…

The men dashed out of the rondavels, shocked expressions on their faces and began running towards us. I continued screaming for my father, my arms stretched out of the window towards him. He was running the race of his life! He knew that he had to reach the car before it was travelling too fast for him to jump onto the runner-board! The black workers were behind him giving chase. It was like a crazy movie! The vehicle was hurtling forward, travelling at speed with the river looming ahead before my big wide eyes. I was hysterical by then.

At the last possible moment, my father jumped onto the runner-board, pushed his upper body through the window and managed to reach over to pull up the handbrake. The station wagon came to an abrupt halt. It jolted us forward. I lost my footing, my head banging hard against the front window, and Antoinette flew forward landing in a heap on the front seat. My father held on to the steering wheel until we stopped dead. The men fell to the ground winded and exhausted.

Once my tears were dry, we both knew we were in big trouble, but in the end the adults were so relieved that we were both safe, except for minor cuts and bruises. Danger forgotten, everyone ended up laughing their heads off! What a memorable day. I have never forgotten that song. It was a wildly happy day at Del-Dar Farm.

About a year after that visit a mysterious fire swept through the farm buildings. To this day I do not know if the horses were saved because my father would never answer that question when asked. The fire was only mentioned in hushed conversation. *I do know* that the cause of the fire was never discovered. My father sold the property soon after that incident.

That was the very last time I ever saw Cousin Antoinette. Throughout the years that stretched ahead of me, Antoinette's life in Cape Town was concealed, even her wedding day. I knew little about her life; it was manipulated by Uncle Mac and Aunt Helen. We were kept in the dark. Of course, there was the gossip. I overheard that Antoinette's mother, Madge, was a 'Coloured woman',[18] which could explain why her life had been concealed.

Such were the laws of the country at the time: that a liaison between whites and those classified as non-white, was illegal by law. Adding to the family shame was the awkwardness of Antoinette's darker skin tone, compared with the fair Greek aristocratic skin of our family blood line.

As Antoinette got older, her holidays spent with my aunt and uncle were mentioned quietly in passing, although we were never invited over during her stay. As cousins, we never got to know one another. The family never arranged for us, the four cousins, to spend weekends, school holidays, birthdays or Christmas together. We were always separated. This may have been unintentional or by design. There were too many secrets, too many lies. To this day my aunts, and more recently my second cousin, Alexia, have kept us apart, for reasons I have never understood.

As life unfolded, there were to be few happy, carefree days.

PART 1

Chapter 8

Parkview via Port Elizabeth

*'Since one cannot have truth,' cried Sebastian,
struggling into his evening shirt,
'let us at least have good manners.'*

Vita Sackville-West, *The Edwardians*[19]

What would the next chapter of our life hold? Little did I know then that there would be a rapid succession of changes including several moves. That meant starting over and over at new schools, with physical and emotional adjustments for both me and my brother. The events that accompanied those changes could never have been envisaged. Even then, I felt that a shadow had been cast over me, and it sat directly above my head.

Without any warning we were taken out of school and whisked off to Port Elizabeth for a long 'holiday'. My father decided to take us down to the Eastern Cape himself, driving his new 4-door Hudson Hornet, which he drove too fast, his eyes glued to the miles of road ahead. A silent intensity hung over us in the car during the twelve-hour journey. There was little conversation between my parents for the duration of the journey. It did not feel as if we were going on a happy holiday.

We drove through the night at great speed, stopping briefly when my brother and I became restless and fidgety with constant requests for the toilet. Even then my father stopped reluctantly. We finally arrived very early the next day and were off-loaded at a sprawling guesthouse in Humewood, a suburb of Port Elizabeth. My father had planned a business trip to Europe during our holiday and left after a few hours of sleep. He disappeared into the night before the dawn, without a goodbye.

We unpacked lazily, exhausted from the long, hot, dry, journey through the Karoo[20], then sat down to a sumptuous brunch laid on especially for us. The large high-ceilinged dining room was empty; it had gone breakfast time for the guests. We began to relax as we sipped hot tea and ate from platters of fresh exotic fruits, hot buttered scones, toast and eggs. We ate at a leisurely pace, my mother beginning to unwind and chat superficially with my 'Aunty' Joan, her very down-to-earth friend and the nurse who had delivered me almost six years earlier.

That afternoon Aunty Joan took me and my brother to The Willow Tree, leaving my mother to rest. We arrived back to the guesthouse all smiles, having devoured huge ice creams there.

That first evening, my mother led us into the spacious dining room, looking a picture of radiance in a soft, off-the-shoulder sundress in shades of lilac. Everyone looked up as we walked in, and she did so with confidence and ease, floating across the room, her head held high. Her crystal necklace and earrings sparkled in the bright lights as she moved. My brother and I, in our best holiday clothes, walked shyly behind her.

The head waiter dashed forward and seated us at a window table. The bay windows overlooked magnificent gardens with huge palm trees waving in the breeze, bright pink bougainvillea covering walls and trellises, coloured flower beds of 'Vygies' everywhere and the perfectly manicured lawn taking centre stage. The table was set with the finest silverware and a fragrant bowl of fresh Roses as the centrepiece. Everything was beautifully done. During our stay the staff treated my mother like royalty, waiting on her hand and foot. Of course, this was not new to her. It was something she had come to expect.

Tired from the long day, my brother and I went to our room right after dinner. I fell asleep as soon as we got into bed. My mother remained in the dining room, drinking chilled wine and participating in conversation with other guests. Comfortable in any social setting, she was in her element, holding the attention of guests and her friends from Port Elizabeth. She looked relaxed for the first time in months.

It was starting to feel like a strange holiday with little sense of fun or happiness. Without our nanny, Mother had to take charge of us, and she was finding us a boisterous handful. We were unaccustomed to spending time with her, which caused a feeling of discord during the days that stretched before us.

The next morning, after a good sleep in the cool airy rooms and a delicious breakfast, I wandered around the lovely gardens while Mother drank coffee with friends. Then we walked to the beachfront, which was quite a distance, carrying buckets, spades, umbrella, towels and swimming costumes. My mother was disorientated and ill-prepared for seaside outings, having always relied on staff to take care of everything. She settled on a deck chair looking bored, uncomfortable and slightly overdressed as we played happily in the soft, blonde sand.

I busied myself building sandcastles and playing near the water. Running back and forth to the water's edge, I only wet my toes, never venturing in deeper, while Daryl swam out catching waves until my mother looked as pink as an overheated lobster. She was definitely a hothouse plant, rather like a precious Orchid. My mother disliked the sun on her pale English skin; she had never enjoyed bathing or sun tanning. Once she had all the sunshine she could deal with for that day, we packed up and made the long hike back to Aunty Joan's for a late lunch.

After two days of coping with us like this on her own, my mother engaged a temporary nanny who was employed at the hotel. This freed her up and allowed her to relax, unhindered by our presence. The hired help was a sweet young black girl with a wide smile and plenty of energy. She took us for walks further along the water's edge and helped me build sandcastles whilst my brother swam in the shallows. It was the first time our temporary nanny had been on the beach; beaches were reserved for 'whites only'. My mother draped herself on a deckchair in her yellow swimsuit, wearing a wide-brimmed, yellow sunhat that flapped back and forth in the sea breeze.

We spent several pleasant weeks there, perhaps it was months. We visited old friends of my mother's, shopped in town and often went to The Willow Tree, the well-known ice-cream parlour that served the biggest ice-cream creations I had ever seen. My favourite became the ten-inch tall 'Crinoline Lady' in her green, lime-flavoured dress with pink strawberry trimmings. She was a beautifully created tower of the most delicious ice-cream.

Life at home in Northcliff slowly faded from memory. I enjoyed our daily leisure time at the beach, playing in the sand, sea and sun. The freedom and simplicity were refreshing. I loved the lack of structure with less formality and the comforting presence of Aunty Joan. I was beginning to accept being with my mother who seemed more relaxed and approachable, as if a new ease had come over her. The days drifted, the sun shone, the wind blew, the waves crashed and life was effortless. I began to feel happy.

Early one Sunday morning, before we had gone down for breakfast, my father appeared at our door. It was a surprise to see him so unexpectedly. He stood in the doorway, hands on hips, while my mother stared at him looking startled. It was obvious that she had not expected him, but my father came bearing gifts for her: an exquisite bottle of expensive Worth Je Reviens Perfume and a pair of sparkling diamond-drop earrings, set in white gold, bought during his recent trip to Amsterdam. She was delighted, but I was disappointed that we had been forgotten, yet again.

After a few hasty words between them, my mother looked perturbed and immediately began packing. My brother and I stood wide-eyed, unsure what was happening. My father took us downstairs and quickly settled us into the 'old' car: the sleek Chrysler Windsor, for the dusty 1000-mile drive home. The car journey was long and frequently silent. I sat staring dreamily out of the car window with the hot, dry wind blowing onto my face. I became dreamy, my eyes blurred and my head dropped over onto my shoulder. I positioned my droopy head comfortably in the corner of the soft leather bench seat and fell into a deep sleep.

As the fierce African sun began to set, we stopped to stay overnight at a hotel, about halfway home. We settled into a family suite and I fell onto a cool bed to rest for a while. Then, after long cool baths, we all dressed quickly to be ready for dinner. Before dinner we strolled around the small town. We rarely did anything as a family, so this remains in my memory as a mellow, gentle evening. I felt content and safe.

My father seemed unusually cheerful as we sat together having a cold drink in the hotel lounge. Then he announced nonchalantly that, when we arrived in Johannesburg, we would be going to what he called "a lovely new home." He chatted cheerfully, explaining that there would be a new nanny and my brother and I would be starting new schools. As my father continued, we sat in shocked silence. As his words began to sink in, my mother gasped, my brother's mouth fell open and I held onto the chair, feeling sick and confused.

What would happen to Nanny, William, Abraham and the others? Years later, I discovered that they had been dismissed thoughtlessly, after long, dedicated service, and with no place to go. What of my ballet classes and the school we both attended and loved, opposite our home, where I felt safe and happy? It was as if a bomb had been dropped in our midst. The glorious, relaxed, holiday had gone from our minds, replaced with apprehension and uncertainty. I slept restlessly, waking from bad dreams all through the long hot night. I was awakened abruptly by a firm tap at the door. It was 6 a.m. The discreet, smiling, black waiter came in carrying a large silver tray laden with tall silver pots of steaming hot coffee and rusks.

We had left Port Elizabeth happy; but, leaving Colesburg that morning, there was a shadowy cloud hanging over us. I began to feel anxious as my father sped recklessly towards Johannesburg. I was silent for the rest of the long journey, my young mind unable to grasp what 'change' really meant.

Why are we leaving our home? I wondered, thinking of all my secret places: the snowdrops, glow worms, fairy garden and the precious school that I had waited so patiently to attend. *Would I ever see Abraham again?* My heart ached for it all. My parents were silent, my brother slept and I stared out of the car window as everything whooshed by, my eyes alert, wide and moist from the strong dry wind coming from my father's open window. Soon we would reach Johannesburg and a new chapter would begin. I did not visit Port Elizabeth again, or any of those memories until fifteen years later.

We arrived back in Johannesburg in record time—Not to the familiar, sprawling Cape Dutch mansion, but to a six-bedroomed flat in Parkview near Forest Town where Grandmother Dorothy had been murdered. My father had 'pulled strings' and taken two flats, which had been opened up into a very spacious home. It was a light, bright, airy flat, but still compact, compared to the rambling mansion we were accustomed to, and with no garden.

The new staff—a housemaid and cook who were more mature women, along with a houseboy and chauffeur—were all there in uniform, expecting our arrival. It had been arranged that Uncle Mac would get the staff settled into their roof-top quarters and show them around the flat. They had been hard at work long before we arrived.

The houseboy, who was in his early thirties, continued unpacking crates of household items, while the maid showed us our bedrooms, then spoke with my father at length about her duties.

After walking into this unfamiliar space, dazed and tired from the long journey, I sat down in my allocated bedroom on a new bed and that is where I remained, motionless, immediately feeling confined.

My mother strolled around the flat looking strained as she took it all in. She was expected to create a stylish home for my father, and that is what she would want to do.

Years later, I discovered that part of the reason for the move was my mother's fears. The unfading memory of her mother's murder made her extremely fearful when left alone in the huge house in Northcliff. My father had begun travelling to Rhodesia, Nyasaland (Malawi)[21] and Europe more frequently, leaving my mother alone to cope with everything, with only black staff to rely upon. He had also begun arriving home later and later each evening. Yet, once in the confined space of the flat, she seemed bewildered. Had she even been aware that we were going to move?

My parents sat quietly in the lounge. She stared blankly out of the floor-to-ceiling picture windows, overlooking pretty, landscaped, gardens. My father sat silently, smoking a cigarette. After an hour or more of silence between them, my father then busied himself organising and instructing new staff, who looked as lost as we did. The staff in Northcliff had worked like a well-oiled machine. They were experienced, efficient, well trained and not easy to replace.

Eventually my mother began unpacking her trunks, including her magnificent party frocks and three fur coats, which she cared for herself. Her favourite was the silver fox bolero, lined in pure black satin. On more formal occasions she wore a classic white mink jacket, which was a gift from her mother bought while in New York years before; her ermine cape was timeless. I loved stroking the fur coats. They were beautiful and sensual to the touch.

PART 1

The new houseboy, Jack, brought in a large tray of tea with freshly baked scones and my aunt's homemade fig preserve. Several hours later the basics were unpacked, crates removed and the flat looked more organised. I went exploring, pirouetting into each room.

Over the next weeks my mother got busy. My father was expecting several business associates from Europe within weeks, and they had to be ready to entertain lavishly. The main living room was huge. Long flowing red and gold, regency-stripe curtains were hung, set off by toning Persian rugs. A pair of tall, porcelain, hand-painted lamps from France, my mother's pride and joy, stood on tables on either side of the Chesterfield sofa. Several tall vases of fresh flowers always adorned the flat, looking and smelling beautifully. Leading off the lounge, through glass doors, was the long rectangular dining room, which held an elegant walnut dining table with eight matching high-backed Chippendale chairs. Deep cream brocade curtains were softly draped across the windows, and a magnificent chandelier hung over the table.

When the flat was finally done, we sat around the table together on that first Sunday afternoon having a proper tea with cakes, sandwiches and scones. It was strange to be at the same table, eating with our parents, and it was an enormous adjustment, especially for my mother. Having us on top of her, without a team of servants hovering around attending to her every whim, she felt somewhat lost. It was a swift reality check, and a lifestyle she would *never* accept.

Our lives continued, but it was a big change for us as a family. We were living in close proximity to one another with less space and privacy, which none of us enjoyed. It felt strange, awkward and intrusive. Neither of my parents had ever lived in a flat. They were both accustomed to living in large family properties. This may have been the start of my mother's mental and emotional issues. She felt that she was losing her identity and her position in society. She was forced to accept living amongst working class people, to which she was totally unaccustomed. She did not fit into it naturally, nor did she wish to.

In the months that followed, untold pressure was placed upon my father. My mother was unable to come to terms with the smaller space and what she saw as a limiting existence. Oh, she smiled demurely and pretended to friends, but her past and its memories developed into an angry silence. From the very day we arrived to live in that flat, my mother never referred to the 'old house' or the past, not any part of it—it lay buried somewhere deep in her memory.

A gentle rift developed between my parents. My father was away more frequently, often travelling to Nyasaland (part of the colonial Rhodesian Federation) for business and to see his brother Robert who had settled there a few years before. My parents played a perfected 'social game', and no one noticed the changes. What was missing were the tennis afternoons, the much talked about Saturday night soirees and being surrounded by hordes of charming society friends. There were no Wednesday card nights with Chef William on hand for whatever was decided upon. There was no walk-in refrigerator, no wall-to-wall larder, no space for an unlimited supply of exotic food and beverages.

Each morning my new nanny would bring me tea or hot milk in bed before I needed to get up. She then cooked our breakfast. This nanny was not a good cook. Our meals were very basic and unappetising. We had relied on Chef William to prepare wonderful meals and to shop, bake, make jams and preserves and plan weekly menus.

Christmas

My father's position in business was changing. The affluent social circle in which my parents continued to move encouraged friends and associates to send Christmas gifts for my brother and me. Each year since being back in Johannesburg, everyone who knew my parents sent generous gifts.

I can remember standing knee-deep amongst the festive packages in brightly coloured paper covered in bows, cards, tinsel and ribbons. It would take several hours to open them all; but by the following morning, known as 'Boxing Day', the happy feeling and festive wrapping paper was cleared away. *All* of the gifts were gone!

Daryl and I would search everywhere, asking where our presents were, but it was never explained. My parents were dismissive of our nagging, and we were in complete dismay. Eventually I became accustomed to the excitement of opening all the Christmas gifts but never having any of them to play with. I would open the gifts mechanically, knowing the excitement would soon be taken away from me and deep disappointment would follow. Where did all those gifts go?

My mother was overly particular about tidiness and having the perfect home. It's possible that, in her desire to create perfection, she stored all our Christmas gifts somewhere in the flat, perhaps gave them away, or returned them to stores. I was always curious but never found where our toys disappeared to. For my brother and me, it remained a miserable Christmas puzzle.

Living in Parkview—Life Unfolds

My parents, more especially my mother, took no interest in how we were settling at our schools or in the new neighbourhood. Although it was towards the end of my second year at school, I was only six and felt shell-shocked to be attending a different school. On entering the unfamiliar gate at Parkview School for the first time, I felt terror grip my tummy and throat. My new nanny did not pick up on my apprehension. She was oblivious to the fear I felt and just walked away before I was safely inside the school grounds. I remained standing at the gate, stiff as a post, daunted by what was ahead of me. Eventually I walked in, dragging my heels, tears in my eyes and dread squeezing my tummy.

This continued day after day. Often I remained standing at the gate, daunted at the thought of another day there. I was deeply unhappy at that school. Nothing made me feel settled or less apprehensive as time went on. I had begun late in the school year. The other scholars in my class had already bonded and formed friendships, and so I was ignored, leaving me lonely and nervous. My health was soon affected. I was often ill in bed with tonsillitis, fevers, headaches and more serious illnesses like whooping cough.

One morning I was lagging behind, already late for school. My father's car was waiting, and he decided to drive me to school. As we got to the school gates I burst into tears, sobbing and sobbing as if my heart would break. I was inconsolable, screaming at my father through tears and a runny nose.

"Please don't make me go! Please don't leave me here... *please don't, please...*" My body, wracking with sobs, exposed my anguish and all my feelings that came from the deep sense of loss of all that I had held dear.

My father's heart melted; he was shocked to see me so distraught. He scribbled a note for the class teacher and coaxed me to walk into the school gate. He did not look back as his car sped away, leaving me to dry my tears and step into the very place that I dreaded.

My father never mentioned that day, nor did he, to my knowledge, contact the headmaster to discuss my inability to settle at the school. My parents, with their busy social calendar, had their own events foremost in their minds. I have no idea what intimidated me at that school. It is one of the few sections of my clear childhood memories that still has a veil covering it.

From that upsetting day onwards, I became withdrawn, secretive and intensely shy. Each afternoon, I roamed around the huge block of flats and large back garden, alone and hungry. There were many children living in those flats with whom my brother had made friends, but I kept to myself. By chance, two older girls befriended me. They would stop me and walk and talk as I roamed the extensive communal gardens.

One afternoon, as I waited outside the flat of my new friends, Penny and Beverly Goldblatt, I could smell food cooking. As usual, I had not had lunch and was hungry. The door was ajar, and I sheepishly walked into the kitchen and stood close to their mother, Norma Goldblatt. She was standing at the stove over a hot pan frying thick succulent slices of Kingklip fish.

"My mother never cooks, and she never makes fish," I said coyly, looking at the floor while swinging my leg back and forth, holding onto the kitchen counter as if at a ballet barre.

"Oh!" she replied looking surprised, "Would you like to try a piece?"

"Yes, *please*," I replied eagerly.

Norma handed me a small slice of golden fried fish that I gobbled down quickly. She gave me another piece that I ate less hastily, enjoying every morsel. I stood with my big eyes on the pan hoping there would be a third piece on offer, but my friends came rushing into the kitchen to find me, and off we went.

PART 1

I am not sure how they got talking, but my mother invited the Goldblatts to dinner a few weeks later. During the evening, after several glasses of good Cape wine, Norma Goldblatt told my mother about feeding me fried fish. Naturally, my mother was taken by surprise and tried to hide her embarrassment.

"Oh, that's ridiculous!" my mother stammered. "The children have fried fish often, I fry it *myself*," she replied in a highly strung voice. A probing black look from my father shot across the table at my mother.

The truth was, since moving to Parkview we were rarely fed when we arrived back from school. I spent much time as a child feeling hungry for love *and for food*, in spite of all that my parents could afford. My mother rarely spent time in a kitchen. Throughout her life, there had always been an experienced cook employed to take care of food ordering and preparation. She had never done such tedious chores.

After moving, with less staff, she failed to take responsibility for my brother and me. It had always been left to the nanny and chef to care for our meals. Feeding us never entered her mind. Unless our new nanny had time in her day, with the many extra chores my mother expected her to complete, we were forgotten. My brother filled himself on Coca-Colas from the fridge and ate spoonsful of sugar out of the sugar bowl.

My father, on the other hand, was a genuine food gourmet. On the few evenings that my mother attempted to prepare dinner for him, the meal was never to his liking. He would be genuinely put-out and annoyed by her poor effort and silly flustering about having to be in the kitchen at all. They would go to a local restaurant for a quick meal, or my father would prepare a simple cold platter of delicacies from the well-stocked fridge. Most of the specialty foods which filled the fridge would spoil. My mother had no idea where to begin. In this 'new life' there was no chef on call. This way of life did not suit her one bit.

During the months following that dinner party, Norma, a down to earth motherly sort, had a subtle influence over my mother, but only for a while. Norma encouraged my mother to be more domestically inclined and taught her how to sew dresses for me, taking her shopping for pretty fabrics, guiding her step by step with cutting out of the pattern and sewing. Soon my wardrobe was full of pretty new summer dresses made by my mother rather than a designer or dressmaker. I was never encouraged to wear them; however they were on display on pretty hangers to proudly show to my father. My mother quickly tired of Norma's domestic ideals and saw less of her once the dresses were done.

In my mother's world my brother and I were her 'show pieces', always to be seen by friends, or anyone for that matter, looking perfect. We were well-spoken, well-mannered and perfectly dressed, even at playtime. Once we had made our appearances to guests, we were sent to our rooms or out to play, putting her strict 'seen and not heard' policy into action. Since our move from the 'big house,' she became obsessed with how I was presented. She wanted to show herself and her daughter off, to be better than the other flat dwellers. She was not outwardly snooty or unfriendly, but definitely knew she belonged to a more distinguished social set. Living here, amongst such 'ordinary folk', her intention was to stand out and set a very stylish example.

Mother would dress me up after school, taking care of every detail, more so on the weekends. I was 'displayed' looking perfect, more akin to a living doll. My mother sat me down at her dressing table to brush and comb my hair into two perfect pigtails or plaits, or to curl it with hot tongs. If she noticed one hair was out of place, she would smooth it down with lemon juice (before the days of hairspray). Those strands of hair would become hard as a rock and painful to comb out, but she wanted me to be immaculate! I would walk around the room and do a twirl for her to take a proper look. When I looked like 'Little Miss Perfect' she was satisfied. She selected the perfect dress for every occasion with matching shoes and fancy socks. Only then, did she allow me out to play. I would strut around feeling stiff and uncomfortable. She had completely lost sight of the fact that I was her child, not a doll or marionette!

I was encouraged by Norma Goldblatt to visit Penny and Beverly as often as I wanted. They were several years my senior but included me in many of their afternoon activities, treating me like a little sister. I do believe that Norma became aware of my mother's lack of interest in all things domestic, even her children, and that she was concerned. They were all kind and gentle towards me, and I felt cared for. I had never experienced such genuine caring. It gave me a newfound feeling of joy.

Norma encouraged my parents to send us to tennis lessons on a Saturday morning with all the other school children and to Cecil

PART 1

Colwin for swimming lessons. Norma and her husband were aghast to learn of my near drowning and that I was unable to swim and even more surprised to hear that my parents were first- or second-league tennis players, yet had never taught us to play. My parents were unperturbed by their surprise and shrugged it off.

My mother took my brother along to have lessons with Cecil Colwin, a young, respected, professional swimming coach. He had learnt to swim at Northcliff School and was overjoyed to be back in the water, learning new strokes.

My mother was nervous about the idea of getting me into a swimming pool but had carefully explained my misadventure and my extreme fear of water. Cecil assured my mother that he would be in the water with me during my lessons. She was eventually convinced that I would be safe.

Cecil made a grave error of judgement with my first lesson, which led me to endure years of terror if I was anywhere close to water. Most of that day is a blank, but I was told later that Cecil began to tease me about my fear. Then, without warning, he lifted me up and threw me into the pool. To Cecil this was obviously the best way forward, but for me it was *terrifying*. I went under. I came up choking and spluttering and became hysterical, my arms flailing about frantically. My mother with other mothers at the poolside jumped up, gasped and all screamed out. Cecil jumped into the pool to lift me out, while there was a stunned silence around the poolside.

Once I had been rescued, shock set in. It was serious. I was hysterical and uncontrollable. On this occasion my mother took me in her arms, wrapped me in a huge towel and held me close. She shot angry stares at Cecil before rushing me to the car. I remember my newest nanny, Patricia, putting put me to bed and holding me while my mother called my father and a doctor.

The doctor arrived soon after and sedated me. At that stage I was still screaming. I remained in bed for about a week and stayed quietly at home for several weeks. I could not go close to a swimming pool until many years later. My brother took over my pre-paid lessons and became a brilliant swimmer.

Several years later when living in Hillbrow, my mother met Barney Barnett. One afternoon their conversation led to his professional swimming career. This was followed by my mother sharing my dramatic experience of near drowning and the alarming lesson with Cecil Colwin, whom Barney knew personally. Barney, with his golden all-year tan and piercing blue eyes, was short but extremely well built for a man in his forties. He was softly spoken and kind.

Barney suggested we go over to the Summit Club indoor swimming pool. He took my hand and off we went together to the club across the road. There we sat watching the swimmers in training. Over the next weeks he gently enticed me into the shallow end of the pool with him, taking the utmost care. Barney held my hand while we jumped and splashed in the shallow end, having fun. We returned to the pool every afternoon for many months, until he eventually took me into slightly deeper water, swimming on his back and holding my body on his chest while talking to me reassuringly. Slowly he taught me movements in the water and gradually taught me how to swim. Barney continued to hold me as I swam around a small area.

Months passed. Then, one day, when I had become more confident, he held me with just one finger hooked into my swimsuit strap. Finally, I felt safe enough for him to let me go. *It was a huge day for me.* I was elated. I swam away from Barney, who had tears in his eyes, towards the deep end. I swam and swam and swam around the side of the vast pool, round and round again. I continued to swim each afternoon until we moved. I have loved being in water ever since and Barney's kindness and patience have never been forgotten.

One Saturday while still in Parkview, my brother and I were sent to have our very first tennis lesson. Children's tennis lessons were held on private courts a few doors away. Before I had learnt to hit a ball over the net properly, or serve and volley, the lessons stopped abruptly.

All too soon the Goldblatt's were moving; their newly built home in Parkwood was ready. Norma encouraged my mother to visit or drop me off for sleepovers. This happened once or twice, by which time we were also moving from Parkview. Norma kept in contact with my mother for a while, but it was never reciprocated.

PART 1

Chapter 9

Parents—Out and About

The memories of those sparkling, glamorous, jewel bedecked nights seem like snapshots from someone else's life.

Once we were established in the new Parkview home, my mother resumed her day-time social whirl with mornings in town shopping, taking tea with friends, lunch dates and having various beauty treatments and regular hair appointments. My father travelled abroad frequently and also entertained international visitors who were in South Africa on business. My parents went out of their way to show the guests an unforgettable time whilst in South Africa, which meant they were entertaining day and night, often for weeks.

My mother had the occasional evening meal to prepare for her husband (now that they no longer employed a chef). My mother was constantly reminded of her lack of skill in the kitchen. A skill she had no intention of cultivating! My father was extremely particular about what he ate and had good knowledge of the preparation of fine food. Her attempts were a disappointment to him. My father became impatient and disgruntled with her efforts. It was not something she had ever had to do, nor did she ever expect to be standing over a stove. Hence, she made weekly visits to Thrupps where she found delicious, cold meats, cheeses, olives and seafood: tempting morsels for my father—to compensate for her lack of desire to become domesticated.

Thrupps became my mother's favourite store. The upmarket grocery store had a branch close to John Orr's in Pritchard Street. My mother, often with my grandmother, would complete their morning tea date at Stuttafords, Ansteys or John Orr's by calling at Thrupps to buy specialty foods. She never considered cost when ordering the finest quality and took home several parcels filled with delicacies for my father. She wanted to please him. Nothing was ever brought home for my brother and me. By then it was obvious that we were rarely considered. I began to feel abandoned and detached.

During this period my mother and grandmother began having clandestine meetings at the vast Zoo Lake, which was within walking distance from our home. Granny had to travel right across town by taxi, or take several buses, which would have been a huge undertaking for her. She had never travelled that distance alone or on public transport. It must have been serious. They would find a bench far from other day-visitors and engage in long, secretive discussions. My grandmother carried a small, engraved, silver hip flask of brandy, with two tiny silver cups. It was for medicinal purposes. After their heart-to-heart conversation they would sit a while in silence and sip from the silver cups. We were taken along with Nanny Patricia to play on the swings some distance away.

Was my grandmother warning my mother of my father's plan to leave, or did she share information about his dubious financial investments? Were they making plans or working out a strategy? Was my father in some sort of trouble? I believe that much of this may have been the case. Granny had become disenchanted with her sons and, perhaps, knew of my father's plans. To this day, I cannot say what the meetings were about, but they went on for several months prior to us moving again, very quickly, and soon after that move my father left for Rhodesia.

Living in Parkview gave me an opportunity to spend Saturday mornings with my father for the first time in my little life. This was so exciting! We would leave home at 7.30 a.m. on a Saturday morning, travelling by car into central Johannesburg to the Multiflora Flower Market. My father bought masses of flowers every week for my mother. We always returned home with boxes and boxes of flowers, never less than ten dozen bunches. In the entrance hall stood a magnificent French Majolica jardinière with a tall column base and wide-rimmed urn. The urn required, at the very least, three or four dozen Gladiola for a perfect display.

I loved the massive flower market where hundreds of flower varieties were on sale: the smells, the bustle of activity and loud excitable auctioneers in action. I felt rather small in the vast warehouse, at six and seven years old, so I kept close to my father, hanging onto his trouser leg because he often forgot I was with him. He would stride around briskly, making swift bids for the flower lots he wanted, with me running behind trying to keep up. When we left the market, the Chauffeur would pack the car boot and back seat with the flowers. The car would be brimming with boxes of colourful, aromatic flowers. Once we arrived home the maid and my mother had the job of arranging all those flowers. When done, they looked magnificent.

After the flowers were loaded into the car, we would drive to Braamfontein, to Father's favourite German bakery, famous for apple-strudel. A large strudel would be pre-ordered for Saturday mornings. From there we would visit Granny. On the way to her house, I would sit in the car with the warm strudel on my lap. My father customarily took flowers and gifts to his mother each week: a few special delicacies such as quality cuts of beef, fine chocolates for my aunt and a generous cash 'present' for my grandmother, which she expected from her son. We would sit around a beautifully set tea-table with the slab of apple-strudel in the centre and a small plate of iced petit-fours set out for me. The adults would eat large portions of warm apple strudel with lashings of thick fresh cream while I enjoyed my little petit fours with bright pink icing and chocolate centres.

My father enjoyed the long, leisurely morning speaking Greek with his mother. For me, it was a comforting, familiar, loving atmosphere. My father was more relaxed and laid back with his family, which was nothing like the formal home we lived in. My mother disallowed Greek to be spoken in our home. For that reason, I never learnt to speak it fluently. I treasured those mornings. They showed me the strong bond my father had with his family and a true reflection of my father's character and my ancestral roots. It would be lunch time when we left for home and, on arrival, my mother always looked peeved if we got home later than expected.

On several Saturdays during the Parkview days, we took a different route home from Multiflora. I would be taken along to visit a pretty blonde 'friend' of my fathers. I was too young to understand who she was, but I was a curious child. My eyes and ears wide open, and I was fascinated by her. She was very different from my mother or any of her friends. It would be early on a Saturday morning, yet the petite blonde would be dressed in a glitzy cocktail frock and would be expecting him. My father would present the pretty blonde with a bottle of French Champagne and perhaps a gift of fine jewellery.

One Saturday my father gifted her with an expensive pair of silver, sequined, stiletto-heeled shoes. He popped the champagne cork and she filled one of the shoes with champagne, giggling uncontrollably. They sipped from the sparkling shoes as she sat perched on my father's lap. In between giggles and sips, they kissed gently. I stood wide-eyed, my little body pressed against the far wall. I remained standing shyly in the corner, my very presence ignored. I knew something different was happening, perhaps *not even allowed*, but I was mesmerised by their actions. I stood there wondering if I should tell my mother about the pretty blonde lady sitting on my daddy's lap. *How reckless he was!*

My father was a ladies' man through and through. Not openly flirtatious, but his natural charm oozed. He constantly had women falling under his spell, much to my annoyance, puzzlement and irritation when I grew up. There were many eye-rolling moments from me. As the years went by, there were more beautiful women for him to enjoy and invest his time and money on. This would eventually be part of his downfall. I do believe my father thought that he was invincible; and, when I became an adult, his hubris astounded me.

My mother spent Saturday afternoons arranging flowers while my father escaped to the golf course or horse racing. He would return with just enough time to shower and change before they left for Ciro's nightclub. His late arrival home irritated my mother, and it showed. Every Thursday, Friday and Saturday evening my parents dined at either Ciro's nightclub, The Colony, or their favourite Chinese restaurant, Little Swallow. They enjoyed the authentic food at Little Swallow, and there was the added excitement of 'slumming it' on the wrong side of town.

Since moving to the Parkview flat, they no longer entertained at home. Though spacious by normal standards, it had limited space for the crowds they usually entertained. Perhaps they did not wish their affluent and influential friends to know exactly where we were living or pry too deeply into why we had moved from the 'grand' Cape Dutch mansion. Instead, my parents invited large parties of friends to join them at the famous Ciro's nightclub.

PART 1

In the 1940s and 1950s, Ciro's was one of the most talked about nightspots in the country. Ciro's was a venue for the rich and famous. With its magnificent chandeliers, sophisticated atmosphere and fine food, it gave everyone an evening to remember. The members-only Club was also noted for the quality of the band and vocalists. There would be dancing all night and my parents would be the first to take to the floor and the last to leave. My mother left home on those evening looking stunning. She was a follower of fashion and loved dancing. Her good taste won her many admirers, both male and female. She was happy and gay socially, but perhaps lonely, and often melancholy, in private.

Ciro's launched countless artists and musicians. After hearing their music, my father became very fond of a Spanish trio, 'Los 3 De Santa Cruz'. They became regular weekend guests at Bertie and Anne's farm, along with my parents. Pepe, Luis and Miguel doted on my father. He supported their career, assisting them financially and helping them find their feet in Johannesburg. He was instrumental in getting them an extended contract as Ciro's. 'Los 3 De Santa-Cruz' (I knew them as 'Los Tres') missed their family and children and loved being around my brother and me. On a Sunday they would bring their guitars and, with me sitting on Miguel's lap, would sing and play.

1950–60s: 'Ciro's was the flashiest and most expensive night club not only in Johannesburg, but probably in the entire southern hemisphere. And the people who frequented it were the flashiest and wealthiest South Africa had to offer. All of Jo'burg's glitterati made their way down its wide curving staircase into this basement of all the earthly delights money could offer. And so did newspaper reporters to see if there was any scandal they could pick up for their morning edition. And there was always plenty of that!

'It was a crazy, amoral, bejewelled paradise—for people of the night at any rate. We all knew that a couple of hundred thousand people couldn't live on this high forever at the expense of the twelve million or so black South Africans, forced to live in conditions of semi-slavery.... It was a wild place where the good times rolled like never before.'

Dave Lee, jazz musician at Ciro's[22]

Chapter 10

Interesting Friends

*Oh, the middle classes!
Aren't they so 'quaintly moralistic'?*

Anonymous[23]

Jack Bryant

Jack Bryant was a celebrity. He was the popular quiz-show host on Springbok Radio 'Pick A Box'. "The money or the box?" was his well-known catchphrase. The show ran from 1955 until the '70s. It was hugely popular on radio and, even more so, for the live studio audiences. The contestant who successfully answered a set of questions was invited to choose a box by number or accept a cash prize. After much hype, the box would be opened. If lucky, the contestant won a prize. Most were unlucky and wished they had accepted the money. Jack Bryant had a very polished sales pitch. He also sold quality used cars and his radio show was another advertising medium to get people to buy cars from him.

How my father met this flamboyant game-show host, I have no idea. I do believe that Jack introduced my father to a different calibre of women: the doting female fans, show girls, models, actresses and hundreds of 'wannabes'. The two men, exuding confidence, enjoyed many of Jack's women friends. The theatrics of drinking champagne out of silver slippers, showering lavish gifts on pretty gullible women, often taken from the show's prizes, was their modus operandi.

My mother and I received several lavish gifts from Jack's boxes, usually when my father got home late from attending the after-show parties. My father never suggested that my mother go along, but his reasons must have been believable. Jack took me up onto the stage one evening when I had waited for my father in the auditorium longer than expected to go home. The two of them sat drinking with an audience of female 'fans' behind closed doors. He offered me any prize box I wanted. I remember a beautiful lilac chiffon nightdress, one of the many gifts Jack gave me, when my father took me along to a live recording of the show.

Later, I understood that my father took me along to add an air of innocence to his early evening outings. I was left sitting in an empty auditorium while my father joined Jack and his fans for drinks.

From his connection with Jack, my father met Yango John, impresario and nightclub owner of the famous, or infamous, Diamond Horseshoe in downtown Johannesburg. Yango was also Greek, which instantly bonded the two men, although they were from very different backgrounds. Yango, a loveable rogue with dark slicked-back hair, twinkling eyes and boyish charm was a shrewd businessman and a chancer, prepared to take massive risks to make a deal. No matter what was at stake he agreed to financial deals with cunning charm.

Yango was what would be called today an agent for entertainers, cabaret artists and stage shows, investing huge amounts of money and often taking a chance on new artists. My father and Yango were soon in cahoots and who knows what they got into for the pursuit of fun and fame, looking for a huge return on their investments.

His wife, Margo, a tall elegant laid-back blonde, with a very affected 'posh' accent, dressed in demure classic style, unlike all the glamorous female artists that were constantly around them. Like my father, Yango loved women, but he was essentially a dedicated family man.

As my father became acquainted with Yango, he sometimes took my mother dancing at the Diamond Horseshoe, although he would have preferred Ciro's where he was known and got excellent service. The Diamond Horseshoe was rather seedy by comparison, with a very different sort of clientele.

Margo was a friend of my mother's from year's back, who had often come to play tennis at Northcliff. Their daughter, Felicity, was my age, but we never became friends and were always slightly indifferent to one another.

"'Flicka' daaarrling...." Margo called to her daughter Felicity on an occasion when we spent a Sunday at their stylish home on Bompas Road in the upmarket suburb of Illovo, where Felicity and I were fed dainty watercress sandwiches. Felicity was spoilt and precocious and I more reserved. We saw each other late at night, well past a suitable bedtime or at very adult Sunday cocktail parties held at Bompas Road for celebrities and entertainers, which usually became rowdy and slightly risqué. Once we moved to Yeoville I rarely went out with my parents and it would be years before I saw Felicity again.

Bertie and Anne Blum

At about the same time that my father was socialising with Jack Bryant, my parents became closer to Bertie and Anne Blum, an affluent couple who were very well connected. Anne and my mother were good friends and frequently met in the city for a luncheon.

Both Bertie and Anne had taken 'early retirement' (or so the story went) and lived on a magnificent 100-acre farm, Zonnehoeve, twenty miles north of Johannesburg. The farmhouse was a substantial rectangular thatched house of grand proportions. It had an open plan living room the size of a grand hall. There was a sunken fire pit in the stone-walled snug[24] and formal conversation areas leading off to a variety of bedroom suites, dressing rooms, game and hobby rooms, offices, guest suites, and a kitchen with walk-in refrigerators and a pantry. On the grounds were thirty-five stables and a tennis court. This magnificent property was later purchased by professional golfer, Gary Player.

My brother and I found the place heavenly. We were able to roam freely on this huge property through orchards where we would stop to pick and eat fruit from the trees, view open fields, then stroll by cattle sheds to watch the milking and drink milk warm from the cows. Close to the cow shed there was a neat well-ordered stable block where a few magnificent horses were kept. I often wondered if these had been my father's racehorses.

It was obvious that their home catered especially to adults. Bertie and Anne had one daughter away at university who rarely came home. There was an obvious absence of children in the social circle. I was born ten years after my parents married; their friends had children already in their teens who had been whisked off to boarding school in England at an early age, so as not to limit their parents social activities and to keep up family traditions. They were rarely home for school holidays, which were usually spent with other family members and friends around England, on Safari in Africa, or skiing in Switzerland.

On weekends at Bertie and Anne's home we were left on our own whilst the raucous mélange of friends kicked off the weekend, packed into the cosy bar room. They would drink heavily while having unrestrained, self-indulgent, fun. It was sophisticated yet flirtatious, suggestive and occasionally slightly improper. This hedonistic crowd, including my parents, thought of us as an intrusion to their shenanigans. Conversations were explicit and uninhibited—far too adult for our tender ears.

After several pre-lunch pink gins, our presence no longer stopped them from having unbridled fun and naughtiness, which was typical of their exclusive set during that period in South Africa. They were a tight-knit group, including civil servants, ex-officers of the British military with wives who belonged to boozy book clubs and garden clubs, all behaving badly, egging each other on.

With a keen interest in everything and sharp ears, I heard too much and remembered it too well. Of course, back then I did not understand half of what was being said. We were there, yet never considered. We felt sheepish and out-of-place in a very adult environment and knew that we were in the way, amongst very intoxicated adults. My brother and I would go back and forth into the vast rooms trying all the chairs out of sheer boredom until white-gloved, black, male staff appeared to summon us to a late lunch. A sumptuous buffet would be set outside on long tables. The obedient staff ready to serve. Often there would be spit-roasted pig, which my father liked to oversee, turning the rotisserie at regular intervals.

On one of those Sundays, during lunch service, we were interrupted by a cacophony of sounds and a commotion coming from the driveway, a short walk from where we were seated. The three Boerboel[25] dogs had run ahead, and we could hear them barking. Loud piercing screams followed, and the dogs' barking became deafening. It was awful! A few stopped to listen, the others continued to eat and drink gaily. The driveway was a winding sandy road that led from the entrance of the house to the main road. My father and Bertie got up immediately and headed quickly towards the driveway. The other men remained at the tables, sipping beer, enjoying the company and the sumptuous feast.

After what seemed like hours, the men came back looking shocked and pale. They announced that Anne needed to call an ambulance for the resident Chef who had been employed there for many years, and we all knew him. He had entered the property as usual, but for some reason one of the dogs had not recognised him. He was savaged by the three powerful dogs, his right arm torn from his body.

My father and Bertie poured themselves a large Scotch and drank it down, then carried on with the lunch party and enjoyable company, as if nothing had happened. I could feel the tension in my father. The boozy social afternoon continued unhindered. It was more large tots of Scotch for the two men, while the critically injured chef, left lying on the driveway with other black staff summoned to watch over him, waited hours for an ambulance.

Chef was never mentioned during the afternoon but, months later, at Sunday lunch I overheard Bertie telling the guests that Chef had sustained severe injuries to his upper body, which had led Bertie to dismiss him. He was of no use to them with his injuries; he could no longer carry out his kitchen duties with one arm. I was unable to forget that shocking day. I found it deeply disturbing, especially the indifference from the grownups and I developed an irrational fear of large dogs from then on. Such was life for black people and the colonial white attitude in South Africa back in the 1950s.

As the friendship of the two couples became more familiar, my parents spent most of their social time with Bertie and Anne. They began taking frequent holidays together to Lourenço Marques (now Maputo Bay) on the East African coast.

Initially my Grandmother came to stay with us for the ten-day period, but my parents soon became carefree and irresponsible. The thrilling exotic holidays had my parents throw caution to the wind in several ways. We were left alone for weeks at a time with inexperienced staff and often an untrained nanny, who lacked the confident to take on such a huge responsibility. My father left no contact details in case

PART 1

of emergencies or ready cash for unexpected expenses. The staff were left to manage with what my father left in the fridge and larder.

I do believe my father kept the frequent getaways to Lourenço Marques from his family intentionally, especially from his mother. We should never have been left alone. The neglect and abandonment of his children would have caused my grandmother to protest loudly. She would have been outraged, and he knew that all too well. My father obviously juggled his professional life and commitments in order to indulge in the countless holidays to Lourenço Marques each year.

My parents would arrive back home unannounced, looking worse for wear, tired, moody, and probably hung over, which made them indifferent and disinterested in our excitement to have them home. We would be jumping up and down with joy, wanting to chatter and be noticed.

If their arrival home was late in the evening, the housemaid would quickly prepare a tray with a pot of tea, extra hot water, milk and a plate of hot buttered toast. My parents usually went directly to their bedroom to laze on the bed whilst drinking tea from my mother's favourite black and white Shelley teacups and nibbling at the toast.

If they arrived in the afternoon, a fresh soda-water syphon was prepared and brought to the lounge with a silver bucket of ice and two crystal glasses. My mother draped herself on the couch, still wearing one of her off-the-shoulder summer dresses that she traveled in. My father relaxed in a high-backed easy chair, looking suntanned and content. They both drank a large gin and tonic before doing anything else. Then my father went through to the kitchen to have words with staff. My mother remained on the couch sitting in silence enjoying her drink, ice clinking as she sipped. We were ignored or sent to bed.

Once we were put to bed and alone in our bedrooms, I would tip-toe along the passageway, hover at the lounge door, watching, listening, hoping. I would be eager to see them, pleased that they were home again, but neither of them ventured out of the lounge to see either of us. I would eventually go back to my room or sit with Nanny Patricia in the kitchen, who would give me a quick motherly hug in her soft black arms and make hot milk with honey while I sat feeling forlorn and miserable.

During the days that followed their return from Lourenço Marques, my mother would get her hair done, have facials and massages and laze on her bed while the maid unpacked, washed, ironed, and sent other items to be dry-cleaned. My mother supervised from her bed where she lay resting, reading magazines, eating chocolate or taking short naps. I would bounce and skip brazenly into her room and look longingly at the box of Black Magic chocolates. She would let me choose one and, turning her back to me, would continue reading her magazine. *She had certainly become a prima donna.*

My parents had acquired a taste for life without children, and it was clear that they preferred it. After the second or third holiday, my mother began to change her look. During the time we lived in Parkview, she reinvented her style completely. She had her beautiful shoulder-length blonde hair cropped to a short sharp style, emulating the less feminine style of Anne's short dark hair. My parents became less formal, yet more pretentious, when with Bertie and Anne. Their friendship was unusually close. We began spending every weekend at Zonnehoeve, rather than with my father's family.

Looking back, I do believe my father found my mother less attractive from then on, without her long bleached-blonde hair and fashionable classic style. There was a distance between them; a coolness had developed, and they rarely spoke to one another. It was noticeable even to me.

Yet Anne seemed to find my mother rather appealing. Originally from Slovenia, Anne's high cheekbones and olive complexion gave her a strikingly exotic look. She was a feminist with a bohemian fashion style and a liberated attitude, far different from that of my mother and her group of friends. Bertie and Anne were involved in human rights activities. Before taking early retirement, he had been a leading human rights barrister. Bertie never mentioned his professional working life, even to close friends. Whatever he did, or who he represented, was kept very hush hush.

My mother began to wear less make-up, using more muted tones of rouge and lipstick, but her evening wear became very daring: off the shoulder, strapless, low cut gowns, allowing the natural appeal of her body to be highlighted. She had her gorgeous blonde hair cut short in the latest style, copying the work of 'Teazy Weazy' Raymond of London, who was the talk of high society ladies.

She chose more provocative outfits for the holidays to Lourenço Marques, including vivid hand-printed fabrics made up into full circular skirts worn with off-the-shoulder, fitted bodices. When back in Johannesburg she continued to dress stylishly, but in a less classic way, which had been her style in previous years.

Had a liaison developed between the two women or had the holidays, far away from family and friends, become a wildly exciting experience that liberated my parents but threatened their relationship? Something had changed. My mother became more relaxed in speech and demeanour and less restrained by my father. It was noticeable, and I did not like this 'new' mother.

Once my mother had settled back into her daily routine, she would take time in the morning to dress carefully, including hat and gloves. She would be driven to the centre of town by the chauffeur who was still at her disposal while my father was at the office. She shopped, took tea, attended luncheon dates at elegant places, before returning home in the afternoon to nap. Mother found life in a flat painfully dull, she felt tethered to domesticity with servants under her feet.

While living in Parkview I was frequently ill in bed. I would watch my mother from my large bedroom window as she waited on the kerb for the car. She looked striking and glamorous in her favourite black felt hat, which had a large bow set at a jaunty angle across her forehead; her waist-hugging black coat had a flared cut that set off her waistline. She looked a perfect picture, and I felt proud of her, but it made me heartsore and lonely too. It was as if she was someone in the distance, never close enough to know, to feel, to touch, or to love.

The mood at home felt different. After, perhaps, too many holidays and taking his eye off the ball, my father's general mood changed. Life was not as it once was between them. Mother appeared to be more assertive, taking on Anne's feminist ways, and my father no longer met with trainers or jockeys on a Friday night. There were no Wednesday night card games, and he stopped attending race meetings altogether, since the time of the fire on the farm. What was *the truth* about the fire and the racehorses? Life began to slowly collapse around us.

It was obvious from the continual change in our circumstances that something was happening, planned or unplanned. Had he lost money on the land deal? Was money being siphoned off to Rhodesia? Had my father been planning to leave us? I have wondered if he took advantage of my mother's inheritance and spent a substantial amount of it, or was their lavish lifestyle funded by him alone.

My parents' carefully crafted social image became less discerning and more pleasure-seeking. They were intensely selfish and greedy for life, with no interests other than parties, dancing, fashionable outfits, enjoyment and excitement. It was a fickle existence.

My mother was accustomed to being 'The Belle of the Ball' and the prettiest in their exclusive social circle, yet my father was easily distracted by gorgeous women or any glittering damsel who offered herself to him. Their lifestyle was stylish, luxurious and extravagant, and their values were put aside for an even more giddy, superficial life. It was a deliciously enticing time for them, filled with excitement and risk. How did he maintain it all and be away from business so frequently? That I do not know.

My mother was not aware then that my father had several glamorous women living in swanky 'love-nests' around Johannesburg. He supported his women and their lavish lifestyles. He was living a scandalous life of a self-indulgent playboy with my elegant, bejewelled mother on his arm and other beautiful women hidden in plain sight. His hubris carried both of them along a dangerous road.

Mickey and Lavinia

Mickey Marais and Lavinia Buchner were an avant-garde couple with an unorthodox lifestyle. Mickey never wore suits or a tie; he preferred gaudy billowing shirts. Lavinia wafted about in kaftans and other long, flowing, garments. Yet, they were actually very sophisticated.

Mickey and Lavinia lived together, which was a huge 'no-no' in the 1950s. It may be the reason they kept to themselves, entertaining a select few at their home. They were not into crowded venues or pretentious social events. They declined invitations from my parents, preferring their laidback low-key lifestyle. The couple lived at the top of Northcliff Ridge in an unusual modern house built almost into the rock face on the hill. Mickey owned an emerald mine in Zambia, as well as a quartz crystal mine somewhere in Africa. People often whispered that he was 'filthy rich'.

His pride and joy was not Lavinia, or his beautiful gems, but a Tretchikoff painting of the famous 'Green Lady'. Mickey claimed that it was the original bought from Vladimir Tretchikoff, even though Trechikoff announced to the media that the original had been destroyed in a fire in Cape Town.

Guests spent hours sitting at the bar staring at the captivating painting. I did the same. I never forgot her: the slanting eyes, the mysterious green face. As a child in a segregated society I had never seen an oriental person and presumed they all had skin that colour.

Lavinia had been married to the infamous Dr. Gerhardus Buchner who in 1949 was charged with providing illegal abortions at Castle Mansions on Eloff Street in downtown Johannesburg. Buchner, a South African doctor who received his medical degree at the Sorbonne, then spent several years in prison with hard labour.

My father met Mickey through their mining interests, and they became firm friends. Their bond was linked by a desire for money and mischief, in which they both indulged, together and separately. We spent many relaxing Sunday afternoons at their home. My brother and I climbed the surrounding rocky land, though I was cautious, aware that there would be deadly snakes amongst the rocks.

George, a mature well-built black man, was their houseboy and cook. He made sure that the fire was perfect and would see to the basting of the spatchcocked chickens with his special hot sauce. For some reason red meat, which was usually eaten at a braai, was never served at their home. George also prepared a variety of salads, baked fresh rolls and ran in and out with orders for drinks and refreshments. He set a beautiful table inside using sprays of flowers picked from the exotic garden and placed the lunch table close to the floor-to-ceiling glass doors that offered a full view of Northcliff.

Mickey had an African Grey parrot who was a real chatterbox. The parrot was able to mimic Mickey's call for George perfectly.

"*Georrrgggge...,*" Mickey would lean back in his wicker chair, yelling for service. The parrot would copy his call, repeatedly., "*Georrrgggge...,*"

A bewildered George, his face gleaming with sweat, would run in and out of the house, much to the amusement of Mickey's guests. Each time George dashed out to the parrot's call, the adults would shriek with laughter.

"I never called you," Mickey would say mischievously.

George would shake his head, looking hot and bewildered. He never guessed that it was the parrot, and he was never told. They found it far too amusing making fun of the hardworking man.

I watched from afar and never found it funny. Even as a young child I thought it unfair.

Mother's Style

Mother's Style – Dior Coat

Black Magic Chocolates

Apple Blossom Perfume

PART 1

High Society Ladies

John Orrs Store – Lifts

PART 1

Ansteys Store

Ansteys – Rooftop

Little Swallow Restaurant

89

PART 1

Eloff Street Tram

OK Bazaars Store

90

Willow Tree – Port Elizabeth

Los Tres

PART 1

White Society

Debutantes Ball    *Eve Boswell – Singer*

Polana Hotel, Lourenço Marques

Polana Hotel, 1920s

PART 1

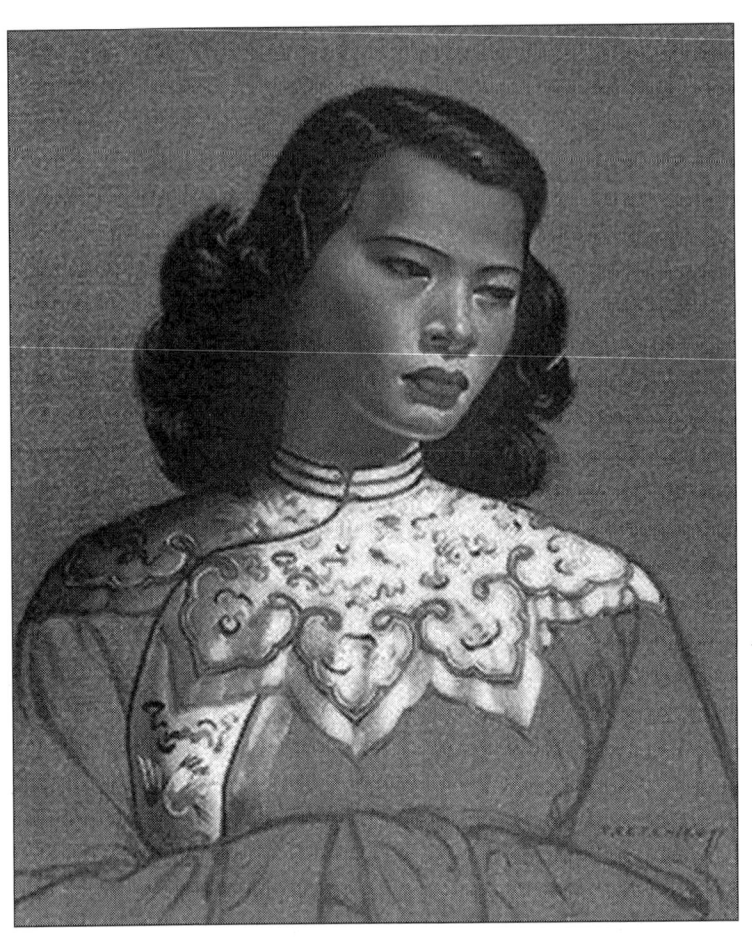

Trechikoff Painting

PART 1

Northcliff Ridge

Port Elizabeth Beach

95

PART 1

PART II

*All the bright precious things fade so fast,
and they don't come back.*

Daisy in The Great Gatsby[26]

PART 2

Chapter 11

The Penthouse

*Nothing is so painful to the human mind as
a great and sudden change.*

Mary W. Shelley, Frankenstein[27]

This was an emotionally challenging chapter to write. The memories from this time in my life had been deeply buried. They were an upsetting and unpleasant reminder of a time when I felt lost, alone and without a secure foundation to hold onto.

It was too soon to be moving from Parkview, a place which I had initially found difficult to adjust to. The mention of yet another move came as a shock. It unsettled me. From that period onwards, I began to blank out life events that were painful or difficult to deal with. I was seven years old.

Our move to Yeoville was unexpected and swift. My brother and I were whisked away with our nanny, Patricia, in a chauffeur-driven car, far from familiar places, faces and friends. We were driven at high speed to a different location, arriving at an 'empty shell' sort of place, and left there for many hours.

And so, our time in Parkview ended abruptly on a Monday morning. That day is a blur of haste and bewilderment. I woke earlier than usual; it was barely light outside. Nanny dressed me as if it were a normal school day, but the kitchen was in disarray and no breakfast was offered. We stood huddled together in the kitchen until my father came in to give instructions. It was as if I were not there. I stood pressed against the kitchen counter next to Nanny.

PART 2

Once there, I was puzzled by the long wait in an empty flat while my mind filled with fear. *Have we been abandoned?* My brother and I sat on the floor while Nanny hovered, pacing back and forth as we waited in the empty shell for our parents, hoping that we would pick up our lives once they arrived. Bewildered, we began wandering from room to room without saying a word to each other. I felt as if my wings had suddenly been clipped.

At the front door there was a spacious, partly enclosed, patio with a highly polished stone floor. It was bare, cold and unappealing. For some reason, my mother never furnished it with patio furniture. It could have been a useful play area, but it remained empty and ignored. The corridors were narrow, the building of a basic design, that lacked character. It was not a happy feeling place. The sprawling penthouse was lifeless, the rooms vast but lacking in warmth, comfort, or style. The outlook was onto a busy road and it overlooked a small Catholic Church. I felt stifled and disturbed by the constant noise. There were no trees, grass, flowers, plants, or prettiness. No gardens, birds or butterflies. No green spaces where we could play.

My mother was certainly not suited to change either. She seemed perplexed by my father's actions. He had effectively removed her from friends and a life that had become familiar: the butcher, the baker, the local grocer, greengrocer, her hairdresser, to mention just a few. She was born to a life of privilege and had always been materially comfortable, but life with my father was becoming less socially acceptable and the atmosphere between them, less agreeable. I have wondered if her hasty marriage to my father was partly rebellion, feeling trapped by her parents' plans and expectations.

As part of an elite society in the 1930s, my mother had her 'coming out' arranged for her eighteenth birthday. I do not know the details, but I understand that she received a dowry, or 'trousseau de marriage', a carved chest filled with all she would need when she married. Her mother spent a year organising and arranging the dance, dresses and guest list with other ambitious society mothers.

The tradition of 'coming out' at a Debutantes' Ball is aristocratic. Well-connected girls were introduced to the monarch and then to society as eligible ladies who expected to 'marry well'. This began in England in 1780. During my research I found that Johannesburg debutantes in the 1930s were part of a huge pageant, but my mother's memory of the event was vague. Who attended such an event in South Africa I am not sure, but I do know that the purpose of a formal 'coming out' was to introduce well-bred girls to eligible young men.

Her stepfather had quietly arranged for my mother to marry a British Baronet. The plan was for her to marry and settle in England. On turning eighteen she also received an opal ring surrounded by diamonds that had belonged to her grandmother, plus several unset diamonds, a trio of rose-cut diamonds and a solitaire diamond ring set in platinum. I still have the rose-cut diamonds.

As my parents' marriage continued, my mother's life with her colonial traditions was slowly being eroded. She was often out of her comfort zone and living a life unlike any she had expected. Yet, because of her deep love and loyalty to my father, she hid her distrust and feelings of trepidation.

1930: The Pageant of South Africa emerged out of the Arts & Crafts movement and Masonic Lodge ceremonies in Edwardian Britain and had flowed into S.A.

My mother made a less lavish effort with decorating the penthouse. It was as if her inspiration and creativity had dried up. She lacked enthusiasm for starting over yet again. Her stylish flair and ideas had gone into the furnishing of our home in Parkview to compensate for the move from her much-loved Cape Dutch home in Northcliff. Her love of beautiful interiors seemed to have dimmed.

Many of her precious pieces were never unpacked. The oriental rugs and French Majolica jardiniere were nowhere to be seen, the beautiful china and glassware, no longer on display. The glorious vases filled with fresh flowers every Saturday were no more. My father no longer went to Multiflora, claiming it was too far, yet it was actually a shorter journey from Yeoville.

The move was to be a huge adjustment for all of us. My father's chauffeur no longer drove for him. He drove himself into the centre of

Johannesburg, leaving my mother stranded. She would not consider using public transport, nor did she ever do so throughout her life.' Thus, her daily life was instantly curtailed. She was trapped, alone all day and bitterly disappointed in my father.

While we lived in Parkview my brother had attended extra lessons and was seeing a child psychologist, at the insistence of the school. The lessons ceased once we moved, and he began to behave erratically. He was drawing on the walls, making holes behind doors with his steel compass and refused to get into bed without a bottle of Coca-Cola. He was addicted to that stuff! I have no idea where he was sent to school. He would be gone before I had my breakfast.

I began at a new school a week after we moved. My first day at Observatory Girls' School required that my mother go along to enrol me and pay the annual fees. She dashed from the school building as soon as she could, leaving me standing in a cold, unfamiliar corridor. *My heart sank.*

I attended my first day in the navy-blue Parkview School uniform and that was how it remained for the duration of my brief time there. A new school uniform was never ordered. I felt like a fool—a conspicuous misfit.

Each day as I walked onto the school property and headed reluctantly towards the large, paved central courtyard, I would be amongst a profusion of olive-green uniforms. All the pupils were milling about in their distinctive green uniforms before school began. I knew that all eyes would be on me as I walked amongst them. Within days I had isolated myself from the girls and none of them attempted to talk to me. I heard them sniggering and whispering constantly:

"Oh, look at the new girl in her Parkview uniform!"

"Ooooh, listen to her! She thinks she is *so posh*."

I was targeted and became the 'outsider'. The girls were not kind. It was painful. I was no longer as frightened as I had been at Parkview School, but I was totally excluded. It was with a heavy heart that I attended school each day, but it was more than that, *much more...*

I endured each day as new challenges presented themselves. I absorbed nothing, learnt nothing. I was in a fog, desiring to run far away. I longed for a friend and a loving family. In the early evening, I would stand on one of the balconies that overlooked the Catholic Church, watching groups of young nuns happily entering before service, their long black veils blowing in the breeze made them look as if they were floating. My little heart felt pain and great longing. Silently, I would cry out to them and to God. I begged to be taken away from the 'empty shell' life and to be accepted into God's big heart.

Nanny Patricia moved with us. She was given a small, cold, rooftop room amongst strangers, mostly men whom she did not trust. She seemed unhappy and unsettled. She took on the roles of nanny and housemaid and did whatever my mother asked of her. Her presence was a relief to me. She did her best to take care of me, but my brother was left to fend for himself.

My memories of regular meals during this period are vague. They were certainly less structured and far less varied. Perhaps my father was less generous with a cash allowance for my mother or she was forgetful about basic food supplies and our daily needs. For most of my young life, beginning with the move to Parkview, I spent many a day feeling hungry.

For breakfast, there were no boxed cereals or porridge as before, or anything suitable, yet imported delicacies filled the fridge and cupboards.

With hands on her generous hips, Nanny would stand peering into the fridge each morning, clicking her teeth. There was no fruit, juice or yogurt unless my father had wanted it. Amongst the array of exotic items there were usually eggs and tomatoes.

"Tomatoes or eggs?" she'd ask herself with a cynical look on her face, all the while muttering in Xhosa, "*Hayi! No... no... no... no...,*" with much rolling of eyes. She varied the two for me each morning, served on toast.

For herself, Patricia was given a weekly brown 'servant's loaf' plus an extra ration of sugar for her tea. She would have a huge chunk of bread and butter with a mug of tea at some point during the day, depending on her duties. Otherwise, she would eat the leftovers after the family had eaten; and *that*, in our home, had become very irregular.

If mother did not tell Nanny to feed us, she was not allowed to go into the fridge and take out whatever she wanted. I also do not recall my mother ever eating during the day, except a few chocolates.

While we were at school, Nanny would run herself ragged with constant instructions from my mother. She was effectively doing two jobs plus other tasks my mother began to expect of her.

PART 2

When we returned from school, tired and hungry, there was not a hint of food. Nanny would be off duty for a couple of hours. There was no place to play and after-school activities were never resumed. We had no friends, no books, toys or games. Our few familiar toys were never unpacked. We became withdrawn, remaining in our rooms. Our parents never bought us books to read, and it was not until a few years later that I joined a library myself. There was no radio played in the house, but occasionally my mother would play records on the gramophone, usually opera, once she was dressed and waiting for my father to return home. She would play Mario Lanza or the music of Italian tenor Beniamino Gigli, who were her favourites.

Patricia would come and get me for my bath, and I would be in bed before my father arrived home. I would lie awake waiting to hear his voice, but I never saw him. My parents dined out most evenings, or my father would conjure up a delicious meal for the two of them, leaving an unbelievable mess for Nanny to clean.

Whenever my parents were out, Nanny would lie on a blanket on the floor next to my bed or sit curled up with her head and arms on my bed sleeping until my parents returned home in the wee hours.

On several occasions my father went food shopping early on a Sunday morning before we were up. He would arrive back with baskets of food and then take over the entire kitchen to cook a huge breakfast of eggs, bacon, sausages, steak, mushrooms, sautéed kidneys and tomatoes. My mother never joined us in the dining room for these casual Sunday breakfasts, but Daryl and I tucked in hungrily with my father, enjoying every morsel. Patricia would bring in a tray of tea, take a cup to my mother in her bedroom and then begin the huge job of cleaning up the mess my father had created in the kitchen.

On several such occasions my father's Spanish friend, Jesús Urunga, would arrive unexpectedly to have breakfast with us. Jesús was younger than my father, good looking, loud, gregarious and fun. He always took time to talk and joke with my brother and would make a fuss of me. After a huge feast the two men would remain at the dining table, sipping something stronger while talking business. I was under the impression that Jesús worked for my father but don't think anyone was clear what Jesús did. He was the only business associate who ever met with my father at the penthouse. They would speak in Spanish for most of the conversation, and it always seemed to me that they were plotting or planning something.

For years after this, Jesús would reappear in my life at random locations, either by design or pure coincidence. We would greet each other warmly and share a brief, superficial conversation before going our separate ways. I have since wondered if he was instructed by my father to keep an eye on me.

My mother teetered between confusion and irritation, while my father ignored the family problems. During the months that followed, my mother was silent, expecting my father to eventually 'fix' everything, but he was rarely home. After dressing beautifully especially for him, Mother waited patiently and *never* ate a morsel without him.

She never wavered in her trust, her blind faith in my father's ability to fix everything in life. She had high expectations yet never interfered with what he decided. She *did* expect him to take care of her like a porcelain doll, to organise the household and discipline us when needed. Whatever came up, he was expected to deal with it. My mother's fragile disposition and desire to be well-cared-for must have become tiresome and, perhaps, beyond my father's capabilities

My parents had heated discussions on one topic: religion. They were both dogmatic in their opinions and argued about it openly. My father was brought up Greek Orthodox and my mother in the Church of England. In all their years together, neither of them attended a church service, nor did they introduce my brother and me to either of those religions. Yet, my mother was adamant that she would 'never set foot into a Greek Church' and my father refused to walk through the doors of a Church of England. Strong determination and stubbornness led to many heated discussions that filled the room with hot air. Their arguments were power games, using God as a pawn. Neither one of us was ever christened or baptised.

From that time onwards, and through most of my life, I was irresistibly drawn to religion. I was curious. Up until I was thirteen, my grandmother tried to convince the family that I should be baptised in the Greek Church. It seemed to bother her that my parents had not done this. Her requests fell on deaf ears. By then they felt that it was too late to bother. My grandmother disagreed.

I took it upon myself to investigate what occurred during a church service. There were two churches within easy walking distance: the St. Francis of Assisi Catholic Church directly over the road and St. Aiden's Anglican Church in Regents Street, a few minutes away. I began to attend services on a Sunday. Early in the morning I would slip quietly out of the front door and disappear. I would walk into one of the churches coyly, then sit and listen. I loved singing hymns and the warm cohesive atmosphere. I did not understand all that was said, or what I read, but being there gave me a sense of belonging. One Sunday, I was noticed by the mother of a girl from school. When she approached me, my face flushed in panic, but she was kind, aware that I was there alone.

The woman invited me to attend service with her the following Sunday. I did so from then on. She asked no questions and never mentioned my parents, which was unusual. I can still remember the hymns and verses from those days. I felt a deep stirring in me during the services; *being close to All That Is God,* was what I wanted, even then.

One Saturday afternoon when Nanny Patricia was on her lunch break and my mother was taking her usual nap, I opened the front door and simply strolled out of the building, with my half-crown weekly pocket money held tightly in my hand. I walked out onto busy Cavendish Road and wandered along towards Rocky Street. My idea was to find a café and spend my money on sweets and Wicks bubble gum.

Brazenly, I walked towards the local café. As I was about to enter, I noticed several adults hovering impatiently at the counter and two shop assistants serving customers at a leisurely pace. Directly in front of me at the entrance, a thin black man, perspiring profusely, pushed a frail black woman to the ground. They had been arguing as I approached the shop. I felt fear rise in my tummy and stopped dead in my tracks as the man began to hit and kick at the old woman on the ground. I was frightened and upset by what I saw. It was an unprovoked attack on a feeble, defenceless old lady. The man continued his assault on the helpless woman who uttered not a sound. The effect of watching such a violent attack left me paralysed with fear.

PART 2

Everyone in the shop remained exactly where they were as the angry black man began jumping on the frail woman's head with both feet, over and over again. I winced as she screamed and screamed for mercy. He was unrelenting and continued to kick and jump on her head. She became limp and silent, froth and blood seeping out of her mouth. Not one adult attempted to stop him, nor did they shout warnings of the police being called. And so, the attack was allowed to continue.

I began to feel dizzy, a sick feeling in the pit of my stomach was rising up, my mind reeling, but the horror kept my eyes riveted. I watched unwillingly, frozen, eyes wide, unable to breathe, choking back the sick in my throat. I stood trembling and petrified at the shop entrance, my head dizzy. Yet I felt guilt that I was doing nothing, saying nothing. I became shaky, limp, wanted to vomit but eventually found the strength to move.

To the tragic end, nobody intervened, nor did anyone attempt to move me away from the scene at the shop door. With six adult men in the shop at the time, it would have been easy to stop what occurred that day. It seemed unimportant to the white males; to them it was simply two troublesome blacks 'having a go' at each other. They gave the skinny black man a wide berth as he continued his savage attack. Not a word was uttered. The brutal death of an elderly black woman had no meaning to them. It was business as usual.

I stepped backwards away from the scene, then stumbled and fell onto the kerb. I lay for a moment, stunned, but courage lifted me and I fled. I ran for my life, frightened that he might follow me. I ran until my chest was burning. I wanted to stop to catch my breath but was desperate to reach the safety of home.

When I *did* get home, I went directly to my room and sat huddled on the floor in a corner, numb, wide eyed, in deep shock. By that evening I had a high temperature and began to vomit. Nanny was instructed to put me to bed. As she tucked me in, I looked into her gentle eyes and felt deep shame. I remained in bed for several days with a fever and an upset tummy. I said nothing of what I had witnessed. The horror and circumstances of that day lived with me for decades. My head often screamed at me, *Why didn't they stop him?*

Such was life in South Africa. *All aspects* of interaction between blacks and whites were done with contempt and disrespect. The indifference and cruelty shown towards black people during those years was shameful and abominable. Yet, it was how we were taught to behave by our parents and teachers. The violence of tribal people towards one another was puzzling to a young child and even more disturbing to witness.

Months passed. One weekday morning I woke before dawn, needing the bathroom. Rubbing my sleepy eyes, I stepped out of my bedroom, my pink floral pyjama bottoms dragging on the parquet floor. As I stepped into the passageway I stopped, rubbed my eyes in wonder and looked again. I heard voices. I peered sleepily up the long passage towards the lounge and noticed that it was filled with people, yet dawn had not broken.

I was puzzled to see my grandmother looking sombre while Uncle Mac hovered anxiously. Members of the band 'Los Tres'—Pepe, Luis and Miguel—were there too. I was flummoxed. *Was I dreaming?*

There were also people I did not recognise, even though I had seen or met hundreds of people because of my parents' lifestyle. I rubbed my eyes again, stumbled up the passage towards the doorway and looked inside inquisitively.

Everyone was very serious, milling around stony-faced. One group of men in well-cut suits stood together engrossed in a deep discussion, sipping small cups of strong coffee. They spoke in hushed tones in a secretive manner. The general mood in the room was clandestine.

Who are these people? Am I dreaming? I asked myself.

I walked through the doorway of the vast sitting room and glanced towards my father. He looked ashen. My mother was sitting on the cream brocade settee with my grandmother. Both women were weeping quietly, and my grandmother was wiping her nose elegantly on a fine embroidered handkerchief. I turned my eyes in the other direction and noticed suitcases and my father's leather briefcase at the front door.

Uncle Mac walked over to me quickly with half a smile on his thin lips. "Everything is all right, go back to bed." Nanny Patricia walked in just then and rushed over to get me. It was extremely early for her to be on duty, but she immediately took charge. She locked eyes with Uncle Mac for a fleeting moment. It was a worried look I saw in her eyes. Gently, she led me back to my room.

PART 2

I lay in bed alert, wide-eyed and motionless. Nanny brought me a glass of hot milk and wrapped me in my warm, red dressing gown. The morning had a chill to it, I shivered, but my ears were alert. I heard people leaving and sensed that my father had left with them. My mother, grandmother and Aunt Helen remained. I heard hushed conversation coming from the lounge.

What transpired that morning or prior to that day, I have never managed to discover. My mother never spoke openly to me about her life, not even years later. I have no idea how she felt about my father's departure, and it remained a tight-lipped secret within the family. For all the business plans that were put in place for Rhodesia, the real truth was that my father had been spirited away at dawn in hushed secrecy. Few people knew that he had left the country; many friends and colleagues thought he had simply disappeared.

We did not go to school that day; nor did we return to those schools ever again. Nanny Patricia eventually got me out of my warm bed and dressed me hurriedly. Two removal trucks arrived soon after. The team of men set about their job of efficiently packing up the contents of our 'empty shell' home. Without a word my mother and Patricia packed three cases of clothing, one for each of us. Within a few hours it was done. My mother, with a distant look in her eyes, said goodbye to Patricia, handing her a brown envelope.

Patricia hugged me close, tears running down her brown cheeks, her soft, generous body ice cold and shaking. We held each other and said a tearful goodbye.

What about Patricia? Where was she going? Thoughts flashed through my befuddled mind as Uncle Mac guided us briskly out of the building. He whisked us away from the 'empty shell' home in his sleek black car. Yet, it was the only way of life I knew, and *that life* was well and truly over!

My father left without a 'goodbye' to me that day. He never did like goodbyes. It would be approximately seven years before I saw him face-to-face again, except for one brief visit. There was something about him leaving that morning that nagged at me. I was concerned for my father's safety. I had a strong sense of foreboding.

Chapter 12

Parktown via Roosevelt Park, 1956

It is strange how vividly memory can be stamped into the soft wax of the very young. The impression is deep and hardens over the years, never to be softened and erased by time.

Clare Leighton[28]

After weeks of waiting and ever-changing plans at Aunt Helen and Uncle Mac's home in Roosevelt Park, it became clear that we would not be following my father to Rhodesia for some time. He wrote several times per week, telling my mother that he was 'working all hours and making good progress' to establish himself, but that it was taking longer than anticipated. She was disheartened, of course, but did her best to be understanding. Well, that is what I was told.

It was rumoured that one investment in Rhodesia was for an exclusive nightclub aimed at the upper echelons of society, the colonial set, predominantly British elite: tobacco barons, mining magnates, diplomats, big game hunters and farmers—the admired, the affluent the infamous, the aristocracy.

The nightclub was to offer impeccable service, cuisine and entertainment, similar to the Rand Club in downtown Johannesburg or the Muthaiga Club in Kenya, where, it was said, "The elite drink champagne and pink gin for breakfast, play cards, dance through the night and generally wake up with someone else's spouse in the morning."

My father boasted that it would offer privacy and elegance for his crowd, all of whom wanted membership. If there were other investors that my mother knew, it was never mentioned or explained to her. Who were the group of men in dark suits that I had seen the morning my father left? Was the nightclub a cover for something, or perhaps a money spinner for all who invested, perhaps even for something illegal?

While we waited patiently to leave South Africa, believing that my father was setting up our new life, he was in the process of building a luxurious mansion without my mother's knowledge. The project had commenced soon after his arrival in Salisbury (Harare). The spacious interior boasted imported marble tiles, fixtures and fittings from Italy and hand-crafted furniture from England. This is where he planned to live, but not with us.

We later discovered that the mansion was for his young, beautiful auburn-haired lover. His new young mistress had celebrated her twenty-third birthday in style within weeks of my father's arrival. Her generous forty-two-year-old sugar daddy, 'Georgy-Porgy', had shown her a wonderful time. His birthday gift was extravagant: a pair of flawless pear-shaped diamond-drop earrings, suspended from cabochon-cut emeralds. They were, apparently, magnificent.

There was something unspoken about my father and his brother Robert's purpose for being in Rhodesia. There was definitely secrecy involved. Copper, diamonds, platinum, coal and lithium were plentiful resources in Rhodesia. It was all a 'big boys' game, an exciting gamble to the cunning investment brokers and financiers.

I discovered years later that my father was well-informed about world copper markets. Some said he was "an expert". When he moved back to Johannesburg in 1964, after six or more years as an invalid, he was soon dealing with the copper mines in Southern Rhodesia and Nyasaland working for a company that offered him a lucrative position 'out of the blue'.

It took several more years before my mother was made aware of my father's many lovers and mistresses; all part of his 'other life' in Johannesburg and Salisbury.

What of us, his legitimate family?

We had been completely forgotten.

Aunt Helen and Uncle 'Mac'

After six weeks of living with my aunt and uncle it had become uncomfortable. My mother and Aunt Helen had never seen eye to eye. Aunt Helen was in her early forties and a striking woman: tall, naturally elegant, with thick wavy hair that fell to her shoulders. Her fine olive skin needed no makeup, and her large dark eyes sparkled behind long black lashes. Her posture and figure were perfect, and she moved with dignified arrogance.

The arrangement was for us to stay until our departure for Salisbury, but those two weeks had come and gone. Aunt Helen was displeased and made us feel unwelcome from the day we arrived. Since her marriage to 'Mac' when in her mid-twenties, he had groomed her to become the perfect wife with little trace of her traditional Greek upbringing on display. She had become anglicised and snooty. Aunt Helen was spoilt. She placed herself on a lofty pedestal with little love or compassion for others. In later years, after Mac's death, she mellowed slightly.

Aunt Helen and her younger sister, Alexandra, were very close, yet complete opposites. My aunts had been brought up in an educated, well-to-do Greek household, but a woman's place was still at home. Unlike most Greeks in South Africa back then, the four siblings were home-schooled by a governess or tutors. There is no record of any of them attending local schools. My grandmother mentioned in conversation that she was the only woman on Corfu to have five servants. My aunts became embarrassed by such comments and told friends that Granny was 'romancing' about her past. Aunt Helen had been allowed to marry outside of the Greek community *and* in an Anglican church. That would never have happened had Grandfather Constantine been alive! Mac had charmed and cleverly persuaded my grandmother.

I discovered that Mac had been brought up by the Salvation Army in Johannesburg along with his older brother. As soon as he was old enough, he enlisted into the army. During World War II he served with a Scottish regiment and suffered a serious back injury that caused him severe pain throughout his life, though he never spoke of it. He later left the army to join the South African Police (SAP) as a Traffic

PART 2

Policeman, which was considered a rather glamorous division of the police force in the early 1950s.

Cruising around on shiny black motorcycles in smart black uniforms, knee-length black boots and elbow-length leather gloves, they were a handsome sight compared with police officers who wore dull khaki uniforms and spoke Afrikaans. People stopped as the traffic officers rode by. They added a touch of glamour to the city. Many women found the very sight of these men exciting. Aunt Helen was pleased by all the fuss over her husband.

Very soon, discreetly and graciously, he began to accept bribes. Gifts would be left inside the front gate each day: crates of alcohol or soft drinks, parcels of meat, baked goods, sacks of fruit and vegetables. The larder at their home bulged with supplies. Mac would deliver a sack full of fruit and vegetables to my aunt Alex and to my mother each Friday evening.

Uncle Mac had developed a polished façade of politeness and courtesy, as had Aunt Helen. He came across as a 'good man', willing to offer a helping hand. His well-built body was unnaturally erect, his demeanour military, his sandy blonde hair cut extra short, combed down flat. His appearance was severe. The Harris Tweed jacket and well-pressed flannel trousers hung perfectly on his rigid frame; a smell of whisky and mothballs hovered. He never allowed his mask to slip, even after several whiskies. I often wondered if Aunt Helen knew who he really was behind the mask. Mac was unable to relax. Even amongst friends and family, he was stiff, formal and patronising. None of us got to know the man who wore the mask.

When my father left for Rhodesia, Uncle Mac immediately took it upon himself to act as head of the family, as if he had been waiting for the opportunity. He became a charming, but forceful, patriarch to the women in the family. He took control of my aunts and my cousin Norman. A few years later, my grandmother fell into his trap. They did whatever he told them to, without question. Uncle Mac was a dedicated Freemason and remained a member of the Lodge throughout his life.

My aunt and uncle were a perfect match. Theirs was an impeccable double act. My uncle definitely hid secrets relating to his past, which he took to his grave. He never spoke about himself or his life growing up; he had a clever way of deflecting any questions about his past.

Aunt Helen had dedicated her life to becoming the perfect wife and homemaker, always competing with my mother, whom she despised. Unlike my sophisticated mother, Aunt Helen baked, made jams and preserves, cooked for the whole family every Sunday, tended a perfect garden, arranged flowers, sewed her own clothes, knitted, darned and embroidered. She looked the part with a glowing complexion, frilly aprons, big straw sun hats and pretty floral frocks.

My aunt acted her role to perfection, but behind closed doors she was unbelievably judgmental and nasty. On the surface she portrayed the perfect housewife with, "Yes, my dear. No, my dear. Let me help you with that, my dear. What can I get you, dear?" She was the perfect example of a dilettante. She knew little about most things, and conversations were superficial, but she was proud of the life she lived, often boastful about it, especially to her sister.

Aunt Alexandra had experienced a grim marriage to a wealthy older man, arranged by her parents when she was not quite sixteen. She met Peter, with whom she was to spend the rest of her life, three days before the wedding. Aunt Alexandra soon discovered that her husband was physically abusive and a bully. It left lasting emotional scars on her and on my cousin Norman. For a time, the family turned a blind eye, but eventually my grandparents came to realise that she and Norman were at risk and allowed her to leave Peter and divorce him. Norman was a toddler at the time.

At the beginning of our stay in Roosevelt Park, my aunt bluntly told my brother and me that she did not like children and preferred dogs. Her stash of Cadbury's chocolate bars was for her and her two Collie dogs, Jenny and Laddie, and not us. During our first week there, she warned us, "Don't you two expect a single square of this chocolate! It's for the dogs."

We stood at the open fridge as she pointed out the chocolates we were not to touch, feeling awkward. *Why was she so mean to us? Why was she so nice when my father was around?* I felt hurt. I stepped out into the pretty garden, pondering on why we were living with them at all. Since my father had left, she openly displayed a strong dislike for my mother and preferred to ignore me and Daryl, which created an unpleasant atmosphere. I withdrew and rarely spoke as we crept quietly around the house.

PART 2

During those unpleasant weeks, my mother was astonished to discover that her demure, strait-laced sister-in-law, was having an affair with a ruggedly handsome police sergeant, who lived next door. My mother and I arrived back early from the local hairdresser, and she discovered the lovers in the bathroom. Jack ran out, jumped the fence and disappeared swiftly. A few scathing words passed between my mother and Aunt Helen as I hovered in the long passageway; from that day my aunt was cold and aloof towards my mother and never spoke to her again.

There was a more sinister and disturbing reason why I was unhappy and withdrew into myself. It was Uncle Mac. It began soon after we settled into their suburban home. One day Uncle Mac took us for a ride on his gleaming black motorcycle, ending up at Emmarentia Dam. The dam was a ten- or fifteen-minute fast ride from the house on Anreith Street.

I was placed on the petrol tank in front of him, my brother on the passenger pillion seat behind. Laughing loudly as he steered the big bike with one hand, he began to grope at my body with the other. He invaded me harshly, entering my most intimate and sacred place. I felt my anger rise inside me, I screamed loudly into the wind, wriggled and squirmed violently. At the same time, terror filled me as I saw the tarred road flying by below. I expected to fall face down onto the hot black tar at any moment. I was terrified!

Mac sped recklessly towards the dam, controlling the motorcycle with one hand. I was petrified of falling to my death. I squirmed as he continued invading my body, violating, hurting, prodding, with peels of laughter as he did so.

I cried out loudly for him to stop, my voice lost in the strong wind. I felt helpless and outraged, my body raw and exposed. I also felt ashamed. I knew it was wrong, and it hurt. I wanted it to stop. I kept wriggling and moving my body as much as was possible, going from side to side, to be out of his reach.

He held me tighter, more determined and even more forceful. I do believe he hurt me deliberately. I sucked in my breath, my chest closed, I could not breathe. Fear overtook me; shock held me frozen, making it easier for him to 'play'.

At the dam he left me alone near to the motorbike, leading my gentle brother off along the water's edge. I can't say for sure what happened with Daryl, because we never spoke of these 'joy rides'. I stood close to the motorcycle waiting for them to return, feeling panic and pure terror, my mind reeling. I felt disorientated and soiled, which caused me to cough up and wretch over and over. I was completely helpless.

Returning to the bike with Daryl, my uncle leered at me, his thick bushy eyebrows meeting in the centre of his forehead. His look was menacing, one which he used often. I was just as scared on the ride back to the house because he rode dangerously fast. I was so ashamed and fearful that it never occurred to me to ask for help.

On every 'joy-ride' after that I would object by shouting loudly into the wind, my body tense and aching, my fear of falling, overwhelming. He would laugh wickedly as I resisted. I was completely traumatised by these motorcycle rides.

Each time I refused to leave the house with him, but my mother and aunt would insist. Little did they know that each afternoon a ride on that motorcycle became my worst nightmare.

I became frightened of my uncle and confused. Somewhere deep inside I understood that what he was doing to me was wrong. What would he do to us next? I was sure of one thing: I knew then who he really was. I no longer liked or trusted him, nor did I ever like him as I grew older. He was a wolf in sheep's clothing, a predator.

During my young life and well into adulthood, I blocked those afternoons at the dam from my memory, yet they left an invisible shadow in my heart, robbing me of a carefree childhood. So deeply had the horrendous motorcycle trips to Emmarentia Dam affected me that I buried it deeply, only to be recalled in my early forties.

I was listening to a client who had been violated by a family member. It was a cruel rape by someone she loved and trusted. Suddenly pictures of those awful experiences at the dam flooded my mind like a movie running through my head. I was stunned and shocked, but managed to keep my composure, enabling me to continue listening to my client. My own healing journey was about to begin.

PART 2

Chapter 13

Doris and Nicholas—San Francisco

This life?
Sweet baby Jesus, it's a wonder.
It's an intense, magical, steal the breath from your lungs,
bring you to your knees roller coaster ride

Jeanette LeBlanc[29]

Out of the blue came an unexpected call from Doris Supkis, offering my mother a lifeline. With perfect timing my mother was invited to dine with two of her dear Jewish friends, Doris and Nicholas, who lived in the quiet leafy suburb of Parktown. They had been part of the group who attended Wednesday night card games at Northcliff. The small group of well-turned-out friends would arrive early for supper, followed by an evening of cards. Those friends contributed to my father's reasons for employing Chef William, who had been trained to prepare special recipes cooked in the traditional Kosher style.

Over dinner, Doris and Nicholas Supkis offered my mother accommodation in their block of luxury flats in Parktown until we left for Rhodesia. We had been rescued. A small, furnished flat was available immediately in the vast modern block called 'San Francisco', extending from Park Lane to Clarendon Place, set amongst Parktown's tree-lined avenues. It was the perfect stopgap and a huge relief.

Little did we know that we would live there for more than a few weeks while my father prepared a home for us. Whilst we waited, my father was living the 'high life' in Salisbury. The accommodation was an adjustment, but each of us dealt with it as best we could. I was still reeling from the effects of the horrific afternoons at the dam. Being away from my uncle was a huge relief, even if it was a small flat. After living with my aunt and uncle it was a safe haven.

We were accustomed to having servants do everything, plus a lot more space, privacy and independence. It was the first time that my brother and I had been without a nanny, and we had never lived that close to my mother for an extended period of time. I was accustomed to having rather remote parents. I was eight years old.

In the days that followed the move to the San Francisco complex, I found it difficult to deal with everyday life after what had happened over the past few months. Uncle Mac—in whom the women in the family put their faith and trust—was not whom he seemed. I began to dwell on him. I did not really understand what had happened, what it had meant, yet I was ashamed. I never thought of confiding in anyone, not even my brother who may have endured similar abuse. I felt physically sick each time I thought of *that awful man*.

My trust in adults had been corroded. There were days when I was numb, stumbling through or living in my own world. For a long while I was fragile; my body ached. I was bruised from the forceful intrusions when I tried to get away from Uncle Mac's grip.

Months passed and I was still scarred and in shock. My heart ached constantly for my father to come and fetch us. From then on, and for most of my life, I was haunted by a feeling of inadequacy and fear of being close to men, but I hid it well.

As life continued at our temporary Parktown home, my mother began to realise that she had few close friends to call upon for advice or comfort. Socialites, after all, never did get close to anyone; it was all about appearances. Perhaps they knew more about my father's 'other' life and his fickle playboy ways. Later, when his secrets and escapades were exposed, it was a shock too great for my mother to bear. The society friends whom my parents had entertained regularly soon became a trickle, perhaps bored with my mother's situation or simply wishing to remain impartial. Many slipped away without a word. No dazzling parties to attend, no tennis afternoons, no sumptuous afternoon teas at the farm or glamorous occasions where women were draped in diamonds and pearls, with food and drink flowing. It was a giddy untamed lifestyle that my parents had cultivated during those days of plenty. They had lived a grand, yet superficial, life; my mother was captivated by that risqué, extravagant lifestyle.

PART 2

Day to day my mother was oblivious to our inner struggles. She was inept at looking after us, even our most basic of needs. She had never been up in the morning to send us off to school, nor had she needed to feed us. She had grown accustomed to having tea served to her in bed most mornings and was usually out when I returned home. Staff had taken care of us, but suddenly we had no one. My mother had no idea what was required. She would be out of her comfort zone once she needed to organise us for school each day, with school uniforms and breakfasts needed. She was unhappy with very basic domestic chores which almost killed her!

We did our best to muddle through. She was slow, exasperated and found caring for us tedious. She frequently had her hand to her forehead, knees buckling, like a wilting flower, and would declare repeatedly, "Oh, God! I can't do this!" as she hacked away at a loaf of fresh bread. This was her first experience at doing anything domestic. Even more disagreeable to her was the fact that it was totally 'beneath' her.

Quietly she wept, "How could he…?"

She had no idea how to cut a slice of bread from a loaf. Watching her was astonishing, even to my young eyes. Being left-handed, she found such a menial task extremely difficult. It had her in tears when cutting a slice, as the loaf became slanted and unmanageable. My brother and I said nothing, dealing with our own inner anguish. It was a learning curve for us all.

My brother and I wrote often to my father who was reassuring and kind. He sent money-orders or cash in each letter of reply. Money was his answer to everything.

Mother found the domestic routine unduly tiresome and was completely overwhelmed by the responsibilities. Puzzled by the most simple of chores, mother began to rely heavily on the muscular black 'flat boy', Themba, who willingly did everything for her. Following her instructions, he cleaned the flat daily, including carpets, windows, floors and removing garbage.

There was no privacy in the small San Francisco flat. While my mother daydreamed of exotic holidays, dinner dates, expensive shopping trips and a team of staff, we muddled along. There was no chauffeur-driven Cadillac either.

"How could he do this to me?" she would wail, patting her damp pink-tipped nose with a small lace hanky. Of course, her life would never be the same again, but *she did not know that then*.

Dearest Mother had been thrown in at the deep end as my brother and I wandered around aimlessly, bewildered by our parents' actions. For months we lived on the edge, waiting to travel, while a feeling of discord prevailed. The smouldering displeasure she tried to hide was palpable. Tormented by his bad planning, bewildered by his excuses and the gradual indifference in his letters, she became concerned about his true feelings for her. She loved and adored my father naively and became wistful and weepy whilst writing letters to him.

My mother had given up everything to marry my father: her family, including brothers Cuthbert and Clarence, her society friends and a privileged lifestyle. She felt completely let down by my father and was deeply ashamed to have been deserted by him. The many months apart and lack of togetherness had become a living nightmare for her. She felt socially embarrassed and her patience was sorely tested by my father's escape from his responsibilities.

What was evident was that neither of them had their children's interests at heart. We were more of a hindrance. To an outsider it would appear that they were ill-matched as a couple. My father, the charming Greek, a dashing extravagant 'wildcard' and she, the traditional English Rose, having had a strict Edwardian-style upbringing.

My mother's choice of a school for us, after several months of absence, was a considerable distance from Parktown. There were better options for us, but thinking it was for a very brief period of time, she selected a small government school that was neglected and rather down-at-heel. Unlike most of their friends, my parents had never considered the best schools for us but did what was convenient for them. Our education was never discussed or deemed of any importance. They were too self-absorbed.

Twist Street School no longer exists. It was a poorer school without the facilities that were offered at most other schools. It did not even have a sports field. It was crowded to capacity with untidy children, which jolted me and immediately I felt out of place. I was bewildered enough, and this was yet another adjustment.

Daryl and I struggled to catch up with our studies, more so my brother. His exam results indicated a lack of concentration, and

PART 2

he never regained focus from that time onwards. It was towards the end of the school year; so, initially, there were no places in the classes appropriate for us. Yet the headmaster had taken us in after a generous donation from my mother. I was placed in a small class with children who were 'backward'. These days we use the phrase 'learning difficulties'. My brother missed lessons due to overcrowding and was often left sitting outside the headmaster's office. Places in the correct classes needed reorganisation to accommodate us. It took a week or more before we were settled into our correct classes.

Looking around, I wondered, *Who are all these strange children?* I sat at my wooden desk wishing the floor would open and swallow me up. I kept imagining that, if I slipped down low enough in my seat, I would disappear into the floor and be gone forever, *hopefully to a magical place.* I longed to go back home to Northcliff, to my 'proper school', to dance classes, snowdrops, glow worms, the giant Oak and my friend Abraham. *He would take care of me. He would!* I was distraught and very lonely at Twist Street.

Doris and Nicholas invited my mother to take tea with them almost every day. They were a gregarious, propertied couple, yet I do believe they understood my mother's delicate position. They had known her since my birth. Doris and Nick were in their sixties and had lived interesting lives. Doris and Nick had experienced terrifying times during the war and eventually escaped to South Africa. Life had been good to them since. After going without basic foods for several years in Russia, they developed a taste for the finest food that money could buy. They ate ravenously and frequently and rarely left their home. They had made themselves very comfortable and felt safe there.

Doris was exuberant and spoke even when her large mouth was full, with the overspill spluttering across the starched white linen cloth onto the table where they both spent most of the day. At eight years of age, having had strict table etiquette impressed upon me from an early age, I was fascinated by Doris's table manners and eating habits. Curious by nature, I studied her as she took in big mouthfuls. I would sit watching her large soft mouth chewing and speaking simultaneously, something I was never permitted to do. On the very first occasion, as I sat watching Doris's busy mouth chewing and talking, I decided, *I will keep my own mouth shut.* I watched wide-eyed as large chunks of matzos shot across the table. Later she would pick her teeth to ensure not a morsel was wasted. My eyes remained riveted. Doris often lapsed into a Yiddish dialect, obviously talking about us to Nick. He sat quietly at the head of the table, a gentle smile on his face. He was softly spoken and kind, while Doris was bombastic and had a lot to say about everything.

On other afternoons my mother would take me along to visit the dressmaker, Irma. She had been introduced to my mother by Doris. Irma was a thin, fragile, Dutch woman with a kindly manner. She hobbled around awkwardly with an exaggerated limp, her face creased in discomfort. Irma was obviously always in pain. I became very perturbed by her suffering and what I heard, which was even more horrific. I was too young to hear such things; her stories remained with me for years.

As Irma's life story unfolded, I realised she was not just a dressmaker but someone who had big secrets. Irma had been in a Japanese concentration camp in Java for three years. She spoke of the injuries sustained from beatings with wet bamboo until blood poured. She showed my mother the deep cavity on her left thigh. I did not see the wound, but by my mother's shocked facial expression I knew it was awful. I do believe it was sobering for my mother. At night I would imagine a hole in her leg and for months afterwards I saw Irma's wound in my mind's eye.

Irma never left her home either. She coped well with her little life, provided she was safely indoors. She took in alterations and occasional dressmaking for extra money. Her tall, slim, fair-haired husband was equally reserved and fragile. The left side of his face was badly scarred, his right cheek completely sunken, the cheekbone destroyed from constant beatings with a rubber cosh.

When her handsome son, George, arrived home from Parktown Boys High School during a visit, I swooned. George was taller than average with golden blonde hair that fell low over his eyebrows, hiding his piercing blue eyes and long lashes. His athletic build and striking good looks had me dazzled! George spent nights on a settee; they could only afford a one-bedroom flat. Without any fuss, they made do. This fascinated me after the life I had known up until then, which was one of privilege and plenty. It was the only world I knew until I met Irma and her family.

Irma altered dresses for my mother who had lost weight, her once curvaceous figure, now slimmer and less shapely. Irma made a few dresses for me to keep me going until we arrived in Salisbury. Few clothes had been packed that day we hurriedly left the penthouse. Irma's hands were bony, with long thin fingers that were always ice cold. She constantly apologised as she quickly pinned and rearranged fabric across my body. She hobbled around me, wincing as she moved.

I remember listening closely with eyes wide, transfixed as she spoke of her life in a concentration camp. My mother sat quietly, being a good listener, yet showing little compassion on her pretty, well-made-up face. Irma spoke very openly because she finally had an audience, someone who had time to listen. For her to share her loneliness and inner torment was cathartic and comforting.

At each visit she offered a little more, telling of the constant beatings with wet bamboo and other unimaginable methods of torture expressed in graphic detail. She spoke of the constant terror, of the cruelty: The half cup of gruel per day included maggots, leading to constant hunger. The filth, stench, illness and body weakness, and the dysentery women suffered in her camp while rats gnawed at their dirt-ingrained toes at night. Irma droned on. The stories tumbled out of the fragile woman's mouth, her face tight, her eyes dim, her emotions frozen back in time. Irma relived every moment, her memory clear and alive. Soon my head felt fuzzy, my tummy twisting, the stories conjured up images that burnt into my brain, to be recalled during the night as bad dreams.

Irma continued her story every time we visited. I remembered every detail. I wanted to cry for her, to make her feel better, I wanted to fill the hole in her leg, I wanted her pain to go away, but I was happy she had handsome George to take care of her.

For many years after we left San Francisco I thought of Irma. I felt pleased knowing that the fragile war-damaged humans had produced such a handsome son. He was indeed their gift. They were the epitome of a good, decent family, and yet they had suffered desperately and endured. She showed me what humility looked like. She was grateful for life itself. A valuable lesson indeed.

Time moved swiftly and my mother finally began to accept that the delay of our departure to Rhodesia had to be extended, and we needed to manage as best we could. In those days women did not have a voice, and my mother was complacent in allowing my father to make all the choices for her, without question. She was at heart a gentle soul and quietly accepted what he decided, even though it was not easy for any of us. My father kept sending huge cheques, which kept her reasonably happy.

PART 2

Chapter 14

Russian Royalty

*I am a princess.
All girls are.
Even if they live in tiny old attics.*

Frances Hodgson Burnett. A Little Princess[30]

Nicholas Supkis died quietly in his sleep one night. It was unexpected and a terrible shock for Doris. Two weeks later Doris spoke with my mother about being unable to find a place of calm during the night. She was restless and unable to sleep. The sprawling luxurious flat was empty without Nick, and it no longer felt right to Doris.

Unknown to me, my mother suggested to Doris that I sleep over for a night or two to see if it helped having someone with her.

Doris was delighted. She declared that I would make a perfect companion.

I was nine years old by then, but how could I possibly know how to comfort a grieving widow? How would I know what to say or do? What would be expected of me, living with a devout Jewess in mourning?

The first evening, as I arrived at their top floor flat, I immediately noticed that Nick's single bed had been moved to the lounge and left with crumpled sheets and bedding that I imagined he had died in. The 'death-bed' was pushed into the far corner of the spacious sitting room and looked out of place, a rigid, unwilling object creating a sombre feeling in this usually cheery, bright room. I froze, imagining that I could see the outline of his dead body in the bed.

Doris welcomed me into her home and directed me into the middle of the living room. Walking through the archway into the room, she motioned to the bed, casually telling me that it was where I would sleep that night.

Panic gripped at my throat. Nick had been lying on that bed before he died! *What would happen to me if I lay on his deathbed? Would I get sick and die too?* Fear gripped me. *Would he come back in the dark of night to find me there?* I was petrified and endured a grim sleepless night while Doris snored her head off.

The following afternoon I was sent back to her. Again, Doris slept well with me there while I lay awake with wide, terrified eyes staring at the ceiling, expecting Nick to come back and haunt me for using his bed.

Even in grief, Doris was loud, bombastic and bossy. I felt awkward, shy and uncomfortable being alone with her. She ordered me around like one of her servants. One thing was for certain: Doris had not lost her appetite. From her imposing position sitting on a high-backed dining chair, she would shout commands to me in the kitchen, her voice echoing down the long passageway.

"Do you know how to make a Prawn Cocktail?" she bellowed on the first night.

"No," I whimpered.

Eager to be fed, Doris shouted out how to put together a 'proper prawn cocktail'.

"Oh, don't forget to add the capful of brandy to the mayonnaise!" she shrieked. "Then make sure you set the table properly."

"Don't forget clean napkins for us both!" Instruction for our meal together continued.

Following her precise instructions, I actually managed to put together two cocktails in beautiful crystal champagne saucer glasses. Each glass was filled to the top with prawns coated in the pretty pink sauce.

Then Doris invited me to sit next to her at the table. I placed the starched white linen napkin on my lap, and we began to eat. Doris finished the rich prawn cocktail before I was halfway through mine. It was very rich, and my tummy felt unsettled. Then, I was sent back to the kitchen to cook our fillet steaks.

PART 2

Standing with my chest in line with the sizzling hot pan, I was filled with panic, choking back the tears, overwhelmed and frightened by the intense heat of the stove. I swallowed my tears, took a deep breath and got the job done. I finally sat down with another plate in front of me and watched Doris devour a tender steak, talking as she chewed large forkfuls of rare fillet.

My dining experiences with Doris continued. Each evening we indulged in an elaborate three-course dinner, overseen by Doris from her high-backed chair. She never once rose from her chair to help me.

It did not take many nights with Doris for me to realise that I was becoming some sort of replacement for Nicholas. Doris wanted me to go everywhere with her, treating me like an adult companion. I would have preferred to be at home, but each day I was sent back there.

Fetch this, get me that, sit down here, make me tea. Is dinner ready? Doris would command. I often thought of dear gentle Nick, and how he must have endured her bossiness.

My mother was never invited to visit Doris during the weeks that I stayed there, which was strange. Doris and Nick had been friends with my parents for many years. Since living in their block of flats, my mother had had tea with Doris most days. My mother presumed she was grieving, but Doris never let up using me, either for comfort or cooking for her. Of course, my mother never guessed. I know she would have been horrified. I was, after all, her pretty daughter, not a servant.

Each night Doris would instruct me on how she wanted her meal prepared. While she sat waiting at the carefully laid table, Doris would shout step by step instructions that I had to follow to the letter. Then we dined together. Finally I would creep into Nick's crumpled bed, exhausted, my tummy stuffed with rich food.

On the Saturday of the first week, I was sent upstairs to Doris *for the entire weekend*. I do believe that it suited my mother. One less responsibility. She was unperturbed at my plea to stop sleeping over. Sitting obediently, I listened as Doris spoke endlessly of her life with Nicholas. During these storytelling hours she was larger than life, expressing herself in an animated manner with arms and hands gesticulating and thrashing around in the air, her fleshy body wobbling like a jelly. She would become breathless then slump over the walnut dining table, emotionally spent. I would sit wide-eyed, stiffening as each chapter of their life exploded out of her.

I was a silent, unwilling participant to Doris's life, offering as much interest as any nine-year-old could muster. I was a child. I got bored, confused, and often she made me feel sad. I could hear children gleefully playing in the large garden below as I sat staring longingly towards the huge window, straining to hear every sound, wanting to join in. I had a desperate desire to run away from this bizarre world, from this person I was meant to comfort. Doris was an old woman from another era, another country and a very different world. A world and a time I did not understand.

Later that day, she turned to me and asked, "Have you got something pretty to wear, Delyse? Go down and change. Be back at 5 p.m. because tonight we are dining with a Princess!"

I gulped, my eyes shining at the thought of meeting a Princess! I had a sudden vision of glistening tiaras, diamonds, rubies, sequined ball gowns and regal processions. *Would I need to curtsy?* I skipped along the corridor and down to our flat to make myself worthy of a grand occasion. I was excited. It was a night I would *never forget*.

I arrived on time at Doris's door, dressed in a crisp white blouse with pearl buttons, a gift from my Aunt Alex. A pastel-pink pleated skirt hung softly around my tanned legs. My mother had pinned a small diamond and pearl brooch to my blouse and put small, delicate, pearl earrings on my ears. The finishing touches gave me a more grownup look than my nine years.

I entered the spacious living room of Doris's home through the engraved glass doors. Before me stood the Russian Princess, poised statuesquely, her stature erect, her elegant right arm draped across the marble mantelpiece, her sable-trimmed, shimmering, brocade coat hung to the floor. Her presence exuded grace and dignity. I paused on the threshold of the room and felt my cheeks burning. In my childlike innocence the Princess appeared to have a golden hue around her. There was something in the way she stood, in the way she carried herself that I had never seen before. It was obvious that even living in untamed Africa could never strip away her royal birthright.

The Russian Princess seemed to glide across the thick pile carpet towards me, extending her hand in a warm greeting. I curtsied. She smiled graciously. Then leaning forward, kissed me on both cheeks. I flushed with joy, my tummy in knots of excitement and awe.

"Well, Doris, who is this pretty young lady?"

"This, my dear, is the granddaughter of a Venetian contessa." that is how she introduced me. I have no idea how she knew that. They smiled into each other's eyes amusedly. After the Princess had said a few warm, encouraging words to me, they began speaking in Russian as they ushered me out of the building to a waiting chauffeur-driven car. We got into the long, sleek, black car and sped away into the African night.

There was an air about the people I saw in the magnificent room. Doris casually mentioned that some were Russian nobility in exile. That did not mean anything to me, yet I noticed that each of them carried about them something unique. Was it aristocratic class, style of dress, culture, education? I was not sure, but I was captivated. I was in a *very different world*. It felt like a distant era, one that felt strangely familiar to me. It became clear that they were accustomed to an opulent life that none of them had either forfeited or forgotten.

I was never told who the guests were, nor given the name of the hostess. It was an unnecessary detail for a child, but I was in awe, my eyes big and bright. I was the only child there, and everyone appeared to be slightly amused by this. They addressed each other with genuine affection and gracious gestures. There was sincere courtesy, which was a pleasure to watch. Something about that night touched me. I was deeply moved by it all.

The vast main room with a high-vaulted ceiling filled quickly with elderly guests wearing gold, brocades, velvet and fur, perhaps remnants of lives in Russia and Europe. The splendour before me was like walking into a famous opera house. I stared closely and noticed that their clothes were well worn, as if from a time long gone. In their eyes I saw great sadness that held secrets they would never share. It was as if their minds held a past so different, so troubled, it had to be locked away forever. Conversation was discreet, diplomatic and certainly not conducted in English.

In a smaller adjoining room several large golden icons of holy images hung on the walls. A long row of tall, flickering candles stood on a magnificent carved chest. It looked beautiful, sacred and felt special. There was a golden glow to the room, and the icons were magnificent; yet, to my young eyes they looked sad. The room was draped in heavy, purple velvet curtains tied back with thick gold cords. Most of the guests spent a few quiet moments in that golden hue.

I was then ushered into a banquet hall and guided to a red velvet, high-backed dining chair where I was propped up on a matching cushion. I looked across the long, walnut-inlaid dining table, overwhelmed at what I was about to face. The evening proceeded with decorum and elegance. Doris was in her element, enjoying the conversation—but in a more dignified tone—and every morsel of the elaborate feast.

There was a long interval following the time that caviar and vodka had been served. Guests showed signs of discreet restlessness as they waited for the main course to be served. A whisper in the hostesses ear, and her graceful long neck turned slowly, her eyes smouldered and, in a husky Russian accent, she replied in English, "Dhaarlink... you can't rush perrrfection!" With that, everyone laughed, sipped more champagne and relaxed.

Suddenly a never-ending procession of staff entered the magnificent dining hall, bearing large silver salvers and platters with piping hot food of every description. As the team of smart black servants entered the room, dressed in red jackets trimmed with gold, their ebony skin glistened in the light of the tall candelabras. They were followed by the resident butler, an efficient looking Russian woman; her black hair scraped back off her face, her slanted cats-eyes narrowed as she watched every servant. I watched with some trepidation, expecting her to reveal a leather whip if the hurried servants did not carry out their duties to her liking.

The platters kept coming until the table groaned. It was a feast good enough for a Tsar. I was offered a beautiful glass goblet, embossed with gold, filled with crystal clear water and a splash of sweet wine. My cheeks quickly flushed as I sipped. I was served graciously by the silent team of well-trained staff, eating heartily, using engraved silver cutlery, some with mother of pearl handles. I felt completely at ease amongst the guests.

That night I did not feel as if I were a child. At nine years of age, I felt ancient and wise, with a deep sense of belonging to that world.

PART 2

The evening proceeded, filled with genteel laughter and fine food, but soon after the lavish banquet, along with the diluted wine, I became very sleepy. I rested my head on the padded armrest and fell into a deep sleep.

My mother never asked how the evening was or whom I had met. I never offered details of that most fascinating and mysterious royal night. It was *my secret.*

Chapter 15

Father Comes to Visit

Crying is for plain women.
Pretty women go shopping.

Attributed to Oscar Wilde[31]

My life had changed rapidly since my father left suddenly on that grim morning at the Penthouse in Yeoville. We had survived those hellish weeks living with Aunt Helen and Uncle Mac. The sexual violation would leave me scarred for the rest of my life. It affected me more than I could ever imagine then, surfacing into my conscious mind many years later. The traumatic experience left me suspicious and nervous of any male that came close to me. Those scars remain with me even today. I have worked constantly with my own healing and forgiveness, yet I will never condone the violation of two vulnerable children left in my uncle's care. To him it was only a bit of fun.

By the time we saw my father again, my brother and I were traumatised and disillusioned. We had endured my aunt's insensitivity and coldness towards us and been subjected to nightmare motorbike rides to the dam with my uncle. Living in that unkind environment disturbed me deeply.

On the same day that my father left us, we had been removed from our home to stay with my aunt and uncle for ten days, which quickly became six weeks. From there we had moved to a bachelor flat in Parktown, no larger than a hotel family suite. My father wrote to my mother regularly and sent cash or cheques in every envelope. The accommodation was small, but we believed it was temporary;

PART 2

and financially we were well-cared-for. I had lost count of time. *How long had my father been gone? When had we moved into that flat?* It was vague in my mind, one day blending into the next. I drifted, in a clouded state of mind, as if in a faraway dream.

Without any indication, my father knocked at the door one Friday afternoon. I was bowled over with surprise and delight. I was over the moon with excitement, but my father spent little time with my brother and me once emotional greetings were done. Looking back, my parents showed no outward signs of joy or affection towards each other that day. There was distance and tension between them.

After his warm greetings and our excitement had settled, my parents went into the small kitchen and closed the door. They spent hours locked in intense conversation, their voices droned on late into the night. I am certain that neither of them slept. I slept in fits and starts, waking frequently to hear their voices talking urgently in the distance.

By the following morning it was obvious that my father had acquired a taste of single life and thrived on it. He barely noticed us. He had always been a kind, distant father who was frequently absent. On that occasion I felt an indifference towards me. Or was his mind simply preoccupied? I already knew that I would never be loved, noticed, or understood, by either of my parents.

My father left the flat early that Saturday morning 'to take care of business' and to visit his mother. We were not invited along.

Later in the day my mother began to prepare for a glamorous night out. I had not seen her taking that much care since the Northcliff days. She dressed slowly, did her make-up carefully, considering every detail in the mirror. She chose a classic-cut lilac georgette frock, lightly beaded at the neck and shoulders, the skirt falling in soft folds around her well-shaped legs. Once ready, she stood elegantly in high-heeled diamanté-trimmed sandals. The long drop-diamond earrings she wore, a gift from my father, looked stunning. She was poised and ready for an elegant evening.

I watched her as she stood at the large gilt mirror, her arm resting casually on the carved mantelpiece. I gasped and grinned as she turned. My mother looked beautiful; the magnificent diamond earrings sparkled with her every move.

When my father returned at about 6 p.m., I was sitting on my bed eagerly awaiting his arrival. He kissed my brother and me mechanically and turned his attention to my mother. He walked across the room towards her and stopped, looking at her critically. His words to her were: "Stand up! Don't slouch so."

My mother moved forward a few paces and stood directly in front of him, her blue eyes blazing with rage "Don't you dare compare me with your twenty-year-olds!" They both froze where they stood. I held my breath, too afraid to move.

My brother looked tearful, his big eyes glued to my father.

None of us moved a muscle. No one spoke for what seemed like forever. In those brief moments of utter silence time stood still. *Why had he said that?* My mind was reeling, I felt sick. I sensed that something terrible had happened. The air was thick with tension, my mother rigid as tears collected in the corners of her eyes and slowly rolled down her cheeks. She stood glaring at my father without uttering a word.

I watched them closely, my heart racing, missing a beat as I unconsciously held my breath.

My parents never went on a glamorous dinner date that Saturday night, but retreated to the kitchen with the door firmly shut. Food was forgotten that night, for us all. I lay rigidly in bed, my tummy gurgling and my ears straining to listen. My father's muffled voice could be heard talking persuasively. All she wanted was for him to love and reassure her, soothe her trembling body until all doubt left her and emotional exhaustion disappeared. None of that happened.

Early the following morning my father slipped out of the flat and out of our lives. He was gone before I awoke. I never saw him again until I was almost sixteen. It was never made clear to me or my brother why my father had travelled down from Rhodesia that particular weekend, but I knew that morning: our life as a family had changed forever.

PART III

Time moves swiftly but we feel heavy and slow.
Life and its complexities puzzle us.
We reach for the stars and end up still on the ground.
We feel fooled, frustrated and tired of waiting—
Yet all around us life is shifting:
The world, the people, the government, the very earth and sky.

PART 3

Chapter 16

Edith Vermeulen

*Tell me, what is it you plan to do
with your one wild and precious life?*

Mary Oliver, "The Summer Day"[32]

Soon after my father's swift departure back to Salisbury, life took on an air of uncertainty. Mother was confused and in a fragile emotional state. Although she had the support of Doris and Nick while living in a nearby flat, she was lost without the well-structured life she had enjoyed with my father. Soon, Edith Vermeulen and her henpecked husband, Johnnie, became mother's constant companions.

'Aunty' Edith and 'Uncle' Johnnie had been regular guests at functions held at my parents' home in Northcliff. They were also part of the afternoon tennis crowd. During those days, Aunty Edith was in awe of my parents. She and her sister Molly emulated my mother's fashion style and mannerisms. To them she was 'the belle of the ball' in any circumstance. Edith's three sisters and their husbands were overjoyed to be included in my parents' social crowd.

With my father gone and my mother confused and bewildered, Aunty Edith took the opportunity and stepped into my mother's life to steer her ship. She took my mother, brother and I firmly under her wing, taking on the role of a *de facto* custodian. My mother, with her gentle manner and fragile state, was easily led into things she did not actually want and quietly buckled under Edith's forceful personality. Edith was domineering and could be a bully, but she was also great fun, albeit rather gossipy and talkative. She had an adventurous attitude for her age and was rarely daunted by anything or anyone. But her habit of interfering was to become our nightmare. She often arrived unannounced and wanted to be part of what my mother had planned, or she simply invited herself. She would correct my brother and I, usually wanting us out of the way.

Aunty Edith began arranging *every* detail of my mother's life. Apparently, Edith had tried the same tricks with others; her sisters had become wise to her and steered clear. This new challenge, after my father's hasty departure and the harrowing weeks spent living with my aunt and uncle, was just too much. It began to expose my mother's distress.

The four gregarious sisters—Edith, Molly, Gertie and Tiny—were from good South African stock, a staunch Afrikaans family, possibly even descending from ancestors known historically as the Voortrekkers, the original Dutch–German pioneers who explored and settled in uncharted territories of South Africa. The sisters were a force to be reckoned with. They were tough characters. All of them were physically and emotionally strong and unflinchingly forceful. Of the four sisters, Edith was the most overbearing.

Gertie, the 'plain Jane' of the sisters, appeared to take little care of herself in the way that most society women did. The other sisters, Edith, Molly and Tiny, though heavily built, were glamorous and well groomed. Gertie was quite the opposite. She was a workaholic, giving herself a punishing regimen of fourteen-hour days, never taking time for herself or time to be with her two attractive daughters.

On weekends Gertie's sisters made full use of her home in the affluent suburb of Birdhaven, close to Sandton and the Wanderers Club. On Sunday afternoons Gertie would arrive back from the large residential hotel she owned, slump into a chair and remain there for the rest of the day while the guests already gathered played tennis, swam, prepared food and generally enjoyed a wonderful day. Her husband, Harry, would arrive later from the Wanderers Club, smelling of alcohol, yet always perfectly polite to all the uninvited guests enjoying his luxurious home.

Their youngest daughter, Mandy, a year or two older than myself, had taken on similar qualities to her Aunt Edith, adding to the mix precociousness that had other children running in the opposite direction. She emulated her mother's toughness as she observed her mother managing a successful hotel single-handedly. Gertie commanded discipline from the all-black male staff and could be heard shouting in a high-pitched, steely voice from the kitchen, passage or office. She fooled many with her reserved manner and frumpy looks. She was fearless.

Mandy was tall for her age and looked anything but childlike. From a young age, her parents dressed her to look older in order to gain entry to various clubs, restaurants and licensed eateries. When Gertie ended her long day at Longford Hotel, at approximately 8.30 p.m., they would go to a restaurant or private club to eat and drink. From as young as nine, Mandy was encouraged to wear lipstick, high heels and get her hair professionally styled. She was strikingly attractive and looked well into her teens.

Mandy was a very bright child and an extremely mischievous one! She would bully her friends, children like myself, whose parents socialised together. She was inventive in thinking up weird games for us to play, all for her own amusement. She forced us to do as she commanded and, very sheepishly, we pandered to her demands. From the age of seven I spent frequent weekends thrown together with her at Birdhaven. We became 'friends' by default. In her teens Mandy spent most of her afternoons and evenings waiting for her mother, swanning about the hotel passages and lounges, seeking attention and making mischief in every way possible.

Once my father was no longer in the picture, our lives began changing. For example, when my mother and Gertie's sisters were playing tennis at her home in Birdhaven, Gertie began ignoring me and my mother.

As we moved from pillar to post, finally ending up at Del Monico Mansions, a few minutes' walk from Longford Hotel, I reconnected with Mandy, again by default. She also treated me with indifference and often ignored me when she saw me at the hotel. I presumed that, because of our new lesser position in her mind, I had become inferior to her, but perhaps she was unkind towards others too. I learnt as I grew up in our changing circumstances that the old adage 'money talks' ran deep in South African society. It was a fickle world with no heart.

As time went on, Aunty Edith convinced my mother that we should not continue living in the cramped accommodation that Nick and Doris had kindly offered. At the same time, it must have occurred to Doris that we would not be leaving for Rhodesia for many more months, perhaps longer, and she was vacillating about having us stay on indefinitely.

Within days of having a long, exhausting conversation with my mother about moving, Edith secured a charming furnished flat for us in Hillbrow that looked as pretty as a picture. Before my mother had time to consider moving, Edith had arranged the lease with the owner, collected the keys, bought pastel-coloured paints (a new craze), pretty curtains and set Johnnie and a few casual labourers to work.

Without a proper goodbye to Aunty Doris who had been very good to us, we left San Francisco. For some reason, my mother never visited Aunty Doris once we moved away, and I never saw her again.

They decorated the big, spacious flat beautifully. Using shades of mint-green and neutral brocade fabric for wingback chairs and a two-seater couch, the effect was soft and elegant. Carefully selected antique pieces were arranged in each room. Aunty Edith made the most of the space. Seeing it for the first time, I was delighted to be in such a beautiful big place but could not understand why we did not stay on at San Francisco.

In spite of this positive move, my mother became despondent. Hillbrow was *not* where she had ever expected to find herself living, nor should she have agreed with Edith. She certainly did not belong there. Hillbrow could be harsh, jarring, and daunting. It was totally unfamiliar to us, the wide-eyed newcomers. It was a packed-to-capacity concrete jungle, a new world, and a far cry from the serene, comfortable start I had, or the elegant life my mother had been accustomed to from birth.

My mother's parents had protected her from the harshness of life, living in gated, luxurious, surroundings. Later, for convenience sake, with the two of them living alone in a huge mansion, her parents moved to a more manageable home in Forest Town, close to 'Brenthurst', the 45-acre estate of the Oppenheimer family.[33] Sadly, it was the home where my grandmother was brutally murdered.

Thus, my mother was *way* out of her comfort zone in Hillbrow. Initially she found it impossible to relax in the untamed place, but Aunty Edith encouraged and prodded her to accept a new way of life. For a while my mother was bewildered and directionless, as if on a runaway train going in the wrong direction. She was unprepared for what was happening to her life and ill-equipped to deal with it. These changes had come upon her quickly and without warning. I do believe that she was terrified.

We began to spend too many weekends with Edith and Johnnie Vermeulen. Even our school holidays were often arranged by Aunty Edith. My mother seemed to have no voice where Edith was concerned. Her forceful personality unnerved my mother. Edith soon began checking *our* behaviour and became overbearing. I was already nine going on ten and did not feel this was necessary at all. My brother and I were utterly exhausted, needing to be constantly on guard and on our very best behaviour. My mother became a shrinking violet in Edith's company, and I disliked watching the power Edith held over her. This caused me to treat Edith with caution. I became defensive, my brother even more so. Pleasant times were *not* had by all. It felt as if we were in a constant battle of wills.

In that first year of living in Hillbrow, Edith arranged most of my mother's daytime outings. My mother's life was not her own if Edith was around. On a Sunday, especially during the winter months, which are bitterly cold in Johannesburg, it was usual for families and friends to come together for a traditional Sunday roast, and my mother felt obliged to accept those invitations.

We had been accustomed to having a trained chef prepare our meals with the finest produce and ingredients, following menus usually with a British or Mediterranean flavour. Edith was not a good cook. She cooked infrequently.

Her cooking was basic and homely at best. For Sunday lunch she prepared traditional Afrikaans–Dutch fare, known as 'Boerekos'.[34] That type of food was unknown to us. Aunty Edith insisted on sitting at the head of the table and serving us all. She filled the plates until almost overflowing with thickly sliced roast lamb, large chunks of sweet potato roasted in oil, rice strongly flavoured with turmeric and raisins and boereboontjies,[35] then covered it all in lashings of thick gravy. The plates were swimming and piled to the heavens. The first time we went I groaned. My mother's eyes showed a look of horror. My brother cleaned his plate. The meal was often too robust to digest, but the menu remained the same every Sunday. To this day I am not partial to over-filled plates or sweet and savoury flavours combined.

During the summer months Edith took us to Gertie's home in Birdhaven on Sundays. A large group of friends would arrive there for a day of tennis. Children were ignored and left to entertain themselves.

There were also weekends when Edith would book a tennis court at Van Wyks Rust, a resort outside the city. We would arrive very early on a Sunday morning, Edith and Molly, would commandeer the best picnic rondavel close to their assigned tennis court. Once the cars were unpacked, they would open the picnic hampers and cover the table with delicious foods: a variety of salads, breads, fresh rolls and roasted meats. Thick slices of watermelon stood on ice for afters, with melktert[36] and koeksisters[37] dripped in syrup. It was laid out for us to enjoy throughout the day. It was a super summer feast.

The adults played tennis, stopping after every match for a gin and tonic before going back onto the court. My brother and I were left to fill the day lazily, strolling around the huge resort or watching tennis. If we ventured onto the court during a break in play, we were quickly reminded, "Off the court kids! The grownups want to play."

I would lie in the hot summer sunshine daydreaming, imagining my father arriving at our front door or coming back to fetch me. Eventually as the years passed, I crawled into an imaginary vacuum where I did not feel anything about my father being gone.

After tennis the adults sat in the shaded thatched rondavel for a few hours, downing cold beers, or gin and tonic. We would return home after those Sundays, sunburnt, tired and happy after a carefree day outdoors.

Edith loved men, any-and-all men, more than she cared for her 'stick-in-the-mud' husband, Johnnie, who was shy, lacking in confidence and extremely conservative. He wore his dark hair slicked back with Brylcreem and combed flat to his head. His pigeon-toed gait gave him a sheepish appearance, and he looked shorter than he actually was. Edith ordered Johnnie around in a thundering voice, and he meekly obeyed her every command, muttering and groaning as he went.

Aunty Edith began introducing my mother to men who were usually attached. When we arrived at her high-rise flat, she would already be entertaining, mostly male friends. Bols Brandy and Coca-Cola was the favoured tipple in her home, and glasses were rarely empty.

I was a child in a room full of grown-ups and seemed invisible to them. Yet, as I wandered aimlessly around the huge open-plan lounge and bar area, watching and listening, I overheard uninhibited conversations, and observed actions that were certainly not meant for any child. My mother would get up quietly and leave after an hour or two, taking me with her. She clearly did not approve nor enjoy Edith's soirees. When we left, the afternoon party would still be going strong, but her guests accepted that they needed to be gone before Johnnie got home.

One story that was repeated frequently by the same group of Jewish men was that of 'Bubbles' Schroeder. Bubbles had been murdered many years prior, in Birdhaven. Of course, I *knew* Birdhaven. It was where Mandy lived. My ears pricked up. What I recall of the story was not how it was reported in the news.

In short, it was a story of two privileged young men from well-known, influential, Johannesburg families. The men had a drunken party with a very 'naughty girly' one ill-fated night. They joked and giggled about Bubbles being 'vulgar,' 'common', and 'easy' and mentioned that she had drowned in a swimming pool choking on semen. I had no understanding of those words, but the tone of the conversation felt ugly. There was a lewd, sinister edge to the dark tale. It bothered me, but I was more curious to know who the 'seaman' was who had killed her.

I have no clear idea why that story remained in my mind, perhaps because they spoke of her drowning in a swimming pool. My fear of water back then was still very strong. Or was it the memory and whispers of my grandmother's murder in Johannesburg? I am aware that I was a child and could have misheard. The conversation could have been about a different night when 'Bubbles *nearly drowned* in a pool.' Yet, the story I recall was as I have told it here.

Many months later, my mother and one of her society friends, Aida, discussed the conversations that often took place at Edith's flat about Bubbles. It was a very discreet chat about having been at an elegant party many years before that got completely out of hand once Bubbles arrived. It was obvious that Bubbles was prone to crude and flirtatious behaviour, which was frowned upon by the high-society ladies.

I recently researched the murder case and was surprised to find details of the case completely different from what I often overheard during those boozy afternoons. History tells us that, despite intensive investigations, arrests, court hearings and the news onslaught, the two young men were never charged. They died with their secret intact.

It was obvious that my mother did not enjoy these shameless afternoons and often slipped away soon after she had arrived. She was loyal to my father in spite of his upsetting visit. She had no interest in the odd assortment of overweight, lecherous men. She remained Edith's most glamorous friend and had many admirers, but she ignored them. This new idea of Aunty Edith's did not hold any interest for her, nor did she feel comfortable. My mother resisted those afternoons strongly and became disenchanted with Edith's overbearing ways. She clung to the belief that my father would soon be sending for us, but Edith persisted. She would set up lunch appointments with men friends at smart restaurants while Johnnie was hard at work at the vast 'blacks only' Baragwanath Hospital[38] where he was Secretary to the CEO.

Those lunch dates flowed into the late afternoons at Aunty Edith's high-rise flat. Edith began giving me money to get me out of the way, suggesting to my mother that I go to an afternoon matinee at the Curzon Cinema, even though they both knew that sending a child alone was unheard of, or to the local café for ice cream. She also knew only too well that it was not done for a child of age ten to be walking around with a wad of cash and to be unaccompanied. Edith persisted and eventually my mother sheepishly agreed to send me out. I felt insecure as I walked cautiously through the streets of Hillbrow alone. I had no choice.

Edith Vermeulen was easily bored, and mischief was what she enjoyed. She constantly planned mini-dramas and escapades to fill her life with flavour and colour, unknown to her husband Johnnie or her family. There were even occasional interesting lodgers taken in at the spacious seventh floor flat and secret love affairs, about which she spoke openly in front of me. Then there was her habit of sending 'poison-pen' letters to people, especially those who may have taken a fancy to one of her men friends or who had annoyed her in some way. Sending anonymous letters was not unusual in those days. Today it is texting and emails.

The following year, bored and disenchanted with her many male friends and occasional lovers, with their opinionated conversations and unwanted sexual comments, Edith began afternoon tea parties for her lady friends. The teacups filled with gin or champagne and the afternoons filled with poisonous gossip. Aunty Edith loved to compete with my mother, especially the lifestyle in which my parents had lived before my father left, but she was daring and flamboyant, which came across as slightly vulgar. Once again, I was sent away for entire afternoons, my hand filled with paper money. I would wander aimlessly around Hillbrow until the early evening, then return to her flat. I am aware now that I was lucky never to have been approached.

On one upsetting afternoon visit, I was dragged along by Edith and my mother to visit Ruth. Ruth was a very dear friend of my mother's, and I loved her. She lived in an ultra-modern, exquisitely furnished flat in Bellevue. Ruth, in her late twenties, was stunningly beautiful with a warm personality and a tender heart. I was at an impressionable age and Ruth, with her dark, sultry beauty and glamorous home, was like a movie star to me. She was the most beautiful woman I had ever seen!

Dear beautiful Ruth was 'held captive' by her clandestine lover. Hidden from the world in a quiet, discreet block of flats, she was 'kept' in luxury by her wealthy lover until her tragic end. Her lover, an older married man, visited Ruth each weekday evening after the close of business. They spent loving, passionate, time together in lavish surroundings until nine o'clock each night when he went home to his wife and three sons.

This forbidden love made the hours they shared very precious. It pained him deeply to leave Ruth each night, but his duty was to his wife and children. Ruth's charming lover would insist that she take a strong sedative, to ensure she was "never lonely" nor tempted to venture out of her safe cocoon. The truth was, he did not want her to meet other men. He was besotted by Ruth, mesmerised by her beauty and insanely jealous of his 'prize'. I felt her pain; it made me feel sad.

After a couple of years, Ruth began to resist the night-time ritual, even though she was blindly and foolishly in love with her handsome 'silver fox'. She knew that he was a married, Jewish man with deep loyalty to his family and slowly began to realise that he would never offer her more.

One glorious, sunny afternoon, my mother, Edith, and Ruth sat sipping tall, iced, pink gins. They spoke seriously about her love affair.

I sat inquisitively listening and looking on, but soon became upset and confused by what I heard. I loved Ruth, and she was openly fond of me. *Why was Ruth not allowed out with us? Why was she so very unhappy?* I sensed a darkness to the love affair; even at my age, something felt very wrong. There was deep sadness ingrained in her extravagant surroundings that enveloped me as I entered.

My mother and Edith began to stay intentionally until the early evening when Ruth's lover would arrive, expecting to find Ruth alone. At first, he was surprised and unhappy that she had been entertaining during the afternoons. Edith openly accused him of drugging Ruth out of possessiveness. The conversation became heated and unpleasant. Edith did not mince her words, while Ruth and I sat crying gently in a corner of the lounge. She reached for my hand, and we sat like two children in the midst of a parental row, holding on to each other tightly as the tears ran down our cheeks.

In spite of the blatant accusations, this powerfully persuasive man led Ruth into the bedroom to change into a pretty sheer nightdress and tucked her into bed. I stood at the doorway inquisitively. She looked up at him with a childlike expression of unconditional love as he handed her the sleeping tablet. Without a word, looking directly into his eyes, she swallowed it. He kissed her gently and walked out of the bedroom. He strutted arrogantly into the lounge, picked up his bespoke tailored suit jacket, slung it over his shoulder and left without another word. He had won.

The grownups sat in silence, lost for words. I had this strange feeling in my tummy that something 'bad' was about to happen. I felt ill. My mother and Edith sat in complete silence for what seemed like hours. My mother and I peeped into Ruth's beautiful pink bedroom to find her sound asleep, propped up on pillows. She looked beautiful. We quietly left her flat, the adults in a sombre mood. Several weeks later, after another encounter between Edith and Ruth's lover, it all came to a tragic end.

It was an ordinary weekday afternoon when Ruth decided to place her head into the gas oven. The explosion was heard for miles around. The force of the explosion rocked the street and buildings in the vicinity. The destruction was instant, as was Ruth's death. The kitchen wall blew out, along with parts of Ruth's beautiful body. The free-standing cooker flew across the street, landing on the opposite kerbside; the explosion left a large gaping hole in the side of the building. Ruth could never have been saved.

I was not told about Ruth's death that day. My mother thought it best to say nothing. She was aware of how fond I was of her and even tried to stop me visiting my grandmother that weekend. Although my grandmother did not know her, she lived close to Ruth's flat. Granny had called to tell my mother of the explosion. She had heard the deafening blast from several blocks away.

A week later, walking from the bus stop to my grandmother's flat, I passed Ruth's building. What I saw was an area of the street cordoned off. On the opposite side to the building, a huge pile of blackened debris lay silently. A lump of cold, distorted metal, remnants of the burnt cooker was lying on its side; the oven door no longer attached. There was a large, dark, clotted mass of blood, heated by the sun, and a foul odour hung in the air. I also saw the enormous gaping hole in the wall of the flat on the first floor.

I stood with my eyes closed for a moment, my body heaving as floods of tears burst out of me. The tears ran down my hot cheeks, soaking the top of my dress, and *my heart ached and ached*. I struggled in those moments and, when I came to my senses, I realised that I would never see Ruth again. *She was dead*. With a heavy heart and a tear-stained face, I continued walking. I was shocked by what I saw that day. My imagination was in turmoil for several weeks. In the future I no longer took that route. I made a huge detour to get to my grandmother's home. The fear of gas remained with me as did the sad memory of my beautiful 'movie star' Ruth who paid the ultimate price for falling into forbidden love.

Aunty Edith occasionally took up employment if the company was glamorous and the goods for sale desirable. Of course, those periods of employment were brief. Her job as Manageress at a special bridal shop on Eloff Street, known as Treasures, was my favourite. I would spend hours wandering from floor to floor, running my hands across the array of fine fabrics. I loved the feeling of different textures, colours and all the sparkly items. I frequently stood before the floor-to-ceiling mirror, posing in many of the magnificent diamanté and pearl tiaras. Once Edith got bored, or took what she needed from a job, she left.

Then there was Aunty Edith's spontaneous side. She arranged last minute holidays and summer getaways—usually leisurely holidays on the South Coast. She cleverly coerced my mother into going along. Edith would get a 'bee in her bonnet' and, at a moment's notice, tempt and cajole until my mother finally agreed to go along. Aunty Edith would give us no more than forty-eight hours' notice to be packed and ready to leave before dawn. With glazed eyes and sleepy bodies, we would dress and wait for Edith's arrival in her blue Ford Zephyr Zodiac.

We were like one big (pretend) happy family. Aunty Edith loved that idea, not having any children of her own. For some reason she never went on holiday with her nieces, who were similar in age. For me, these holidays to the seaside were an exhilarating break away, even though every moment of our day was managed. I loved the South Coast, being close to the ocean and having a break from the city. These last-minute adventures were without Uncle Johnnie; he rarely took time off work. I recall only one holiday when Uncle Johnnie joined us.

There were occasional surprises, like the time Aunty Edith brought a handsome young man along. After that holiday, Francis travelled to Margate with us several times. He was studying at the University of the Witwatersrand, commonly known as 'Wits'. Francis, born and raised in Mozambique, was handsome and unassuming. He was tall and slim with large hazel eyes surrounded by thick, black lashes and dark eyebrows. He had distinct cheekbones and a strong jawline with soft, full lips. He was indeed very handsome. Once settled in at the hotel, young women swooned when they saw the handsome olive-skinned Adonis. There was an intensity about him, yet he was easy to be with and kind. He was an enigma; no one knew much about him. Francis preferred the company of my brother and me to that of the grown-ups, perhaps because of his shyness when speaking English. He certainly had no interest in Aunty Edith, much to her disappointment.

Aunty Edith always arrived on schedule to collect us. We would quickly force our cases into the overloaded boot and race off as the first orange rays of sunrise appeared, which gave the morning a warm fuzzy feeling. I held my breath as we drove out of Johannesburg, my eyes transfixed by the beauty of the colourful African sunrise. As we drove out of the city, the sun would barely have risen. Town would be silent, deserted, with teams of street sweepers stirring up dust. The drive to the South Coast of Natal was 450 miles. If the journey went well, we arrived at the hotel by mid-afternoon.

On route, we travelled over the precarious Van Reenan's Pass with its steep winding bends, often the scene of fatal accidents due to reckless driving and severe weather changes. Fog could appear quite suddenly, veiling the road ahead with a thick, eery, blanket of damp mist, making it difficult to see other vehicles. Johnnie or Francis and occasionally one of us, would have to walk cautiously in front of the car, guiding Aunty Edith to ensure she did not hit anything hidden by dense fog. It was painstakingly slow and dangerous. We sat forward in our seats to help guide or alert Aunty Edith. Of course, it was exciting for my brother and me. We loved the adventurous journey to the seaside!

Once the drive down to the South Coast was over, and everyone had relaxed, Edith became her demanding self. As we stepped into the hotel foyer she began. Because she was paying the bill, she felt it gave her permission to control everything. My mother would kowtow to her every whim. We had to restrict our enthusiasm, which was little fun for a child at the seaside, but being away from Hillbrow and our startling circumstances, my brother and I relished the adventure and the freedom.

The hotel was welcoming. It was spacious and relaxed; the reception area was light and open, filled with beautiful flowers and plants. Tall sprays of bright pink, purple and red bougainvillea filled the corners of the long reception desk. The effect was exotic. It seemed to blend with the colour of the sea view from the huge, glass-panelled, windows. This was a subtropical paradise. The hotel itself was homely and family orientated. Most families were regular guests. It was informal with smells of homely cooking hovering in the warm air. A delicious afternoon tea buffet was set out, waiting for us. I felt so happy that I did a few twirls and pirouettes, my excitement bubbling over as we were being checked in.

The beach, with its long stretch of perfect white sand was magnificent. Each day we busily explored the rock pools. While I would be paddling at the water's edge, tiptoeing into the water with trepidation, my brother would dive headfirst into the waves, swimming out further. The sea water felt gentle and soft on my feet, but I was aware of its power from my past experience when I had floated away into a weightless void of its silence. I was cautious near water, aware of the danger, yet I loved the ocean's blue beauty.

In the evenings we took a stroll together along the promenade before finally retiring for the night. We walked silently, the grownups lost in thought or admiring the lights on the ocean with the sound of breaking waves where the white sand met the arc of frothy water at its edge. It was heavenly. As we strolled, I loved the smell of salt in the air and in my lungs. I would lick my lips to taste the warm saltiness. I loved being at the seaside. I was a happy child there and fell into deep restful sleep each night.

I have never returned to Margate as an adult, but my memories of those holidays are precious. I did not enjoy another holiday after those few spur-of-the-moment trips with Aunty Edith for more than a decade.

Edith and Johnnie featured for those few years and then disappeared from my mother's social life as swiftly as they had arrived. Once we moved from the pretty flat that Edith and Johnnie had spent time and money decorating for my mother, we rarely heard from them. I can imagine that Edith stepped back intentionally. She had taken charge of my mother's life, rather forcefully some might say, but in her opinion she had done her best to support my mother.

My mother was stuck in a groove of living a certain way, of continuing life with an unwavering set of ideals and principles. She was unwilling to adapt to anything other and refused to move on without my father. It was clear for all her friends to see that the once smiling, elegant, woman was slowly losing her way, and it made friends uncomfortable. They gradually stopped calling. She began to befriend people who asked no questions and did not challenge her.

Each day she was expectant, hoping that it was *the day* that *the* letter would arrive from my father, finally asking her to join him, in spite of *everything she knew about him* by then. She had no idea how to stand on her own two feet. She had been spoilt and privileged all of her life. She expected her husband, for better or worse, to provide for her and to take good care of her.

Managing without my father was a foreign concept to her. The wonderful life she had lived up until that time had been turned into a sort of hell for us all. She loved him blindly. Her heart shattered into too many pieces to mend. My delicate, spoilt mother did not know how to put her life back together. She needed him. She had expectations that no one else would ever meet.

Dearest, gracious, delicate mother left fragments of herself, like rubble, at every home we left. She wanted her old life back, a grand home filled with fun, laughter, dancing, and glittering, glamorous parties. My mother continued her long wait to be rescued and saved like a damsel in distress in a Greek tragedy, but that was not about to happen.

9 August 1956: Women from the Black Sash march to the Union Buildings in Pretoria to protest against the pass laws.[39]

9 December 1956: The Treason Trial begins.
156 prisoners were at the official hearing, including Nelson Mandela.

PART 3

Chapter 17

Hillbrow

*The loneliest moment in someone's life
is when they are watching their whole world fall apart,
and all they can do is stare blankly.*

Attributed to F. Scott Fitzgerald[40]

In the 1950s Hillbrow became known as 'flatland'. The once very flat terrain was quickly filled with tall blocks of flats of varying quality and facilities. The intention behind all the high-rise blocks had been for luxury living in serviced flats offering a wide range of attractive housing for a rapidly expanding white population in that area. Large investments allowed for these buildings to shoot up everywhere, creating a concrete jungle where little sun penetrated, and every open green space soon vanished.

It was an exciting place to be, with a kaleidoscope of shops, blocks of flats, hotels and residential lodgings to suit people from all walks of life. Many happened to be passing through and decided to stay; others were escaping from a life elsewhere. Then there were young 'out-of-towners' seeking adventure at any price. It became a high-rise melting pot!

This area of Johannesburg held extraordinary moments for many. All around there would be music playing: penny whistles, homemade drums, guitars. It was the time when Kwela music was born. The sound of Spokes Mashiyane[41] with his penny-whistle would be in the air with crowds of black and white adults together on street corners listening to these untamed musicians beating out new sounds of foot-tapping music, a mix of tribal and rock.

PART 3

On the weekends impromptu bands would come together on street corners with any number of whistlers, guitarists, and deep bass sounds made from wooden tea-crates, a stick, and a length of string. These self-taught black musicians attracted huge crowds on the streets of Hillbrow. People, young and old, black and white, would stop to listen, feet tapping, bodies gyrating as many danced together wildly in the street.

Whenever I saw a band forming below our balcony, I would run down to join the crowd gathering. The music was so contagious that I could not resist tapping my toes and wiggling along with it. These music sessions were impromptu and illegal. If we heard a siren or saw police approaching in the distance, we would scatter, racing at high speed in different directions, hiding in lanes or strolling away nonchalantly. We would hang about and in less than fifteen minutes would hear music starting up again in the distance. A crowd would collect and run towards the sound and begin to dance again with more people joining in. This would continue for several hours. Oh, it was so exciting!

What an exhilarating but dangerous time it was in Hillbrow. Besides the dancing, there was the fashion and style of the time that had jaws dropping, languages not previously heard, and foods never tasted before. It was totally bedazzling. But there were other adjustments, like the 24/7 noise factor: the general hustle and bustle, loud music, shouting, shots fired, cars speeding up and down Claim Street in both directions at all hours, police sirens, fist fights, verbal arguments and wild screaming. I would lie awake, rigid in my bed, listening to unfamiliar, frightening sounds echoing through the streets, my heart pounding.

Across the street, outside the Hamburger Club, gleaming motorbikes pulled up at the new American-style diner that, for the first time in South Africa, served the finest beef hamburgers with golden fries. This style of food was unique and never tried before. It was all part of the Rock-n-Roll era. The place was heaving every night. Bikers, including the Hell's Angels wearing black leather jackets and chains with peace symbols around their necks, would roar along Claim Street and pull onto the pavement outside the entrance to the Hamburger Club, commandeering the entire pavement. People would stop and stare. The tension with the arrival of the legendary Hell's Angels was palpable. *They were not to be messed with.*

Little did we know that a 'new time' was being born in South Africa and the world. The changes became more obvious by 1958: Brigitte Bardot was the new pouting cover girl, Ricky Nelson was on the cover of *Life* magazine, Elvis Presley had us gyrating to a new Rock-n-Roll beat with his records topping the charts around the world! New music, new fashion and constant liveliness—it was unique, it was exciting, with uninhibited behaviour that had every young head spinning.

By the 1960s accommodations, especially the high-rise flats, were alive with young, white, single people. The night life buzzed. Hillbrow became the wild, beating heart of Johannesburg. For the white population back then, Hillbrow appeared to have been born suddenly, with no strategy for future expansion and development. Almost overnight it became overpopulated and overcrowded.

This period in time was also the beginning of my own realisation that there was more than one level of life going on in South Africa. Firstly, there were the 'haves' and the 'have nots'. You only had to look around to see evidence of inequality and hardship. We young ones did not understand it yet, but it was the beginning of change in the country as a whole. That beautiful land—filled with pain and pleasure—was about to face *radical change at any price.*

Our parents *did not* see change coming. They were living 'the high-life' of 'well off' whites, living in comfort while black people were forced to live a life of deprivation and degradation. Eventually, the black population became driven by a need for money, and their anger led to the emergence of an underworld of crime and corruption in Hillbrow. This made Hillbrow a daunting yet exciting place to live. With its total lack of sophistication, the raw qualities of life were exposed.

What I witnessed was often harsh and difficult to grasp; it had me overwhelmed, with many people behaving in a wild and untamed manner. There were moments when I longed for the days-gone-by when I had felt safe and secure, when life was 'normal'. As a family, we continued a bizarre day-to-day existence in which the three of us still waited for an unknown future in another country with no news of the move to Rhodesia on the horizon. Were we going anywhere, or nowhere? Was this an exciting new beginning, or a dramatic ending? There we were: a mother, two children and our tarnished lives.

My brother and I had no guidelines to follow, no structure in place for that chapter of life, and no explanations of what the future would hold. My mother gave us no support as she herself struggled to adjust to this bizarre new life. She presented herself as a confident stylish mother, showing the world that we were fine, but we were struggling to find emotional stability, and at my age it was easy to conjure up the most awful scenarios. I became a cautious observer of life, taking each step with trepidation, dismayed and perplexed with everything unfamiliar.

Coming from the leafy affluent suburbs and a privileged life, there had always been a rather formal structure in place that held our lives together. Good etiquette, fine manners, and the perfect household management were at its core. Hillbrow was the complete opposite; a contradiction to everything I had been taught. I was unable to grasp where I belonged or how to fit in.

After several months of living in the area, something inside myself told me that to survive I needed to set my own boundaries and make my own rules. With that in my unconscious mind, I slowly began to accept what I saw on the streets and eventually became sensitised to the eclectic mix of people and their behaviour. It was an unsettling chapter in my life, with experiences we could never have anticipated or expected.

My mother in haute couture outfits—even with her limited wardrobe, with her possessions in storage ready for Rhodesia—was still centre stage wherever she went. By Hillbrow standards, she was stunningly attractive, elegant and slightly overdressed. In her mind she was dressing down. Many women stared, brazenly envying her style. She seemed unflustered, often looking as if she had stepped out of *Vogue*. She received constant stares but paid no notice. When we ventured out together, she walked slightly ahead of us with practised confidence.

There was something about the way she carried herself that made her look as if she were gliding along on a thick pile carpet. She would breeze into the local Post Office to post letters to my father, her long silk stole trailing behind her, slightly off the shoulder. She would glance around at the people and smile with indulgent graciousness. The young man behind the counter always became rosy-cheeked and flustered.

My mother was open and friendly to anyone who struck up a conversation with her, yet she appeared to be out of place, overdressed and perhaps too 'posh' for Hillbrow. Those who befriended her were fascinated and intrigued. The glamorous lifestyle continued, but I was growing up fast, becoming more aware of what was happening at home.

Arranging company to share sundowners with her each evening encouraged my mother to make new friends at parties she attended. She was often out, leaving us completely alone. Friends like Edith, Anne, Margo or other friends would send a car for her most Saturday evenings. We were never told where she was going, how to reach her or when she would be home. When a chauffeur-driven car arrived for her, she would sweep her silver fox fur around her shoulders, her long diamond-drop earrings swinging, as she waltzed out of the front door with just a hint of theatre for good measure.

We continued living in the comfortable, pretty, flat with its large, open, third-floor balcony. My mother placed chairs, tables and a divan out there and added tall, lush, plants and dozens of flowering pot plants, creating a blaze of colour in the summer months. We sat out there often, but rarely together. From the third floor we looked onto the Summit Club. I would stand watching the comings and goings in Claim Street and the Hamburger Club, from the safety of the balcony, which was on the corner, diagonally across from our block of flats. I viewed it all from the safety of the balcony.

My brother and I began attending Saturday morning movies at the Curzon Cinema. The children's morning show had rapidly grown in popularity. We had our own pocket-money, which my father sent in his weekly letters. We left home early in the morning, with not a word to my mother, and each took along an armful of comics to swap before the show. There would be a long queue of children dressed in the latest fashions, ready to swap with us: there was Dagwood and Blondie, Little Lulu, Jughead, Donald Duck, Casper the Ghost, Woody Woodpecker and many others on offer. It was the highlight of our week.

Soon after we moved to Hillbrow my mother discovered that, on a dark, stormy night, Mickey had physically kicked Lavinia out of their home. After many happy years of living together, Mickey had found

PART 3

a younger version of Lavinia, which came as a complete shock to her. She had nowhere to go and no cash on hand. It was before the arrival of credit cards, and she was too proud to ask for help. Lavinia spent a few dangerous nights sleeping in her car before contacting her ex-husband's family who moved her into a luxury high-rise flat in Hillbrow.

Lavinia was devastated by Mickey's actions and never fully recovered. I remember the first time my mother and I visited her new flat. She was in floods of tears and unable to pull herself together. Her flawless fine skin was blotchy and red, her eyes puffy and swollen.

Much like my mother, Lavinia had never suspected Mickey of being unfaithful, nor anticipated such a dramatic end. He sent her away without access to a penny. In those days wealthy men held women hostage with tight purse strings and a controlling iron grip. Mickey and Lavinia never saw each other again. My father and Mickey had a cavalier attitude towards those they loved and cared for.

My mother and Lavinia visited each other often. She was a refined woman, a real classy lady. I was captivated by her Nordic beauty, her quietly spoken voice and natural grace. Once over the shock, she began a new life. With her medical background she was able to find an excellent job, even though few women worked in those days.

Slowly, my mother and Lavinia drifted apart. She saw that my mother was attached to the same fickle, glittering, social scene and was prepared to keep on waiting for my father. Lavinia moved on successfully.

Fashion in Johannesburg was changing fast, and it usually began in Hillbrow. In the late 1950s when I lived there, white girls were daring enough to wear skin-tight cropped pants in bright colours or blue Levi denim. Then there were the wide, full skirts with stiff net organza petticoats; girls wore two petticoats for exaggerated fullness. The skirts stood so wide that it was difficult to walk by on the pavement. The wide skirts bounced as you walked. Tight, elasticised, buckle belts were the final touch, showing off tiny waistlines. I had to wait until my thirteenth birthday for my first pair of 'kitten heels'. Other fashionable shoes, with pointed toes and high thin heels, made walking painful and precarious.

PART 3

With every new experience there was a sense of uncertainty in the fast-developing neighbourhood. I kept close to my brother during the initial months of living in this strange place. I needed him by my side. At first, he was a real comfort to me.

2018: Hillbrow is the most feared neighbourhood in S.A. It is one square kilometre in size.

PART 3

Chapter 18

Tea for Two

It is a miracle of a city, especially considering it was founded in a frenzy of greed and oppression.

Di Brown, The Roaming Giraffe[42]

On a Saturday morning, the city of Johannesburg was crowded with shoppers. There was always a lively bustle in the town, with a hubbub of activity as people dashed this way and that. After moving to Hillbrow, my mother took Daryl and me for tea with Granny at the enormous OK Bazaars in central Johannesburg. OK Bazaars had been a revolutionary retail concept. It was the first store to buy directly from the manufacturer and cut out the middleman. It was an instant success, and eventually there were one hundred stores nationwide. My grandmother never shopped in the store but took morning tea there when she was in town. She knew that the manageress of their tearoom would take special care of her.

Mother and I continued to meet Granny once a month after that, but Daryl had no interest in joining us. Once my father's intentions became less committed or honest, my mother slowly moved away from his family, even though she adored her mother-in-law. I do believe my mother's decision to retreat was more out of shame, combined with the disappointment my grandmother and mother felt about my father. My grandmother was devastated by my father's behaviour towards us. She never came to terms with her two sons leaving Johannesburg and having to fend for herself without their financial support, which was customary in a Greek family.

OK Bazaars Tea Room became a regular meeting place for my grandmother and me after my mother distanced herself from my father's family. Although only ten, I had become accustomed to going places on my own, and greatly valued spending time with Granny. We spoke on the phone regularly and made our own arrangements.

When we arrived at the OK Bazaar Tea Room, the manageress would rush forward to greet my grandmother. Her gracious dignity—that of a great lady of the Venetian Court—intrigued everyone wherever she went. Granny would be ushered in ahead of the queue and treated much like royalty.

My grandmother, who had kept to the elegant timeless fashions of the 30s and 40s, wore elegant hats, perhaps adorned with peacock feathers, elbow-length gloves and patent leather shoes. Her clothes, remarkable in their quality and formality, made a grand entrance at the OK Bazaars as we were led to the best table.

I looked forward to those Saturday mornings, always feeling great joy at taking tea with Granny. I felt privileged to be out with her. *I adored my grandmother.* I miss her to this day. She taught me about poise and grace, elegance and moderate behaviour, yet her Greek passion could burst forth in a moment. On those occasions my grandmother became animated, vivacious and vibrant. She also taught me to care about myself, to remember that I was special. She showed me quiet confidence, patience, quietude, generosity and, above all else, kindness. From an early age she instilled in me a strong sense of self belief. My grandmother made me feel proud of my heritage and deeply loved.

The Manageress at OK Bazaars would escort us to my grandmother's special table. Heads would turn and stare. Her usual table overlooked the bandstand from the upper tier of the restaurant, and the resident band would be playing softly in the background. Elegant fashion models did their daily parade. They knew my grandmother and would stop at the table, do a twirl, then stand motionless while she examined the fabric and took a closer look at the style and cut of the garment on display. The fashion shows were a unique way of advertising the store's fashion department; an array of professional mannequins commanded attention with style and flair. Everyone enjoyed it, and it was sheer delight for a girl of my age. I loved the fashion show, the treats, and the understated attention my grandmother received wherever we went.

PART 3

Being amongst stylish and beautiful women from a young age was a wonderful foundation for my early entrance into adult life. It certainly rubbed off on me. Those mornings with my grandmother are amongst my most precious childhood memories.

PART 3

Chapter 19

Carney and John

*They were so awfully rich
but so awfully common...*

Carney and John Steyn were a unique Afrikaans couple. They were adventurous, exciting hosts and wonderful parents to their two children, Peert and Heloise, who were childhood friends of ours. We got on very well as two families.

John was descended from an old pioneering family, well established in Pretoria. His forefathers had been Afrikaner settlers who eventually owned vast amounts of farmland in the Transvaal, soon becoming a wealthy farming family. John's father had been successful in both the city business world and in merino sheep farming. The large farm continued to expand and grow, managed by a white Afrikaner with dozens of black farm labourers at his disposal. The farm was a long, pleasant, scenic drive outside of Pretoria

When John was approximately thirty-five years of age, his father died suddenly, and he inherited a significant amount of money, more than he had ever anticipated, imagined, or dreamed of. Much like my father, Johnny was not a hands-on farmer. He had been involved in multiple business ventures with his father in the Transvaal. The farm was left in the capable hands of the manager and his team.

Once he received his inheritance, Johnny retired and set about enjoying his massive wealth with family and friends. Everything from that day forward was aimed at pleasure and enjoyment, but he took it to extremes with everything too elaborate, lavish and over the top. Each day was filled with glorious fun for adults and children alike. To be part of any event or activity with them was pure theatre. Carney and John were dynamic. They carried an effervescent spirit of fun, with John, a natural prankster, who played boyish pranks at their own parties on expensively dressed female guests. They were both high-spirited, loved life and enjoyed sharing their wealth with others.

After my father had been in Rhodesia for some time and my brother and I felt more settled, we began going up to Pretoria during many of our school holidays. My mother never accompanied us. I did wonder later why she was left at home alone. Was it her choice to remain, giving her space and time to do her own thing, or was my mother intentionally excluded?

A luxury car would arrive to collect us. Once settled, we were taken on a leisurely drive up to their large double-storied mansion in Muckelneuk, Pretoria. The family would be there to welcome us. I loved the Steyn family and felt welcome in that boisterous atmosphere.

Christmas during those years was a magical annual event. A Christmas wonderland was created each December on the extensive back lawn. Christmas gifts were extravagant, often jaw dropping. Meals were lavish, the tables bountiful. Throughout the festive season a banquet was held every evening and always included a surprise. Each meal was a sumptuous treat, offered to young and old alike. It brought so much joy to us all.

The grounds were ornately decorated with thousands of fairy lights, set up the week before Christmas. The colossal Christmas tree seemed to reach the sky. It was placed on the back lawn and expertly decorated. There were copious amounts of tinsel, thousands of sparkling lights, coloured baubles and, finally, priceless decorations. The lawn was covered in 'snow'. It was pure magic, whatever your age.

A second Christmas tree was placed in the enormous rectangular 'entertainment room' with its floor-to-ceiling glass walls and sliding glass panels. The glass panels led directly onto the back lawn, which was overlooked by the main house. The high ceilings and glass walls were a striking backdrop for the indulgent Christmas and New Year events held during those years. The Christmas tree in the entertainment room was also magnificent. For me, it held the real magic. Once that tree was tastefully decorated, the floor space directly beneath was covered with dozens upon dozens of elaborately wrapped gifts.

On Christmas Eve all the children were gathered on the lawn. Overhead a helicopter hovered. By then we were shivering with anticipation and over excitement. The helicopter landed expertly, away from the house, on a perfectly green manicured lawn. 'Father Christmas' and the 'Christmas Fairy' stepped out of the helicopter onto the lawn. The helicopter would lift straight up and fly away while we shrieked joyously and screamed with delight. Father Christmas carried a huge sack filled with gifts. All the high-spirited children rushed forward to greet him, eyes wide, filled with wonder. The Christmas Fairy was dressed in a shimmering white lace gown, covered in sparkling sequins, rainbow crystals and silver beads. The bodice shone like a rainbow as thousands of crystals, sequins, beads and silver embroidery were caught in the lights. It was a magnificent ball gown, perfect for our Christmas Fairy.

My eyes would fill with tears of child-like wonder as the sparkling Fairy ran around and around the lawn, waving her magic wand. I was mesmerised. *I had never seen anything so beautiful.* She shimmered in the array of brightly coloured lights that adorned the majestic Christmas tree; her magnificent diamanté crown glistened and sparkled with every turn. Father Christmas chuckled and laughed as he handed us several gifts each. A while later, we all stood in awe, watching wide-eyed when the helicopter returned and swept them away. *Oh, what fun we had!*

Sometime later that evening, Carney and John would rejoin their guests. Then the adult fun began. It was a raucous night filled with laughter and a warm feeling of generosity and sincere goodwill.

Towards the end of the Christmas party the extended black house staff and their families were invited to come to the entertainment room to receive gifts, food hampers, and toys for their children, who had bright, dark eyes bulging with delight and disbelief. Humbling moments for the privileged white guests, as a hat was passed around to the men and piles of cash soon filled it. A well-earned bonus was shared amongst the hard-working staff who were on duty around the clock.

The delightful Christmas celebrations continued for about three days. We slept when we were tired and, when we woke, got ready to rejoin the party in the entertainment room. Staff were on standby in the dining room where a buffet breakfast was served until midday.

All of the house staff were there to meet our every need. Whatever we wanted, we got. There was fun, food, games, dancing and much laughter. I felt a sense of sheer joy during those wonderful times with the Steyns in Pretoria. After Christmas, I left feeling jubilant. Those Christmas events, even for us, a 'privileged white family' in South Africa, were spectacular and never ever forgotten!

During other school holidays, we would join Peert and Heloise for a farm holiday, unplanned by any adults, allowing us complete freedom to explore, play, swim and engage in childish fun, at times slightly dangerous mischief, but tremendous fun for the four of us. We were a team and did everything together from the moment we opened our eyes. Those holidays gave me a taste of real freedom, which I had never experienced before. They were liberating! My mother's idea of keeping me 'dressed up' in beautiful dresses and with every hair in place was out of the window as soon as we got to the farm. *It was no wonder that I revelled in that environment*, dressed in shorts and shirts, getting dirty and up to a fair amount of mischief.

Long before dawn farm staff would wake us up, wrap us in thick wool blankets and put us in the back of an open truck with a huge wicker basket filled with delicious breakfast food: chunky farm-style meat sandwiches, flasks of coffee sweetened with condensed milk, homemade rusks and chunks of cheese. Off we'd go, driving for miles across the dry farmland, the truck kicking up dust as we sped along and the icy morning air freezing our faces.

A pink and orange sky would slowly appear as the golden sun began to rise. We were able to see hundreds of thickly coated sheep foraging on the land. Their sandy-coloured wool blended with the variety of natural grasses and other plants. The farm workers had keen eyes and would survey the flock, checking them all. Along the way we often came across other animals roaming the land. It was exciting and exhilarating. Hours later we'd arrive back at the farmhouse, fall back into our beds and sleep for a few hours.

Once awake, we would dash out into the bright sunshine to enjoy the rest of that day. We swam, diving into the huge rain-water tanks, or waded into the duck pond, making funny splashing sounds in the heavy water. I was often first into the pond, wading carefully with my toes squelching into the soft muddy bottom layer. On the very first occasion my new white swimsuit instantly became a dull khaki, and I wondered, *What will my mother say?*

We had dangerous bike races on a steep rugged track, daring each other to ride a small three-wheeler down the hill without coming off. *They were exhilarating, dangerous games.* Needless to say, there were many scratches, grazes and often more serious cuts on our knees and elbows. The farm staff were tough men who simply laughed at our bloody elbows and knees.

By the evening, very hungry and dog tired, we were fed on hunks of fresh white bread spread with a thick layer of farm butter, braaied sausages, chops and 'stywe pap'[43] followed by huge slices of juicy watermelon. We always ate the watermelon slices sitting on the lawn, the pink juice running down our arms and faces as we laughed at each other mischievously. After dinner, we sat contentedly around a raging fire with the farm manager and a few of his friends staring into the dancing red flames. Very quickly, our eyes would begin to droop; our beds were calling. We would dive into bed, lights already out, and be transported to dreamland immediately in the pitch-black silence.

A few weeks later, we would arrive back at the house in Pretoria late in the afternoon, slightly battered and bruised but happy to be back with the Steyns who welcomed us affectionately. We were put into hot baths, our wounds attended to by the nannies, our hair, nails and ears cleaned, then we jumped into a giant bed together and, after much giggling and fidgeting, slept soundly.

After several glorious holidays there, I woke one morning back at the house to find that I was the only one left in the huge bed. I wandered along the open-plan passageway to find Heloise. She was sitting quietly with her mother, Carney. She was not feeling well. They seemed distant and aloof that morning and I sensed that I was intruding. There was an atmosphere; and, on that morning, I felt excluded for the first time. Carney was not her usual cheerful self. Nothing was said, but after lunch staff had already packed our cases and, after a cheerful goodbye from the Steyns, we were driven back to Johannesburg rather unexpectedly. We never saw them again.

I have never discovered what happened; but something changed that day. I was puzzled, my brother silent and bewildered. Could my brother and I have been blamed for the rough games we played? I had no idea what I could have done to upset Heloise, but she most certainly did not want to be my friend anymore. Had my brother been rough with Peert, letting his frustration out, or had we simply grown apart as life took us in very different directions? It was a huge loss to me and Daryl. The Steyns had been like a second family. They gave us a sense of belonging and brought joy to our lonely, unpredictable, life. Those times that we spent in Pretoria are memorable and irreplaceable. After *that holiday*, my mother never mentioned the Steyns again.

The four of us were living in very different worlds by then. My brother and I had changed forever. I was beginning to feel that if anyone created any kind of foundation for my life, it would quickly be torn away. Slowly I began to feel fragmented and frightened. I was lonely and unhappy and withdrew from the world around me, never feeling joy or happiness until many years later.

PART 3

Chapter 20

My Brother

*Constantly changing 'home' became a place
where you could scream for help,
but no one was listening*

Life at home began to feel a little harsher each day. There was a noticeable succession of subtle changes. For us, coming from the affluent northern suburbs of Johannesburg where we had been sheltered and protected from lower levels of life, Hillbrow offered up constant shocks and surprises. It had a wild, untamed, slightly uncivilised atmosphere.

There was little news from my father by then, and Mother Dearest shared nothing with us. My brother and I were confused and in the dark because she never discussed when we would be leaving for Rhodesia; perhaps she never knew. Yet for some reason we kept moving house. It was a time of huge uncertainty for the three of us, and I began to feel invisible to her, as if I did not exist. I was not seen, I was not heard, I was an invisible child.

We were living in a very insecure time, with my mother becoming distant and silent when alone with us. She had become noticeably nervous since living in Hillbrow, but her main interest continued to be cultivating a fabulous social life. This included getting her hair shampooed and set and her nails manicured every Friday morning at a top Kotze Street salon, then having her outfits dry cleaned or professionally pressed, ready for the next party or social event. She made sure there was a good selection of drinks in the cabinet for guests who began calling later at night.

My mother's behaviour had become capricious and even more self-absorbed. Daryl and I were beginning to feel the full effects of the constant changes happening around us. Our mother remained oblivious to our needs and we were constantly ignored. Nothing in Hillbrow made either of us feel safe, or secure, and life had an air of impermanence.

There were the dark memories of Uncle Mac hovering over me. I was carrying the unhealed trauma of the sexual abuse that had left me cautious and untrusting. I also carried deep shame and fear and, at times, told myself it had been an awful dream.

My brother was struggling emotionally without our father around; *he definitely needed him*. There was an undercurrent of misery and restlessness about him. He slept on a divan in the sitting room and was expected to get to sleep, even when Mother Dearest entertained, often with music playing loudly and couples dancing. There were nights when he crawled into our mother's bed until the guests left. It was very unsettling for him.

We continued our schooling at Twist Street School, essentially a 'poor' school with raggedy children from underprivileged homes. I felt out of place there. The school had no sports field, swimming pool, or after-school activities. Our walk to and from school was easier from Hillbrow than the long walk my mother had expected us to manage when living in Parktown. That route had taken us around Clarendon Circle, up Twist Street hill, over the rise and down, towards the end of Twist Street, to reach school. On hot afternoons the walk home was arduous. Initially we were given tram-fare, but eventually that, as well as lunch boxes, were forgotten. We walked and went hungry.

Once my father left, my mother no longer employed a full-time nanny because she expected to be leaving. It was a huge adjustment for me and my brother. We were accustomed to staff taking care of us. As far back as I could remember, my mother had never attended to us. My brother and I found ourselves alone in a new world with no direction or structure. Neither of us had any idea how to manage without a nanny and house staff, and my mother had no awareness of how to supervise or care for us. We no longer had our own bedrooms or playroom or a garden. Our school friends and familiar faces from Northcliff and Parkview were gone from our lives forever.

Some may say that we had been spoilt, but up to that point, we knew no other way of life. We had no coping mechanisms in such a different environment, and there was little kindness or comfort shown towards us. Both of us felt insecure in an outlandish world. We were often left completely alone, not knowing where my mother had gone.

My brother began to vacillate between anger and restlessness yet was also showing signs of insecurity and meekness. He seemed frightened in Hillbrow without my father around. My father had been his idol and a strong grounding influence. He was coming up to his teen years and, I suppose, hormones were stirring. He was completely out of his comfort zone.

Our mother lived in her own world and, for a time, Daryl and I were close. Having him by my side gave me a sense of safety. *Together we saw violence on the streets* between the Afrikaans-speaking police and black people that was frightening for children to observe. Such violent actions close to home affected our sense of freedom from then onwards. *We were not aware that we were living in a police state.*

After several months of living in Hillbrow, my brother began to hurt me physically. It began with a random playful punch on the arm, a shove, a swift kick, but it escalated quickly. He began to pursue me. He took every opportunity to get me on my own, even for a moment. He would follow me around the flat or wait for my mother to turn her back, then strike out. He punched with force: both my arms, behind my neck and my head. He was persistent and would punch me again and again. He never uttered a word during or after, but I saw rage in his eyes. I was innocent and taken by surprise at the change in him. Was it my fault?

During those few grim years, my brother became silent, surly, secretive and unresponsive. My arms were black and blue; the back of my neck, where he would knuckle punch me repeatedly, my upper back and head were constantly painful. There were occasions when I was upset by his actions and in pain and lay on my bed in the afternoon, face to the wall, crying softly.

Alas, my Mother never questioned, nor did she ask what was wrong. She turned a blind eye and got on with her life. Her life was all that seemed to matter to her: going out and about with friends or acquaintances, seeing and being seen at all the right places, became all important to her. Perhaps, it was her salvation.

As I recall, during those years of what felt like constant 'punishment', I was saddened and heartsore. With every painful blow the question

Why? was in my heart. I have never felt like a victim but, back then, I was deeply troubled by Daryl's need to hurt me.

He had befriended three siblings who lived in our block of flats. They were many years older than he was. My mother began having sundowners with their parents each evening. Whilst the parents became inebriated, Peter, Louise and Daryl got up to mischief.

They began to 'mess around' after school. Derrick, the eldest, was already working; he was the quiet one. Peter was sixteen and wild. Louise was eighteen and a tomboy. Their British parents were 'ever so proper', but they failed to notice Peter's serious antisocial behaviour. He enticed my brother to join him on his mischievous escapades: stealing books, comics and sweets from local shops, throwing things at passing cars (including ice-cubes), spitting at passing black men and having regular punch-ups with my timid brother, who had no experience of rough boys' games, or fist fights. Peter was a bully, and my brother was out of his depth.

I often wondered if their friendship caused the change in my brother's behaviour. He had become volatile, moody and aggressive. Or had he merely suppressed those tendencies up until then? He may have been a victim of bullying or beatings, but I saw no signs of that.

With hindsight I understand that my brother was venting his rage at my mother, who had never taken charge of her children and without staff around she had no idea how to parent. She also began to disappear into her own inner world from then on.

Chapter 21

Laeticia and China

*Let me tell you this, I am not a loner by choice
But life continues to disappoint...*

My unlikely friendship with an Afrikaans couple, Laeticia and China, began one bright sunny afternoon. The young couple lived in furnished rooms at Sunbeam House on the corner of Banket and van der Merwe Streets. It was a brief walk from our flat, which was then on the corner of Claim and van der Merwe Streets. I could see the building clearly from our balcony. (Sunbeam House still stands today, but the building we lived in no longer exists.)

On that particular afternoon, Laeticia was walking along Claim Street as I was coming out of our building. Innocently I peered into the pram to see her baby. We both smiled and immediately struck up a casual conversation. I had noticed Laeticia from the balcony before. She took her young baby for a walk every afternoon. Her pale delicate skin always looked pink in the dry summer heat, and her curly golden hair would bounce around her face in the sunlight. She had a fresh, youthful glow about her, which made her stand out in Hillbrow.

Laeticia was Afrikaans-speaking and struggled to speak English correctly, even though it was taught at school as one of the two official languages. English and Afrikaans were subjects taught in all schools. She felt comfortable with me. I was a child, which allowed her to feel less self-conscious. We enjoyed being together, and very soon I spent more time with her and her tiny baby than I did at home. She was lonely and bored, away from family and friends and China worked long hours, arriving home after dark.

She made a huge effort to appear positive and upbeat, doing her best to make a go of living in the city of Johannesburg. They were both from Benoni, a small, conservative, Afrikaans-speaking mining town that formed part of the urban east. (It now merges with Johannesburg.) From 1886 the urban east was filled with Europeans who settled in that gold-bearing mining area.

By Hillbrow's standards Laeticia was old-fashioned in style and outlook. She acted older than her age and looked out of place in the vibrant, bustling suburb. She had been a teenage bride and was very immature for nineteen, almost childlike. I had just turned ten but had experienced more of life than she had. My maturity and her immaturity allowed us to converse on a similar level, and we became firm friends.

Until then, I had found it increasingly difficult to make any friends due to moving from school to school. When I became friends with Laeticia, I had already attended four or five different schools with never a chance to integrate, learn how to participate in group activities, or make any foundation friends. I became cautious, shy and detached when I was with other children of my age.

Since my earliest school days, I had become an outsider: independent, aloof and emotionally removed from the mainstream, never voicing what I thought or felt. In contrast, the afternoons spent with Laeticia were filled with light-hearted fun. It was an easy friendship, and I enjoyed being away from my brother, his new wild friends and my mother's flamboyant lifestyle.

Laeticia and China lived in a large, furnished bedsitter. It was dark and slightly untidy, which allowed us to sprawl about wherever we landed. Laeticia placed baby Johan safely on the double bed, clad only in a nappy. We would flop on the bed together and laze about all afternoon. We chatted and giggled, talking about anything and everything, whilst watching baby Johan, who was always happy and content.

On their anniversary, China, a tall, athletic, good-looking twenty-two-year-old, asked me to babysit while they attended a dance to celebrate the occasion. Laeticia was delirious with joy. They had not danced together since their wedding. China had given her money to buy a new gown especially for the occasion.

We had such fun shopping, searching for the perfect ball gown. Laeticia eventually chose a flowing, full-length gown in soft pink tulle. It fell in gentle folds to the floor, the shoulders and short sleeves were embellished with lace, while tiny mother of pearl beads adorned the left side of the bodice, cascading down over the waist, to the hip line. Seeing my friend in a dress fit for a princess was like being in a beautiful dream. She looked beautiful. I daydreamed of going to a dance one day in a dress just like it.

I was apprehensive about the responsibility of babysitting. Both Laeticia and China assured me that Johan knew me well and slept through the night. Plus, they would be at a hotel nearby, where I could easily reach them. I felt far too young for such a responsibility and had no experience with babies. I was scared of taking care of their precious child who was only a few months old.

The evening began well. The weeny bundle was asleep on the bed with me as I lay happily reading my library book. A few hours passed, and I became sleepy. Ever so carefully I rearranged the pillows and lowered myself next to the sleeping bundle, which roused Johan from a deep sleep. He began to whimper, then to cry…and cry he did, wailing and wailing.

I picked him up gently and began to rock him back and forth as I cooed and spoke gently to him. Nothing pacified Johan. He simply would *not* stop crying. His little face was bright red, his lungs and throat exploding with terrifying sounds. I soon became distraught and frightened, *What was I to do?* I kept putting his dummy into his mouth and he would spit it out as he continued screaming loudly, his tiny face red and angry.

After an hour, as I continued rocking him and crying myself, I knew I could not go on much longer. The evening had become a living nightmare!

With shaking hands, I lifted the phone handset and called the hotel. It took a while for staff to locate China and Laeticia in the large ballroom, but very quickly, they arrived back home.

Laetitia swept into the room in her magnificent ball gown and plucked the screaming child from my arms. I was exhausted, upset and tearful and ashamed that I was unable to manage Johan on my own.

China gave me a hug, poured brandy into the cap of the Bols Brandy bottle, and told me to swig it down. I did as I was told. Johan settled in his mother's loving arms after she had breast-fed him, then got cuddles from us all. I began to relax, even though I felt weepy and sad to have spoilt their special evening. I was disappointed with myself.

China made cups of milky Milo and we sat together in silence, sipping our hot drink, watching the tiny bundle. It was very late when China walked me home. I got into bed feeling completely exhausted. It had been a harrowing evening, a shock too, at the fragility of a little human life. I decided then that I would *never* babysit again.

Several months later, my dear friends decided to move back to Benoni. Johannesburg was not for them. At the same time I discovered that we were moving again. Once they left Hillbrow, I rarely heard from Laeticia except for a very occasional newsy letter.

Two years had passed when I received a letter from Laeticia inviting me to spend a long weekend with them. I was taken by surprise but was also excited at the idea of seeing her again. I was aware that much time had passed and my life was very different by then. I was at high school and had grown up a lot. Life had changed me. The time we had shared together in Hillbrow was almost a distant memory. I wondered: *Shall I go?*

Enclosed in the letter was a return train ticket to Benoni that decided the matter. *It'll be an adventure, which I truly need.*

Setting off on a train journey from Johannesburg's Park Station was exciting. *I love trains.* I settled in as the train sped towards the once wealthy gold-mining town on the East Rand.

I arrived at Benoni train station expecting to be met but they were not there. I had the address written down, but was slightly disorientated, arriving at a very different town. I began walking aimlessly around the station, then ventured slowly down the main road. I had never been to the East Rand of Johannesburg and had no idea where I was or where their home was situated. The street was deserted as was the station. I looked around at the sprawling town that was very suburban and the general terrain, totally flat. All the houses on the street were bungalows, the streets wide, bare and quiet. It was not what I expected at all.

In the far distance walking up the road, I could see Laeticia heading in my direction. I took a deep breath, relaxed and felt instant relief.

It was a slightly awkward meeting after such a long time. I was more adult, and she more a young woman than a teenage bride. Living back in Benoni she had become even more old fashioned in her ways, and I had become better educated and well spoken. We took a long, hard, look at one another and realised immediately that we had both changed, matured and grown apart. Life for both of us was no longer the same.

I knew immediately that the reason for my unexpected invitation was to babysit their two children, although nothing had been said in the letter. My heart sank. I was deeply disappointed by the way Laeticia had hidden the true intention behind the invitation.

It was not far to walk, and we were soon at their modest home. They had two children by then and space in the compact bungalow was limited. Neither Laeticia nor China were as playful or friendly, nor did they seem happy as a couple. Life had been tough for them both, as it had been disheartening and challenging for me.

The atmosphere became slightly strained once the purpose of my visit became evident, even though a bundle of money was forced into my hand by China as compensation. I noticed that China was openly flirtatious towards me and Laeticia uneasy having me in their home with my well-developed, womanly figure. It remained uneasy throughout the weekend, but that Friday evening was the highlight. It made the journey worthwhile.

Their new neighbours had invited us to join them for dinner. They were new to Benoni and had no family. The charming young Jewish couple made me feel very welcome. They had been expecting an older person to accompany Laeticia and China, but we took to each other immediately and got on well. Laeticia and China, who were staunch Afrikaners, were stiff and awkward.

I felt very comfortable and relaxed in their new home. The lovely warm-hearted gentleman was the Cantor at the Benoni Synagogue, and the evening proceeded in the traditional manner of a Friday night Shabbat dinner held in Jewish homes. A blessing was offered at the table, followed by a blessing over the loaves of plaited bread. It was beautifully done, reverent and holy. The Cantor sang Shabbat songs between courses and recited verses from his book. I was touched by the sacredness, which continued through the evening. I felt privileged to share food with them, and I have always remembered that special dinner.

The Jewish faith played a big part in my childhood. My parents had many Jewish friends, and it was a very familiar culture to me.

Throughout my early childhood my parents socialised with many such friends. I remembered well the Wednesday night card games attended by a group of them. The card game was taken seriously, being played for high stakes. Chef William prepared special food for them, and I was accustomed to seeing and eating their traditional foods, such as chopped herring, gefilte fish, chopped liver, blinis, and many such dishes.

Saturday evening came and went. I took good care of their two children that evening while Laeticia and China attended an important social event. I woke early on Sunday morning and dressed quietly before they woke. As soon as I was packed and ready, I stepped silently out of the house and walked briskly to the train station.

The air was crisp and fresh and, as I walked, tears ran down my icy cheeks. I was disappointed that we had all changed. I felt a sadness in my heart as the train swept out of the station, racing back towards Johannesburg. I was aware that I was leaving a chapter of my life behind. It had felt different. Long gone were the carefree summer days we spent together. We had been catapulted forward by life with many challenging experiences to face. Nothing would ever be the same again.

Laeticia wrote apologising for not being completely honest and extending another invitation, but I decided to decline. I understood that we had grown apart and had moved in different directions with our lives. We never saw each other again.

Little did I know then that, twenty years later, I would return to live in Benoni where I became extremely successful with several lucrative business ventures.

PART 3

Chapter 22

Weekends

*Yesterday is gone.
and took away its tale.
Today we must live
a fresh story again.*

Rumi[44]

On a Friday afternoon I would arrive home from school, change quickly, pack a small bag and, without a word, leave home for the weekend. When we had moved again, I could walk directly to the bus depot. I walked down into town from Wanderers Street, passing the Johannesburg Train Station. I went through Johannesburg centre, taking a right into Plein Street, then walked the length of Eloff Street, towards the 'whites only' Bus Terminal. From there I took the red double-decker trolly bus to Kensington where my grandmother, Aunt Alexandra and Cousin Norman lived, in a spacious, traditionally furnished bungalow.

Walking down Eloff Street, I loved to window-shop on my way to the Bus Depot. I would gaze wistfully at the beautiful window displays, forgetting that I needed to hurry. It was a long walk, and I needed to be on the bus before dark. Everyone left the city quickly in the evenings; I knew that I would be at risk waiting for a bus alone. I was a child, and children were rarely out alone in Johannesburg.

From my young naive perspective, I never really knew if I was welcome or expected, but I arrived at my grandmother's home every Friday afternoon for years. It was automatic to me: my grandmother loved me, and I wanted to be with her. Once I arrived, she always made me feel very welcome, with joyful demonstrative greetings. I had full use of my cousin Norman's bedroom because he spent his weekends in Highlands North with his father, stepmother and stepsisters. It seemed to me to be an easy, casual arrangement.

PART 3

My aunt spent little time with her son. In fact, the children of our family: Norman, my cousin Antoinette, my brother and I, were never put first or considered. Nothing was even arranged for the children; even birthdays were ignored or turned into an adult party.

I must admit that my father and his siblings seemed to be self-absorbed and somewhat selfish with their time. The children were never a high priority in their lives. When I was younger, Cousin Norman was never around. To my knowledge he was a boarder at a Greek school and spent school holidays with his father and stepmother. He was rarely mentioned. He was never at family lunches and special occasions until he was a young man. I loved my cousin; he was a genuinely nice person. I would have liked to know him better.

During my happy 'normal' weekends, my grandmother and I often sat together, letting time go by unnoticed, sitting in comfortable silences, each in our own wistful daydream. We also spent hours in conversation. I listened intently to Granny's tales. We usually embroidered, knitted or read books—my aunt and I reading in English, while Grandmother read Greek novels. We savoured our favourite chocolates and ate freshly baked cakes and sweet treats with pots of tea constantly being made.

During the autumn months, my grandmother would knit away speedily, making jumpers for my brother, Cousin Norman and me. She cooked delicious dishes in advance for our evening meal, after which my aunt, grandmother and I would sit together contentedly, huge smiles on our faces and a wonderful twinkle in my grandmother's eye. It made her happy to feed me and I *always* delighted to be fed.

The days spent with those women were the complete opposite to my 'real life' with my mother who was never mentioned. I was rarely asked anything of my home life. Even then, this struck me as odd. I wanted to spit it all out: the anguish, the fear, the bewilderment. It was as if my mother did not exist to them. Perhaps they were afraid of what they might hear from me, knowing they were powerless to deal with any of it. Granny was upset by my father's departure and his behaviour towards us, which often had her in tears, but my parents and our home life were an unspoken topic.

Granny had never integrated into South African society. She kept to herself. She was not an outdoorsy type, nor was I. We were happy and content sitting indoors together. Spending time there was a godsend. My grandmother was my saviour, my rock, my light, during uncertain times in my life that often felt so very bleak.

During each hour of those weekends, in the back of my mind, I knew that once Sunday was over, I had to go back to my mother. I never uttered a word to them, holding on tightly to my distress.

Aunt Alexandra became my role model. I looked up to her and loved her dearly. She had one child, my cousin Norman, who was ten years older than me. I was very fond of him and vaguely aware that my aunt had little skill in bringing up a son. She was not comfortable with males or men in general and loved having me around. We chatted and giggled constantly, she was very at ease with me and only comfortable with the women in her immediate circle.

My aunts, Helen and Alexandra, got on extremely well. I don't recall them ever having a cross word or disagreeing on anything; for that reason they never looked outside of the family circle for other friends. They had a very good relationship and spent all of their free time together. During holiday periods the two of them got together to cut and sew new outfits. Their choices were pretty florals and soft fabrics, very different from my mother's well-cut, sophisticated, couturier gowns. They came from two different worlds and lived dissimilar lives.

Except for weekends, my aunt did not keep contact with me to ask how I was, nor did she ever suggest meeting in town on a Saturday morning, even though she went in every Saturday and knew that I would be walking through town to get a bus as she was busy shopping. I never gave it a thought back then, but it was a little strange. Perhaps she needed time for herself. In my mind, my aunt treated me more like a daughter than my mother did and, for many years, we were very close.

Aunt Alexandra unknowingly set standards for me to follow. I wanted to be like her. I watched and I emulated. I loved her reserved graciousness, her soft feminine way of dressing and her kind manner. She had a radiant smile that created a joyful aura around her, yet she was extremely reserved in the company of others. I do believe that I have become a lot like her now, in my 'golden years'.

She was also extremely creative, having inherited my grandmother's patience and skill at needlework and knitting. She always had a sewing needle or knitting needles in her hands and created magnificent garments. She was able to embellish the most simple pattern with wool, silk, or cotton, creating something extraordinary. Her stitching and knitting were so perfect and finely done that her work looked machine made. It was a special gift; one I have rarely seen since.

My aunt lived her life at home with her mother as was customary in a Greek family; she was pampered and spoilt by my grandmother. Perhaps my grandmother carried guilt because of the unsuccessfully arranged marriage my aunt had endured. She was also the youngest. Unlike her sister Helen, my aunt never lifted a finger at home; everything was done for her. This was unusual because it was customary for Greek daughters to do everything for their parents. She sat painting her nails twice a week while Granny did the cooking and took care of their home. Granny and her daughter Alexandra never had a chipped or broken nail. I admired their elegant hands with nails perfectly painted and manicured. Using an old family recipe, my aunts and grandmother made a special hand-exfoliating lotion. The main ingredients were olive oil from Greece, lemons and sugar. Their skin was like velvet.

My aunt worked as Office Manageress/Receptionist in large, bright, relaxed offices at the headquarters of Blue Ribband Dry Cleaners on the border of Bezuidenhout Valley, known locally as 'Bez Valley' and Kensington. Her pleasing disposition, natural elegance, naivety and innocence had men wanting to protect her, and women enjoyed working with her. She was often the centre of attention and the best dressed. She was petite, with a perfect figure, yet ate cake and chocolates most days. Her boss and fellow workers nicknamed her 'Angel' or 'Ang' for short. During the school holidays, my aunt was permitted to take me to her place of work, and I was able to see firsthand, how much she was liked and admired and why she loved her job. She secretly loved all the attention.

My grandmother and aunt's desires for life were simple: to be happy, healthy and live with dignified elegance, as simply and elegantly as the many pretty tablecloths my grandmother carefully embroidered. My aunt embraced whole heartedly the simplicity of her life and never needed more. She was kind and caring to me, yet never intervened in my home life. I looked up to her more than she ever imagined.

There was an innocence and complete naivety in both my aunts. They had been over protected and sheltered by their parents, two brothers, and a small group of Greek friends who were close to my grandmother. In later years, they were strongly influenced by Uncle Mac, who did his utmost to push my brother and me out of the family circle once we were young adults.

My aunts knew little of life outside of their closed circle. They never went out at night to dances, movies or the theatre. Neither of them ever attended nightclubs, parties or concerts, other than suitable functions at my parents' home. Their world seemed to have stood still since the 1940s, after the war. They happily carried that period of time and that lifestyle along with them; it was a time when women were judged by how they kept house, cooked, baked, gardened and stitched. They were always smiling and never offered up an opinion to the menfolk.

My Aunt Alexandra had a provincial attitude towards life; she did not understand the changing world and never questioned her outmoded lifestyle, but both my aunts lived free of stress or pressure, yet with the slightest excuse they could conjure up theatrical mini-dramas and silly gossip within their limited circle.

Once I became a working woman, they took every opportunity to criticise me, especially Aunt Helen. I overlooked their comments because I understood them, and I loved them unconditionally. They remained living in the past, as the world around them changed rapidly. This was commonplace in tight-knit Greek families. My aunts could never envisage, and therefore never asked, how my mother was managing financially or how we were coping without a father. It was beyond their scope of understanding. Aunt Alex would never have imagined that I was unsafe, ignored or neglected, and I never mentioned it. She was completely naive.

Perhaps, because of how my mother was behaving by then, and the unsettling home life I was experiencing, I placed my aunt up on a pedestal. Granny and Aunt Alex set firm unfaltering foundations for my life amongst the confusion, the slow decay of my mother's mind and body, and the instability that she brought to my life.

Every other Sunday morning, Uncle Mac would arrive by car to collect us. Before my father left, Sunday had been 'family day' held at Aunt Helen and Uncle Mac's home. It was a full house, never less that ten or twelve people for a traditional Sunday lunch. It was always an extended lunch, with my Aunt Helen working hard to impress her brother, George, my father. He was extremely important to the two sisters. They looked up to him. Food would flow from the kitchen with my aunts dashing back and forth, seating themselves last.

The table groaned under the weight of the impressive spread: there were several courses starting with a pasta dish, either *pastitsio*[45] or spaghetti with beef *pastitsatha*[46]. Followed by roast leg of lamb, roast chickens with cinnamon, soft roast potatoes, boiled potatoes with oil and lemon dressings, *horta* (wild greens) with lemon, usually foraged and picked by my grandmother. A variety of other vegetables followed by a large platter of Greek salad adorned with '*throubes,*' olives from Corfu, and thick slices of feta cheese with luscious olive oil and lemon dressing.

Much later, desert was served, usually *baklava*[47] and *rizogalo*[48], with fresh fruit. In later years, my cousin Norman's wife, Kay, would indulge us with her mouthwatering *galaktoboureka*[49].

After the extended lunch, the men would remain at the table drinking small cups of strong Greek coffee and occasionally a liqueur. They would spend hours in deep discussions, while in the kitchen a huge clean-up would be underway. When back in the kitchen, my aunts finally began to relax, laughing and joking or talking about one or other of the lunch guests.

My mother never joined my aunts and grandmother in the kitchen but remained with the other guests. She certainly did not expect to carry plates or tidy away the remnants of the lunch table. It was on those occasions that I noticed how my mother placed herself above my aunts in every way.

The kitchen table was covered with leftovers which were soon packed away. My aunts washed every plate, dish and the cutlery at a leisurely pace, happily chatting together. My grandmother would sit at the large kitchen table and enjoy the closeness with her daughters. I would help my aunts or sit with granny, but my mother was never part of that.

Soon after, they would get the tea-trolly ready, laden with homemade cakes: Victorian sponge, *kourabiedes* (shortbread), jam tarts and home baked biscuits.

We would leave there at 6 p.m. on a Sunday evening, each carrying a parcel of treats and leftovers. Aunt Helen packed a parcel for everyone. I became silent in the car on our way back to Granny's home, knowing that once we got there, the weekend was well and truly over. When Uncle Mac dropped us, I quickly packed my bag, then hurried to get the bus back to the centre of Johannesburg, back to my other life. It would be dark by the time I reached the bus depot. I was scared on my own, so I dashed quickly through the deserted streets of Johannesburg city centre. The few loiterers I saw had me breaking into a run until I was over Noord Street bridge. Then I would begin to relax, I was almost home.

Of all the years I am able to recall clearly, my parents never invited my father's family to lunch. Nor was my father permitted to speak Greek at home.

"There will be no Greek spoken in *this* house!" my mother often reminded him. On those occasions he would stare at her with sadness in his big dark eyes, without uttering a word. Yet, she was in love with this Greek—enough to have married him against her parents' wishes. How fickle she was. It hurt my father and confused me.

1960: Assassination attempt on Prime Minister Hendrik Verwoerd at the Rand Easter Show.
David Pratt arrested.

PART 3

Chapter 23

The Ugly Side of Life

The stupidity and selfishness of the average South African in the face of the colour danger is amazing... The patience of the Bantu is equally amazing.

Winifred Holtby—a letter to Vera Brittain[50]

Life in Hillbrow had its own frantic pace. The diverse environment was often a rude awakening, a constant jolt back to the moment. It was a very different reality compared to what I had known before, and I was forced to accept life amongst a puzzling, tangled web, called 'life'. I developed a fascination for what I saw and that helped me to survive. Yet my emotions were trapped in a state of fear and confusion.

I was ten years old and totally neglected by my parents, emotionally and physically, at a time when I was witnessing violence, aggression, street brawls and other outlandish behaviour on the streets. I was in the company of adults living fast and loose, including those who, today, would be considered celebrities. It was disturbing for a child who had, thus far, been protected from the world at large.

What would come next? I often asked myself. The question scared me. *Was there to be yet another new home in an unknown place or land? Were we going nowhere, or was somewhere new waiting for us?*

I began to listen to my mother's conversations. I paid attention to what was said, especially when my father was mentioned. I would prick up my ears and take note. Something felt wrong about his sudden departure, and it nagged at me every single day.

I gradually became aware of a restlessness around me. I heard silent whispers and saw the strong dominant presence of Afrikaans-speaking police, referred to as 'Rottweilers' with their vicious German Shepherd dogs, guns, batons, and sjamboks (heavy leather whips). Then came the 'stop and search' policy that caused more anger and resentment due to the humiliating pass laws.

Extreme crowding in black living quarters, usually at the same premises where they were employed, was a problem. The unfairness of their contrasting life was a puzzlement to me. At times it tormented me. Yet, as an average young 'white girl', I knew nothing of what was really going on behind the scenes with regards to the unfair treatment of 'non-whites'. There was a rough, cruel, manner in the way black people were handled by the South African Police. From a young age, what I saw upset me deeply. There were many occasions when it scared me.

Those who entered the city to work had to endure the laws created for 'blacks only' because the city was where black men could find work. The management of each block of flats, residential hotels, boarding houses, or other establishments supplied these rural men, who kept their buildings and premises spotlessly clean and polished, with live-in quarters. They comprised a small dark room at the back or on the flat concrete rooftops of the buildings. They became known as 'locations in the sky'. The run-down accommodations were shared with other men, allowing no privacy. There were communal washing areas and a toilet with a small communal cooking area.

Black migrant workers, then the backbone of South Africa's labour force, were also lodged in massive single-sex hostels, located close to their workplace, or on the edge of black townships. In many instances, noise, off duty drinking and violence were commonplace. The police frequently raided these areas, and *they were ruthless*. We all knew, saw and heard the stories.

Their living quarters were considered a total 'no-go' area for any white person. Migrant workers found the city way of life a shock. These were men who lived on the land in wide open spaces. Through their ancestors, they understood the sacredness of the land.

One sunny afternoon, a day that has been difficult to bring forth into my memory, an incident occurred directly across from where we lived. At the precise moment it began, I happened to be standing happily on the third-floor balcony that was filled with pretty flowering plants.

A group of black waiters from the Summit Club came out of the back entrance of the club restaurant. The group piled into the narrow back lane. A fight broke out and immediately escalated. *It happened so fast.* From loud shouting and arguing to a group physical fight; a violent brawl erupted, perhaps tribe against tribe.

I stood rigidly looking on, watching the violence. It was soon bloody and frightening, but it held my attention. I was actually frozen to the spot, unable to move a muscle. Then I saw the group turn on just one man. *They began to brutally assault him!* He was punched, kicked and slashed at with knives in a frenzied savage attack.

I was stupefied by the horror, tears streaming down my cheeks, but I kept watching, my eyes glued, my body shaking uncontrollably. I could not speak or move away. My heart was pounding loudly, and I wanted to throw up. *I wanted it to stop!* I tried to scream, but I had no voice. I did not want to see any more, but I was unable to move, my eyes transfixed. *I saw blood flying in every direction.* I began retching.

The men continued, viciously pummelling, stabbing and kicking at the body. Blood was spurting onto the white walls of the building. He was just one man, lying lifelessly on the ground as the group continued the beating, on and on…

Eventually, after what seemed like forever, they stopped suddenly. Staring blankly at the blood-spattered body, the walls, the paving, they turned around without words, and one by one walked back into the club to resume their duties serving customers. Had they killed the defenceless man or left him for dead? They walked away as if nothing had taken place.

I was coughing and retching with shock and sheer terror. *Then it hit me:* Had they seen me watching? I began to shake even more; my body became like a jelly as I slid to the floor. I sat on the balcony floor for what seemed like hours. I was shocked and frightened. I could not move, and I could not stop my body from shaking. Tears flowed for hours, like a gushing river. The men had decided that their victim had to be dealt with, yet his crime may simply have been that he was of a different tribe. I would never know. The deed was done, but it left me completely traumatised for decades.

After a long while I peeped. I saw slight movement from the body. The man began to crawl. He moved forward unbearably slowly, flat on his stomach, inching his body forward, his entire body covered in blood; his white jacket had become a deep shade of red. He crawled painstakingly slowly towards the street, his body shuddering with every movement, leaving a trail of blood, skin and tissue fragments behind.

As I watched his supreme physical effort, I felt silent hysteria building inside me, but I found no voice to scream. My body stiffened with each agonising move he made. The dark trail of blood followed him, and the pool of blood outside the back entrance of the club had begun to congeal in the hot African sun. As the man got to the street, he slumped onto the hot tarmac. It felt final. He had taken his last breath, he never moved again. *He was dead.*

As the thin trail of blood trickled into the street, white people walked by with a quick sideways glance, paying little attention to the blood or the savagely injured black man. It was a bloodied, lifeless, body that only hours before had been a proud working man, a father, a good son, a fellow human.

I was never able to speak of what I had seen that day, even though it tormented me. I could not find my voice to speak of it. I told no one. I became numb, which was easier for me than having to deal with what I had experienced. I suppose I was in shock for weeks, months, possibly years. The vivid pictures of that day came to me most nights and, at times, during the day. The grim bloody picture of that lone man lying in a back alley lived in my memory and disturbed my mind. *I could not shut it out.* The traumatic flashbacks went on into my adult years.

From that day and for several months after, I was unable to stand on the balcony or leave the flat and I was easily frightened by groups of black men. I began to imagine that the attackers may have seen me watching them kill someone and was certain that they would come for me. It was a terrifying time for me then, with a society dominated by strict racial segregation and highly charged energies, ready to explode.

The feelings of unrest on the streets of Hillbrow were palpable. I was too young to understand what was beginning to happen in the country politically and to black people at large, but my body felt it. I was tapping into the imbalanced energy of apartheid through which wealthy white patriarchs with narrow-minded, fear-based ideals, controlled the country. Back then, I was not sure what it was I felt, but I was often uneasy and very sensitive to what took place around me.

I was soon to have a closer encounter with black working men and their living conditions as my life moved forward towards a place called 'nowhere'.

> *The population of Hillbrow is exclusively white other than black men employed as flat-cleaners. They live on the flat, concrete roof tops.*

PART 3

Chapter 24

Jimmy Spills the Beans

*Life changes us.
Sometimes it brings us to our feet.
Sometimes it brings us to our knees.*

Oriah Mountain Dreamer[51]

One hot, dry, summer afternoon, I arrived home from school to find Jimmy, a work colleague of my father's, sitting contentedly in the living room with my mother. She had a pained expression on her face, rather than her usual dimpled smile. As I dropped my satchel in the hallway, I knew immediately that something was wrong.

My parents had often invited Jimmy and his wife, Janet, to their dazzling Saturday night parties held at Northcliff. Jimmy did not move in the same social circles as my parents or that of my father's business associates. His brash, unpolished, cockney manner, along with poor social skills, saw to that. He was an electrician who had done my father and Uncle Mac a few favours. In return, my father had helped Jimmy's small business become known and established.

My father had done a lot for Jimmy over the years and organised a constant flow of work to go his way with good secure contracts. He also offered Jimmy useful contacts in the electrical trade. My father was happy to help him get on, but Jimmy was sly, a chancer, an opportunist and was tolerated mostly because of my father but not liked by anyone in my parents' circle.

I watched Jimmy as he sat casually cross-legged on the wingback chair. He felt no shame speaking about my father in front of me and continued his conversation with my mother, making disparaging comments about my father. He savoured every moment, his jealousy towards my father and our family had grown over the years, and Jimmy had let it fester.

I stood for a long while at the lounge door, staring at him with cold anger, my eyes locked on the awful man. I felt disbelief. It was *my father* he was talking about. My throat became bone dry; it was hard to swallow. It soon became obvious, even at my age, that he was deliberately hurting my mother and discrediting my father. My mother was understandably mortified by what Jimmy was revealing. She was stunned by every word he uttered.

As his tall stories reached an emotional climax, Jimmy's voice became louder. At one point he was almost shouting, the words tumbling out of his big, wide mouth with speed, his thin lips curling around every word. His cockney accent became brash, his lack of refinement more pronounced. Jimmy sat forward in his chair and looked ready to pounce, with glee in his blood-shot eyes. By then, my mother had been reduced to tears. I felt a lump in my throat as I looked on in horror.

After several hours of tears, nose wiping and loud gasps, my mother's bright blue eyes suddenly flashed with rage, something I had never seen before. Jimmy had a smirk across his lips, enjoying every moment as he destroyed my mother's perfect image of her husband and her marriage. He was very aware that my father was her whole world. That afternoon, *Jimmy rocked the very foundations of her life*.

According to Jimmy, my father had numerous affairs and had 'kept' several women over the years. As he announced the cold facts, he seemed proud to have so much information to offer. "Yeah, just around the corner, he set up one of his redheads." He gesticulated wildly with his arm and went on, sparing my mother no detail.

Jimmy was certain that my father had a long-standing affair with a redheaded woman whose place of business was close to where we were living. When their affair ended, Jimmy claimed that my father bought his ex-lover the business as a parting gift. It was a hairdressing salon called Maureen's, named after her. Standing there, listening, my mouth parched, *I knew that my mother would know exactly where the shop was, because I did.*

Jimmy rambled on, enjoying every moment of the vicious gossip, embroidering the stories as he spoke, weaving tales together into an ugly work of art. By then my brother was also back from school. Jimmy showed no consideration towards us. It did not deter him in any way. He did not even acknowledge our presence. Neither of us said a word; we were stunned by the gossip offered so carelessly, telling salacious stories about our father's behaviour. Of course, we did not understand it all, but from my mother's actions, *we knew it was very bad.*

My mother was falling to pieces before our eyes. She adored my father; she trusted him. Jimmy continued with his cache of stories about my father and all his 'other women': women in other countries, other towns, women at horse-racing, women after work, women on a Saturday morning, women, women, women!

"Oh, he is a real bastard!" sneered Jimmy.

Another hour passed. My brother and I, still frozen at the threshold of the living room, all three of us beginning to feel tormented by this man. Too distraught to think straight, my mother's expressions were agonising to watch.

I left the room, feeling deep anguish about what would happen next. I could not help but eavesdrop. My brother came to the bedroom with me. He looked pale and began to cry. *My father was his hero.*

Jimmy's stories became more exaggerated as the afternoon wore on. His manner was flippant, with a spiteful glint in his eyes. He felt no remorse and occasionally even laughed loudly at his claims, while my mother received each thread of gossip as if it were a body blow, her shaking body folding with emotional overwhelm.

He finally reached the finale. According to him, my father was currently living in a luxurious home in Salisbury with his twenty-three-year-old girlfriend. That was the last straw for my mother; she summoned up her strength and told him to leave. As he left, he looked pleased, a wide smile across his deeply lined, sweaty, face.

What Jimmy did that day would prove to be irreparable. It was as if a violent storm had swept through our lives that afternoon. There were no more happy dreams, no sunny days to look forward to. A heavy storm cloud hung over our heads. My mother must have felt very alone, her heart torn apart. The devastation was complete; Jimmy had made her feel unloved and completely worthless.

Had Jimmy *not arrived* on that perfect summer afternoon, our lives may have had a very different outcome. On that particular day, he took my mother's heart and squeezed until it shattered. The deed was done. We never saw Jimmy again.

Months later, once my mother's fragmented mind and shredded heart had slowly begun to heal, she embarked upon a dangerous journey. Little food passed her lips and she stayed up most nights. It was clear that she needed help. She had lost her way. Her actions became unpredictable and her choice of company put us at risk. We did not know it then, but she was travelling speedily towards a complete breakdown.

My love for my father ran cold and suspicious from that day. I was confused and hurt. As a child, I believed he did not love us and wanted us to be unhappy. For a long while after that dreadful day, we were all depleted and sad. It changed us.

I mulled over what I had overheard that day for years and came to realise that Jimmy was extremely jealous of my father. I wondered if the stories were even true. I am sure many were, but Jimmy's long-held jealousy finally erupted that day. He wanted to get back at my father out of spite. It was my father's perfect wife, his luxury life, wealth and irresistible charm, of which Jimmy had none, that he envied. Jimmy felt insignificant compared to my father, yet my parents treated him and his family generously and kindly.

By the time Jimmy left, my mother had begun to turn her shock and grief into hatred. In her mind, every detail was real and true. Without a call to my father or a letter to ask about Jimmy's claims, she severed ties with him immediately, without any real proof; but she was never able to stop loving him. She loved him to her dying day, even though her behaviour showed no signs of that. To the outside world *she did not give a damn* about my father, but I knew. I saw it in her eyes. Their love for each other ran deep.

One afternoon, weeks after Jimmy's visit, my mother dragged me along to bolster her courage to find Maureen's Salon. There it was, but a few blocks away from where we lived. How uncanny. Once my mother found Maureen's she returned there often. She would stand outside the pretty shop and peer in, "Is that her? Yes, I am sure that is…no, maybe it's the taller redhead." She did eventually discover that the tall, graceful, redhead was Maureen. It tormented her for years.

What unfolded that day, and in the days that followed, changed my mother's mental and emotional state *forever*. She was tormented by

Jimmy's stories. She never considered that they may be lies, exaggerated tales, or that he had told them to her for his own malicious pleasure.

Many years later, my mother realised that, after the wonderful years living in Northcliff, my father stopped showering her with lavish gifts, he restricted her spending and kept her stranded at home without the use of a car. She decided that he was obviously spending on other women. My mother had been humiliated, betrayed, ridiculed, and felt completely unlovable. She slowly began to lose faith in herself. Finally, she closed her heart to love. She began to drink more and with that came cynicism. She developed a careless disregard for all of us.

Unknown to my father, when Jimmy came visiting on that hot summer day, he changed our lives forever.

PART 3

Chapter 25

Life Goes On

*Hungry little girl with holy water tears
dreaming of happy summer days of holy love
and forgetting all her fears.*

Early one morning, countless months after Jimmy's bombshell, I woke to the sound of Dean Martin singing 'Volare'. As I rubbed my sleepy eyes, I heard loud voices. I knew that my brother should be asleep on the divan in the lounge, but I could hear laughter, music and voices. I stumbled down the passage from the bedroom my mother and I shared, still rubbing my eyes and ruffling my hair.

As I got to the threshold of the lounge, my mother dashed towards me, grabbing my arm excitedly, pushing me forward and proudly announced: "Look! Look who's here! Say 'hello' to Miss South Africa! It's Norma Vorster!"

Norma was perched on the arm of a chair, her full skirt ballooned around her long, tanned legs. I stood wide-eyed, beaming at her. I was instantly awestruck. There were several other guests there that morning: ladies in fine silk dresses with exotic perfume wafting around and fur stoles draped from slim, golden-tanned shoulders. I stood rooted to the spot staring coyly while everyone laughed at the surprised look on my face. They continued sipping champagne out of mother's best French engraved crystal glasses. It was 7 a.m. on a Sunday morning. My mother was a wonderful hostess. It was what she did best: being the most elegant and gracious, albeit early morning, social butterfly in town. Despite her lack of sleep, she looked vivacious and glamorous.

Life went on in unexpected ways. A few weeks later my mother was invited to attend the Ballroom Dance Championships at City Hall.

Norma was dancing. It was the first big event I had ever attended. I was usually left at home. Edith, my mother's long-standing friend, was being her usual self, bossing my mother around and placing demands upon her. "We are leaving early, and we are travelling in my car."

The glamorous evening began as soon as we walked into the foyer of the City Hall. It was a place of pomp and importance and to me, at my age, it was spectacular. Once the dancing commenced, I was captivated by the glamour, the ball gowns, the elegance and the perfection of the dance steps. It was a lot to take in. By the time the first dance began, I was completely captivated.

Ballroom dancing had been a big part of my mother's young life. It was important for a young lady to dance well; attending balls and dances was always on the social calendar and so my mother was sent to classes during her teens. That night she was thrilled to be part of that world again. She and my father had danced competitively. I was told that they had been crowned champions before I was born. I never saw them dance together, nor did they ever mention their love of dance, which was how they had first met.

Norma Vorster dashed past us in the foyer during the interval on her way to the huge lady's cloakroom used by the dancers as a dressing room. We followed. The room was strewn with dresses, shoes, cosmetics and personal items. There were bags and cases of pretty things scattered everywhere. Norma had to make a quick change before the final of the Foxtrot.

She ran into the centre of the cloakroom, dropped the magnificent full-skirted, silver-beaded, ball gown to the floor and stepped out of it. She stood there in her magnificent nakedness; her perfectly shaped body, with an all over tan, shimmered with tiny beads of moisture. She was *breathtakingly beautiful*. I was mesmerised by her perfect form and surprised by her unabashed nakedness in front of strangers. With my mother's rather formal upbringing, I had *never seen a naked female body* before. I was dazzled by her natural beauty.

Once the glorious evening was over, we strolled back to the car, dreaming of ourselves in magnificent ball gowns, being led around a stunning ballroom. It was a very special night.

PART 3

Chapter 26

Arma Court, 1958–60

*"Give me everything mangled and bruised
And I will make a light of it to make you weep,
And we will have rain,
And begin again."*

Deena Metzger, 'Leavings'[52]

Hillbrow years were an impressionable time; the many occasions of fun were outweighed by the initial culture shock of living in such a place and the dramatic events that we witnessed. There was a dark underbelly to life there. An undercurrent of fear and anger that was smoulderingly obvious. It created a constant rumbling tension in a volatile tribal country. What I often witnessed on the streets frightened me; many of those scenes traumatised me, incidents that have stayed with me.

Without any warning, my mother packed up and we were saying goodbye to yet another home. We were moving away from central Hillbrow to a quiet, green suburb, known as Berea. My head was reeling from all that I had been subjected to over those few years and I felt unsettled by the thought of another new start. I wonder if my mother noticed the huge changes in my brother and me. Probably not!

With the many temporary homes, it was difficult to form any attachments. With each move we met new people and lived in more incompatible areas. I began to feel rootless. My brother and I were sulky and silent as we attempted to settle into a new suburb. There were many times when I suppressed my desire to scream.

Our new 'home' was in Arma Court on Catherine Avenue on the border with Hillbrow. The old grey block of flats was solidly built, a small concrete mass sitting at the corner of Esselen Street. The street was tree-lined and green and very much quieter. My mother had rented a large, soulless, bachelor flat on the ground floor next to the entrance. The interior of the flat was outdated, dreary and uninviting. It was comprised of a good-sized kitchen with an old-fashioned three-plate stove, refrigerator and a table with two chairs. The long narrow bathroom was exceptionally dark. The large square-shaped living area had three single beds placed around the periphery of the room. Standing at the front-facing window was a large Victorian mahogany table with four matching chairs. The interior woodwork had a dark varnish finish, giving the flat a drab, heavy look.

It became more acceptable once my mother had added a few creative touches: beautifully draped curtains, pretty lamps, pictures and ornamental pieces and, to finish, an exotic rug on the floor. But it was inadequate for three of us and far removed from the spacious interiors we remembered. It did not feel homely; it was more like second-rate lodgings.

We were slowly sliding down into a life of poverty. The arrival was gradual. There were subtle changes happening daily, yet we did not recognise them. Our existence was nothing like the life we had been born into. We had been surrounded by luxury, prominent people, captivating individuals who held powerful positions in the city, if not the world. They played an important part in my earliest foundation years, yet there we were, living in a tiny flat, fending for ourselves in a world that was completely unfamiliar and very uncomfortable.

My mother never grew accustomed to 'making ends meet'. Most months they did not. She began to vacillate between cynicism and self-pity. The constant uprooting was distressing, yet there were no outward emotional displays from any of us. We lived alone in our heads in very different worlds.

In the small dark flat I began to experience bouts of deep unhappiness and claustrophobia. My mother remained oblivious. She lived in her own self-created bubble. Perhaps it was her coping mechanism. Four years had passed, and my mother continued to live in the past, dwelling on her perfect life with her perfect husband. Yet every move we made was a rude awakening of how far removed she was from that life.

My delicate mother was losing her way, losing parts of her identity, with no idea how to pick up the pieces and embrace a very different life. Her constant talk of the past, how it was and *how it was meant to be*, kept my brother and me stuck in the past with her.

"It was *never* like this before…"

"I don't think I can *cope* for very much longer!"

"How *could* he *do* this to me?" were the phrases we heard repeatedly.

I had mixed feelings about my parents by then and who was to blame. I began to doubt my father with each passing day. Eventually, I began to dislike him as my mother constantly made ill-thought-out, unreasonable, decisions for the three of us. We were rootless, stumbling and fumbling along as best we could.

My mother had never had to take care of herself. Most women of that era were guided or controlled by parents or husbands. Her expectation was that she would be well-cared-for during her life with her inheritance and by her wonderful husband. Divorce never entered her mind. It was frowned upon socially and therefore unthinkable.

Going out to work was not a thought that would ever cross her mind. When it was casually suggested, she was *aghast at the very idea* that anyone would *expect* her to work. It was not something she ever considered, even when things became dire. Her idea that my father would eventually send for us continued unabated. In her opinion it was his *legal* and *moral* duty.

My dear mother craved her luxurious life with black staff hovering close at hand, ready to attend to her every need. She had been raised in a gentle, colonial, cocoon of wealth with a certain social standing: a life of position, privilege and plenty, which she was unwilling to forget or forgo.

In the years that followed, with our worldly possessions still in storage, my mother continued to hope and remained unable to adapt yet did absolutely nothing to change or improve our circumstances. Her mind fogged over, she drifted and daydreamed while going through the motions of living; sipping wine from pretty long stemmed glasses, dragging elegantly on a lipstick-stained cigarette, or titivated and groomed herself; letting out frequent long wistful sighs. She existed from one foggy day to the next, and still she waited, longing for my father's return.

It was an unhappy time. I wondered if the life I was living was just a bad dream, that eventually I would wake, and it would all be over. There was something very wrong happening to us, but I was too young to grasp what it was. Yet, my mother's outward self-composure never diminished. She continued to have her weekly hair appointment, invested in expensive face creams, her favourite Helena Rubenstein lipstick, Rothmans cigarettes (when pretty pastel Sobranie's were not available) and bottles of fine wine. On the other hand, I was going to school in broken shoes, without a blazer during the bitterly cold winter months.

I began to wonder if it was my father who had wanted to have children and not my mother. It had become blindingly clear by then that our mother had no maternal instincts and was unable to love us or even take responsibility for us. I no longer felt any connection to my mother or my brother. The way we were living brought out cynicism and detachment in me.

I had a very mature understanding of life for my age, yet there were days when I felt as if I were floating in a dream, watching my life happen from afar. I locked myself away from all feelings and emotions. I did not care for the road my mother was travelling. I became more and more removed from her, like a stranger passing through her limited world. Until then, my life seemed to have been a series of dramatic events. *Surely there had been some sort of silly mistake,* I thought.

"What are you doing? What is going on? I want my father!" I wanted to shout out at her. Tears of frustration and fear flowed. It was all such a muddle and so unfair!

At the time of moving into Arma Court, I was having regular flashbacks of the murder I had witnessed from the flat in Hillbrow. My mind insisted on keeping it alive. I had internalised every detail and had become withdrawn and tense, spending too much time in my head, with a running commentary of that event. I was deeply troubled by the violence I had witnessed.

In my final year, Standard 5, at Twist Street School, I faced daily challenges and was unable to focus on my studies. There were the day-to-day practicalities to deal with: my school shoes were broken and worn through from the long walks to and from school. The soles had come adrift from the upper section, and I had to walk with a stiff-legged gait to keep from tripping on the flapping leather sole. I have *no idea* how I kept my composure, dragging my shoe along with me. I did it because I *had* to! Oh, I did mention shoes to my mother *every day,* but she would just stare back at me, blankly with a cold disinterested gaze. Not a word. The shoes could have been stitched at the Shoe Repair kiosk nearby, but she glazed over when confronted with any requests from Daryl or me.

I was going through other adjustments as my birthday loomed. A high school needed to be considered and applied for. The school of my choice, after carefully listening to discussions in class, needed to be applied for immediately to get a place. I took application forms home for the schools for which I was eligible. It required discussions and decisions; there were costs to consider and many other requirements. It meant nothing to my mother. She glanced at the forms for a brief moment, looked up at me with a bored expression on her face and threw the forms down, adding: "Don't look to me! You had better sit down and write to your father."

I lay in bed that night contemplating how to get myself into a good school. I realised that I had to take the next step on my own. In the early hours of the morning I sat bolt upright in bed, filled in the forms and signed them myself. I felt a frisson of excitement run up my spine. I applied for the most prestigious school on the list, Johannesburg High School for Girls (JGHS, known colloquially as 'Barnato Park') with the school motto "Vincemus", 'We Shall Triumph!' It had struck a chord in me.

The school was founded in 1887. After the passing of the diamond-mining magnate, Barney Barnato, his nephew, Solly Joel, gifted the entire estate to Fanny Buckland, the headmistress, and Johannesburg High School for Girls was officially born. The imposing entrance and circular driveway were surrounded by well-maintained gardens and green playing fields with tennis courts, hockey fields, a swimming pool and more. The school held strong traditional British values of Empire, Church and Sport. In those days girls were taught to become 'ladylike'. The insidious changes in Johannesburg altered the school's values over time, yet it gave me an excellent foundation for my future, both academically and personally.

That weekend I mentioned to my Aunt Alexandra that I had filled in the application forms to attend Johannesburg High School for Girls and signed them without my mother's consent. She was aghast at my mother's disinterest but amazed at what I had done. After listening to my wishes to attend a good high school and eventually study medicine, she offered a small weekly allowance towards school requirements, which included books, pens, uniforms and sports equipment. I saved every penny I received from my aunt, without knowing if I would have sufficient by the time school began.

During that year I was accepted into the school and also had a chance meeting with one of my mother's friends, 'Duckie' Orkin. He was a good friend of Edith's and perhaps her lover at one time. He was a plump, pink-faced man with a kind heart who, on meeting me, took an immediate interest in my schooling. He asked questions and, before I realised it, I was telling him about my plan to attend JGHS at the beginning of the next year. It was a rare conversation to have had with one of Mother's friends. My mother sat quietly with a bored look on her face while Duckie focused on my story, nodding as I spoke. Then he smiled and turned his attention back to my mother. Nothing more was said.

A few days later Duckie popped by unexpectedly. Much to my surprise, he had come to see me. He quickly explained that his sister owned the School Uniform Supply Shop on Twist Street. He had arranged for her to assist me with my uniforms. *I was overjoyed*!

I found the shop on the first floor of a building on Twist Street opposite a local branch of the OK Bazaars. In my hand I held on firmly to my savings. I was apprehensive because I was very aware that the money would *never* cover the costs of what was required by the school.

Duckie's sister, 'Kay', a tall, willowy, blonde in her forties with good posture and a kind manner, took me by the hand to the far end of the shop. I immediately handed over the money, including a small bag of coins. I naively asked what I could buy for that amount of money. Duckie's sister gazed directly into my eyes and felt my humiliation and awkwardness. Kay sat me down and pulled up a chair beside me. She spoke quietly and gently, telling me that I had *exactly* the right amount

PART 3

of money to buy everything I needed. How kind she was. I felt tears sting my eyes with relief. *Only then* did I realise how distressed I had been. I wanted to attend a prestigious school *without* my parents' help.

Explaining that her daughter had just completed her final year at the school, Kay offered me all of her daughter's uniforms, including the sportswear. They had been worn but were in perfect condition. She offered me three white summer school dresses, a winter gym tunic, four blouses, a blazer and two hats.

"Leave it with me for a few days," she whispered. "I will add new badges, headbands and blazer trim. It will all look brand new!"

I was utterly bewildered by her kindness and comforted by her gentle manner. Inside I was *thrilled!* I would arrive at my new school looking the part. I skipped happily all the way home and never mentioned a thing to my mother.

The year we lived at Arma Court was 'socially uneventful' for my mother. Or so she said. She made no new friends in the building or in that neighbourhood.

"There seems to be nobody here with any class or any sense of style. If I can't meet anyone worth knowing, then it's best I live my life alone," she muttered, more to herself, as she wandered restlessly around the small flat.

In the mornings she would while away the hours, sitting at the mahogany table, staring out of the window. There would be a pot of tea in front of her and her favourite cup: a black-and-white, gold-trimmed Queen Anne porcelain cup. It was *that fine,* the pattern looked like lace. She sipped slowly and stared.

Mother continued life in the same manner, oblivious and ungrounded, but my brother and I were on edge. The three of us in one large bachelor flat was difficult. My brother and I were teenagers and well-developed for our ages, with no privacy. We had suddenly both become very self-conscious. It felt stifling and uncomfortable, with no space to do homework or school projects.

My mother never saw herself as 'poor' or leaning towards poverty. In her mind, *in spite of everything,* we would soon begin a new life in Rhodesia. The time of 'lack' was, according to her, simply "a nasty little period we have to get through."

I remember one afternoon in particular. It was a turning point for me. I got up from my single bed where I had been sitting studying and said, "I am going to the café, be back in a few minutes."

As I spoke, it hit me, and I burst out laughing: "*You* don't have to tell *anyone, anything.* Just go!" I said to myself out loud.

From that exact moment I accepted that I was on my own. If I wanted to go anywhere, I would go. What was the point of telling *her* anything, since she never responded? I skipped out of the building giggling gleefully. My disconnection was complete.

Once I began at high school, I slowly developed a feeling of being untouchable. Yes, it was false bravado but my need to endure and survive was resolute. There were times over the years that followed when I felt disdain towards my mother or her choice of friends.

It was a few days before my twelfth birthday. I had invited my two friends from Twist Street School, Patsy and Margo, to a movie on the Saturday. A friend of my mother, Michael Levy, Manager of the local branch of OK Bazaar, had gifted me with a pretty, pink dress with black polka-dots, a large stand up collar and a sweetheart neckline. I had saved my pocket money for my first pair of kitten-heeled shoes, trimmed with little bows. *I could hardly wait for my birthday.*

I was living in a very adult world and had developed a mature mindset, yet I was *extremely naive* about the facts of life and becoming a young woman. In those days, intimacy was *never* discussed. To my shock and horror, I woke to find that I had unexpectedly begun to bleed. I had no idea that I had started my 'periods' (menstruation cycle). I had *no clue* that such a thing would occur. It was, indeed, *a huge shock* to me. I remember feeling faint with fear. Such topics were out of bounds; our parents were unable to bring themselves to discuss such intimate matters. My mother had never explained, or mentioned, a monthly menstrual cycle.

In my young mind, I thought that I was bleeding internally and was completely distressed by what was happening. To my dismay it did not let up. I got into bed and lay as still as I could, but soon developed excruciating cramps, as I lay doubled up in a foetal position.

Hours later, my mother stopped for a moment and stared at me lying in bed.

"What on earth is wrong with you?" she asked, looking down at me with a puzzled expression on her face.

I told her I was 'bleeding between my legs'.

She smiled, walked casually to her cupboard, brought out a large white pad and said "Here, put this on," with no further explanation.

I lay there in discomfort feeling mortified. I remained in bed, lying rigidly, for two or three days, dragging myself out of bed as infrequently as possible. Without a word, my mother would hand me another padded towel to use. She would float past my bed, which was against the main wall of the one room, offering no advice, nor did she appease my fears, even though it must have been obvious that I was shocked and frightened by what was happening to me. She was simply unable to discuss such matters with me, ever!

When a new friend of my mother's, Pam Feldman, arrived one evening, I was ashamed and embarrassed to be in bed. She amusedly asked my mother what was wrong with me.

My mother smiled and said nonchalantly, "She has started her 'monthlies'."

They glanced in my direction as I lay huddled under the covers, pale and uncomfortable. Their eyes twinkled with amusement as my mother poured two large glasses of wine.

Life for them continued as usual. My monthly cycle was never mentioned again, but my birthday plans had been cancelled. I was too preoccupied with what was happening to my body to venture out. Finally, after several days, I got out of bed carefully and began to adapt to the new womanly phenomena.

When our first Christmas at Arma Court loomed, I felt miserable at the thought of spending Christmas in that tiny dark flat. My mother had made no plans for us. 'Aunty' Pam decided to treat us to a special Christmas Lunch at the Blue Room[53], part of the Johannesburg Railway Station.

> The South African Railways (SAR) had a showpiece restaurant situated on the east side of the concourse. The cuisine was the finest that the Catering Department could offer.

On entering the Blue Room, I noticed that it was a very formal dining room, adorned with cascades of fresh flowers and gleaming

PART 3

solid silverware. Pam placed my mother and myself at the head of the table and my brother, herself and two other guests sat alongside us.

The silver cutlery spread across the table to my left and right, had at least four or five pieces. This did not concern or faze me. My mother had spent many an afternoon teaching us the art of correct table manners, using an eraser on a dinner plate, to practice with. I remember one occasion when she spent hours teaching us how to eat a chicken leg or wing elegantly with a knife and fork. We were never allowed to pick up food in our fingers. My brother hated those afternoons.

What did strike fear into my heart was that I was left-handed, which posed a problem with the extensive place setting. Having entered my teen years with hormones all over the place, I often blushed bright red for no reason at all.

Looking down at the setting, I knew that I needed to swap over the cutlery to enable me to eat properly. The tables were set with precision, the waiters in starched uniforms hovered. I was mortified at the prospect of anyone noticing me change the setting. I could feel the heat rising up my neck, my cheeks burning at the very idea.

That day I forced myself to eat right-handed. The heavy embossed silver cutlery remained as it was. I ate slowly and carefully and managed better than expected. I was proud that I had done so well and gradually began to enjoy the Christmas celebrations.

The many courses were beautifully presented and delicious to eat, ending with an enormous flaming Christmas pudding wheeled into the centre of the room. It was a joyous moment. Everyone stood, clapping, cheering and turning to wish one another a very Merry Christmas. It was a memorable day and a very grown-up one for me in many ways. I do believe it was on that day that my passion for fine dining began.

A few weeks after Christmas, I began my first year at the 'posh' Johannesburg High School for Girls. My brother had already started high school at Athlone Boys' High. For some reason his uniform was bought with no fuss or comments. Daryl had not adapted well to the constant moves, especially since moving to Arma Court, which felt very confined. To him it was another new home, another place

Chapter 26 • Arma Court, 1958–60   205

to live and another school to adjust to, which included a very long walk to get a bus. His grades were poor that year, but he had taken to rugby and was selected for the team. His study efforts dwindled with each passing week. He was not a conscientious scholar and became despondent and moody. Daryl missed our father terribly.

My mother was changing too. It was subtle but I noticed. She was often anxious and perturbed. The all-night parties had slowly faded away, her busy social life had become less so. New friends disappeared as quickly as they arrived. The beauty queens, the socialites, longstanding party friends, gone; the private dinner invitations became infrequent and the phone rang less often.

My glamorous, socialite mother replaced the lack of social engagements with pre-lunchtime drinks with one or another of her local friends but more often she drank alone. Each day she sat at the mahogany table with a gin and tonic, including lemon slice and clinking ice-cubes, in a tall Waterford crystal glass in the one hand and a Rothmans King Size cigarette in the other. Her lips left ruby red lipstick stains on the cigarette and crystal glass. From time to time she sighed deeply as she stared out of the large window.

After her drink, she occasionally ate a dainty cucumber sandwich on fresh white bread cut into quarters, crusts removed. She sat primly with an embroidered linen napkin on her lap to pat any crumbs from the corners of her mouth. Hours would pass. Another gin and tonic. A melancholy mood would arrive like a dull cloud as she sat deep in thought.

Occasionally, when in a darker mood, emotions would surface and out it came, *"That bastard!"*

I found that word jarring to my body as neither of my parents had ever used slang or swear words. Their language had always been very civilised.

1959: The University Education Act is passed.
The Act sets up separate colleges for black university students.
Blacks no longer attend white universities.

Chapter 27

Father, What Will Become of Us?

The tragedy is not that things are broken.
The tragedy is that they are not mended again.

Alan Paton, Cry, The Beloved Country[54]

One Friday afternoon in 1958, Uncle Mac arrived unexpectedly. He looked tense, with a determined expression on his face. He came with news of my father.

Without a word to anyone, my father had flown down from Rhodesia and had been staying at The Edward Hotel on the famous Golden Mile along Durban's beachfront. It would appear that the purpose of this quick visit was for an undisclosed business meeting. To this day, I have found no information or details of that meeting, not even whom he met with on that fateful day.

As he left the meeting at a hotel on Brickhill Road, he stepped off the curb to cross the busy road. According to bystanders, a car travelling at high speed drove towards my father without swerving. When his body connected with the speeding car, he was hit full on and flung high into the air. The car raced off. Was this accidental or intentional? It was never discovered nor discussed.

Hearing this shocking news, even though details at that stage were vague, sent me into a state of panic that went unnoticed by the adults. *What if he died? What if I never saw my father again? Who would look after us?* I wanted to go to him.

Uncle Mac and my aunts were leaving for Durban immediately and expected my mother, brother and I to travel with them. My mother shocked us all with her slow and measured response.

"No...I am not going with you. Let that philanderer *suffer!*"

I gasped. Uncle Mac scowled, snorted and, without another word, spun on his heels and walked briskly out of the flat.

It needed to be more than a catastrophic accident to soften my mother's shielded heart. In her mind my father could not suffer enough for what he had put her through: the shame, the indignity, the hurt and the intense heartache. According to her, my father had no legitimate excuse for his behaviour or for leaving her stranded but, in the eyes of his family, my mother had crossed a line. She became 'persona non grata' from that day forward. *They cut her out completely.* At no time in the future did they ever offer my mother help or financial assistance. We were left floundering.

We heard nothing from my father's family for a long time after that day. It caused a very deep rift between us. For a while I felt uncomfortable going for weekends until my grandmother and Aunt Alex called me. When I mentioned how I felt to my aunt, she replied, "Now, don't be silly...of course you are welcome." But my uncle made no attempt to share further details of my father's condition and became nasty and facetious towards me. With his influence, my aunts excluded me from many family occasions that year

We were never given the full details of the accident at the time, and I have been unable to establish the real truth since then. Was the meeting at the hotel with another woman, or was it actually important business? To my knowledge, my father never spoke of his reasons for being in Durban on that day with any of his family.

My mother chose not to visit my father during the three years he spent in Addington Hospital in Durban. He underwent several surgical procedures for complex bone fractures, including bone grafts. Later, skin grafts were needed.

There was serious damage to his lower legs. His right leg had been completely smashed; there was an open fracture to the femur and five other breaks, with crushed bones in the fibula or lower leg. There was serious ligament damage to his knee. His arm, head and face had injuries that, luckily, healed without scars.

The fractures were eventually stabilised with pins and large metal screws long after the accident and after several operations. There was a large pin running horizontally through his lower right leg, much like a metal meat skewer. Initially he was in constant pain and later the draining of the weeping wounds around the pins created a foul smell. There were often complications and infections for the surgical team to deal with.

After four or more years, my father was able to walk on crutches, but his hospital days were far from over. Full recovery and mobility took several more years. My father was in hospital for over three years and was still unable to use his legs effortlessly. He was then treated as an outpatient for a further three years. At that stage, the surgical team was considering amputation because his bones had been badly crushed and were 'chalky'; the bones would not 'knit' together.

When I saw my father in 1963, it was nearing my sixteenth birthday. He was still on crutches with the pin through his leg. It took a while for me to adjust to the sight of his right leg.

Six or seven years after the accident, by sheer coincidence or luck, it was suggested that my father get a second opinion whilst in Johannesburg. He had arranged to travel there to discuss future job opportunities with colleagues. One of his old friends who knew an Orthopaedic Specialist personally, quickly arranged an emergency appointment. My father was examined on a Saturday morning by the highly respected surgeon. Soon after that appointment he performed complex surgery on my father's leg, finally fitting a steel rod into it.

Afterwards the surgeon said to my father, "Get up and walk!" That was groundbreaking back then!

A built-up orthopaedic boot with a four-inch elevation was needed. Initially balance was a huge challenge for my father. The very heavy cork build-ups used in those days have become a thing of the past. The synthetic foam and crepe lifts used nowadays are much lighter.

My father's pride would not accept that he was 'disabled', and he did not wish to appear that way. He was determined to train himself to walk without a severe limp. It took him time, with many serious falls—often landing on his head—before he mastered the skill. It was difficult to watch, constantly hoping he would not fall yet again. He proved during his life to have a strong physical constitution and a no-fuss attitude towards his health.

My father was unable to return to Rhodesia or keep track of investments and business ventures until many years had passed. The surgeries were frequent, and he was never fully conscious for much of that time. Although he never said as much, it was obvious that business partners, associates and colleagues had acted underhandedly and unethically. They took advantage of his circumstances to gain control of vast amounts of money. He was cheated out of a small fortune! Yet he said nothing.

He was left with gigantic medical bills, with only a portion paid by insurance. The ongoing expenses took an enormous sum from his coffers. Eventually, funds began to dwindle, but as always, he had made good provision for himself and was able to keep afloat by living in simple comfort, with no trace of his once lavish lifestyle. In many ways, he was a changed man. It was only when I reconnected with my father that I got the true picture of what he had endured. My dear, long-suffering, father had a lot to ponder upon, lying in his hospital bed, and much to reconcile within himself. Until his death he remained very secretive about the past and never spoke of it.

Eventually he moved to a spacious flat in The Gables on Durban's Esplanade close to the hospital. It was almost seven years before he was able to pick up the pieces of his once flamboyant life and illustrious career. I don't know what happened to the family wealth. I presume most of it was transferred to Rhodesia or other parts the world. Nor could I determine what became of the properties he owned or invested in during his time in Salisbury. This includes the mansion he built for himself and his young lover. And what of his beautiful red-headed damsel? To my knowledge she never travelled down from Rhodesia to see him. I wonder if she ever discovered the truth about the accident, or did he seem to vanish into thin air?

Whilst in hospital, my father became good friends with a fellow patient. Eric was an enthusiastic stamp collector. To pass the time, my father began reading through Eric's collection of catalogues and books on philately. Within a year my father became very knowledgeable on the subject and eventually became a respected international stamp dealer. He did this from his hospital bed and later from a small office in his flat. Eric introduced my father to a few kind, decent friends, who kept an eye on him once he left hospital. Eric continued to visit my father daily, helping in any way he could. When our father was in hospital, my brother and I still received brief letters with cash enclosed.

During those years, my mother never wrote to my father to enquire about the accident or his health, nor did she consider what he was going through. Yet she had waited *all those years* for him. *It made no sense.* While he was in hospital, she expected a substantial allowance from him for us to live on and 'pin money' for her own requirements.

Looking back: I have come to realise that things were not good between my parents in the year before he left, in fact with each move they made. While he was with us, my mother began to trust him less. Reviewing those years, it would appear that he may have been winding his life down in Johannesburg while planning a new life without us. Perhaps he had decided to leave her but did not have the courage to tell her. From my point of view, he knowingly deserted us.

When living at Arma Court, I never noticed my mother read a book, a magazine, bake a cake, cook a meal, listen to a radio show, or do anything constructive to change our circumstances. She was drifting, treading water, in limbo. She did enjoy reading The Rand Daily Mail newspaper while sipping her morning coffee but, in general, she was preoccupied with *her own plight*, blaming my father for it all. She gave little of herself to us and was still tormented by the loss of her mother, which she carried like a dead weight. The 'loss' of her precious husband was too much to bear and affected her deeply on every level. She became more distant towards me and my brother, to the point of complete physical and emotional detachment, which others often viewed as neglect.

Days went by, which became weeks and months, when my mother rarely moved from the dining table that had been moved to the centre of the room. She would sit elegantly poised for endless hours, looking wistfully out of the window. Occasionally I noticed a slight quiver of her chin, as if she were about to burst into tears; other times her face would drop, her mind consumed by unhappy thoughts. The only movement was her breath and frequent wistful sighs.

My mother's new friend, Pam Feldman, arrived at our home one afternoon with a cheerful smile and an armful of champagne bottles.

PART 3

From that afternoon onwards, daily visits became a fixed arrangement at either home. Pam lived a short walk away, along Esselen Street in a modern compact flat. The interior was decorated in soft greys and lemon yellow, the furnishings arty and minimalist. Very quickly Pam Feldman and mother became inseparable.

I don't know how she met Pam, perhaps at the hairdresser, but her friendship with Pam and her villainous selection of male friends would take my mother down to another level of that slippery slope. The men included professional gamblers, jockeys, trainers, dubious 'businessmen' and other infamous wealthy gentlemen. Pam playfully encouraged my mother to drink more.

"Come on, have another one!"

"Why the hurry, let's have one for the road…"

They indulged in low toned 'heart-to heart' conversations, huddled together laughing and sipping chilled champagne, from elegant crystal flutes.

Pam used cash for everything she wanted. She invariably had a bundle of notes close at hand. Her neighbour's twelve-year-old son, David, was on a substantial weekly retainer to run errands for her at a moment's notice. Anytime Pam wanted me out of the way, she would flash a wad of cash at me and tell me to go and buy myself something.

David spent many afternoons sitting on her front step waiting for his errands while Pam entertained with lavish lunches, after-work 'drinkies' and evening parties. I liked David, so we often sat together, whiling away the afternoons and listening to the loud conversations that seemed suspect to us naïve teenagers, including talk about the prize racehorse Sea Cottage that was later shot by Johnny Nel in Durban in June 1966. Johnny Nel visited Pam several times with a group of his friends. He reminded me of a mobster I had seen in a Saturday morning movie show.

Edith and Johnnie never visited us once we moved from the pretty Hillbrow flat that they had secured, decorated and furnished for my mother. Edith had spent almost five years as a sympathetic friend to my mother, paying for holidays, days out and so much more. For a few months they continued meeting for drinks or tennis on a weekend, but Edith eventually stopped calling, after meeting mother's new friend,

Pam Feldman. My mother made little effort to keep in contact with Edith once we moved. We never saw them again.

Carney and John from Pretoria, once very close friends of my parents, disappeared from our lives just as suddenly after my brother Daryl and I had spent that last summer holiday with our friends at the farm.

The four of us children, Peert, Heloise, my brother and I, had not got on as well that last year. We were growing up and apart, due to the widening gap in our circumstances and different environments. By then, home life was beginning to affect me more than I realised. I was less carefree and often silent. My brother was moody and on occasion rough with Peert. That may have been one of the factors that decided the Steyns to stop inviting us and to cut loose their long-standing friendship with my mother. It was a huge loss to my brother and me, leaving us adrift with our very aloof mother.

My mother was no longer the convivial social butterfly once so admired and adored; perhaps friends found her company less captivating and they presumed incorrectly that we were well provided for by my father or his family. Bertie and Anne and their grown-up daughter enjoyed having us for extended weekend stays. Theirs was a magnificent property in Honeydew, but they rarely contacted my mother once my father left, yet the two couples had been inseparable for years. It was puzzling.

Was it that Johnnie Steyn and Bertie Blum were on my father's side and aware of his plan to leave my mother, or had Bertie and Johnnie trusted my father as principle negotiator for various Rhodesian 'projects' and lost money? This would have soured the friendship. Very few of his friends knew that he lay in a Durban hospital for years, presuming he had vanished *with an undisclosed amount of money*. Perhaps he did.

On an ordinary mid-week day in 1958, my brother disappeared. It was a few months after we moved to Arma Court. Daryl left for Athlone Boys High School and never returned. He simply *disappeared*. By the evening I was concerned; after all, this *was* Johannesburg and there *were* dangers, especially after dark.

"Where could he be? I asked my mother.

"I have *absolutely no idea.*" And *that* was the end of the conversation.

Days passed with no sign of Daryl and no word. My mother made no effort to find him; she did not call the school or the police to report him missing. She carried on with her life, showing no outward signs of alarm at Daryl's disappearance.

I was too young to know what to do, but I was distraught and stunned by my mother's indifference. I conjured up all kinds of grim scenarios in my head and cried myself to sleep at night.

"Don't leave me alone with her!" I cried in my wakefulness and in my dreams.

Life continued, unchanged by Daryl's disappearance. I went off to school each morning, getting home as late as possible, and my mother's days were unhindered by her children.

Uncle Mac had, by then, become a well-respected Senior Health Inspector, working for the Johannesburg Municipality (Council). When he heard that Daryl was missing, he did nothing either. Daryl was not even mentioned during his weekly visits to my mother that had resumed all of a sudden. Uncle Mac definitely had a fondness for her.

The subject was brushed under the carpet and never spoken about. It was as if *Daryl had never existed!* Uncle Mac should have approached Children's Services and other departments at the Municipality where he worked, yet he chose not to assist in finding my brother. Perhaps his main concern was his unblemished reputation; admitting that he had family issues would have raised eyebrows.

Occasionally my mother mentioned my father, usually after several glasses of chilled Rose wine. She would look deep into her glass as she sat elegantly poised and all of a sudden would mouth off nastiness about him.

"This is all *his* fault!"

On each occasion it took me by surprise because it was so unlike my mother to raise her voice or use harsh words. Her pleasant, well-spoken voice was usually even toned and placid.

Her main interest continued to be herself and her wellbeing. She dwelled in the past, her mind agitated by her circumstances. Yes, she must have been deeply hurt and in distress, but hid that well from everyone. She was unable to grasp the seriousness of the situation we were in or to meet any of her responsibilities. Mentally and emotionally she was incapable of considering others or creating a life without my father. Her mind was more troubled and tormented than I understood at that time, yet she put on a good show socially.

By the time my brother had been missing for close to a year, I was constantly on edge. *How could someone vanish into thin air?* I was disturbed by thoughts of what may have happened to him. Not a day went by when I did not jog my mother's memory, asking after my brother. Her reply became consistent.

"I don't know," she would reply in a bored, monotonous, voice. Then she would turn and walk unhurriedly away from me.

One weekday afternoon, about twelve months after my brother had disappeared, I was staring listlessly out of the large front window when I noticed two women walking purposefully into the building. They looked out of place somehow. Mrs. Russel, with her daughter-in-law Mary, knocked firmly on our door. My mother opened it expecting to see her friend Pam, only to find two strangers on the doorstep. She was caught off guard.

Mrs. Russel spoke up immediately with a well-educated British accent. She sounded angry.

"I have your son Daryl living with me. I have come to ask *why* you have never bothered to look for him!" My mother gasped and staggered back a step, holding onto the door handle. She was shocked at Anne Russel's accusing tone.

"He went missing from here, *over a year ago*," she snarled at my mother.

I have no exact recall of what was said that afternoon, my head was reeling, my mind bewildered. I *do know* that Anne and Mary Russel gazed at me frequently with concern in their eyes and stared with obvious contempt at my mother. Her lack of interest in my brother's wellbeing, her poor excuses and apathetic demeanour, angered Mrs. Russel all the more. She sat opposite my mother, flushed with rage.

The two women left after a stormy visit, perplexed by my mother's indifference. She appeared unmoved by their visit and made no arrangement for my brother to return home.

I was seething that day; I wanted to explode. Her attitude appalled me.

Two months later a feisty Mary Russel arrived on a powerful black and silver motorcycle. I was wide-eyed with surprise and even more surprised that she had come to see how I was. Her visits became a regular weekly arrangement and over several months we developed a warm, sisterly bond.

Mrs. Russel never returned to visit my mother, and Daryl continued living with the Russels. He and their youngest son, Ronald, had formed a firm friendship while playing rugby for the school team. The Russels paid for Daryl's education, clothing, food, pocket money and holidays.

Neither of my parents ever thanked the Russel family for taking care of my brother, even though I encouraged my father to do so in later years. Pride kept him from admitting that he had neglected his family duties during those years and stood in the way of my father doing the right thing.

Over a period of four or five years, almost every friend my mother thought she had quietly walked away. Not seeing familiar faces was upsetting for me. It left me with a feeling of emptiness. They had all been 'Aunties' and 'Uncles' to me, part of my extended family, and had been the core of my parents' social life and my early childhood. My mother's constant criticism of my father may have become a total bore and by then our living conditions were probably unacceptable to her socialite friends, causing guilt and embarrassment. Our situation painted a less than perfect picture. It may have been pride that stopped my mother from keeping in touch with them, yet she refused to consider that she had lost her social position. But I could see that they had discreetly pushed her aside.

Without a word my mother contacted her brother, Cuthbert whom, to my knowledge, she had not seen since she married my father. Out of the blue she announced that he had sent a train ticket for me to holiday in Durban. I was stunned!

I was hastily bundled onto a night train, unprepared and nervous. To this day I have no idea how my mother knew the whereabouts of her brother. It was never open for discussion.

Her brother was a lot like her. 'Collie' had fair hair, a slim build, but was extremely fit. He had served in World War II and, due to shell shock, was highly strung and at times child-like. Aunt Doreen took it all in her stride. She managed and organised Collie and was more like a mother to him. Aunt Doreen had a glorious crown of thick red hair, was down to earth, capable and very kind. She took me under her wing. I was taken along wherever she went. She asked no questions about my home-life, but it was obvious that she was concerned about me.

I spent a pleasant, uneventful, holiday with my aunt and uncle who were kind and caring. Several months later I spent another holiday with them and wrote to my aunt frequently, but never saw them after that for many years. They may have attempted to help my mother but, for some reason, my mother and her brother did not keep in touch.

My mother continued living a life that rarely showed any kindness or consideration towards me. With my brother gone, my other 'uncles and aunts' no longer in the picture, I felt sad and very alone, but eventually became more resilient, even though I was still vulnerable and had a lot of emotional growing up to do. I began to think more of my future and less of having a happy childhood. Then I had an unexpected epiphany: I realised that my mother had nothing emotional, intellectual or spiritual to share with me. All she was able to offer was crushing heartache and an ulcer by the time I was thirteen.

Oh, not again! There was a move on the horizon.

March 1959: A state of unrest In Rhodesia (Zimbabwe) and Nyasaland (Malawi).

British troops moved into Nyasaland, with many arrests. A State of Emergency declared.

PART 3

Apartheid – Whites Only Sign

Apartheid Days - Mandela

Hillbrow – Street Music

PART 3

Hillbrow –Kwela Music

Twist Street School

PART 3

Park Station Blue Room Restaurant

Sea Cottage – Shot

PART 3

Bubbles Schroeder

Norma Voster – Beauty Queen

White Hair Salon

60's Hair Style

222

PART 3

Clarenden Circle – Hillbrow-Parktown Border

Rissik Street Bridge

PART 3

Hillbrow – Johannesburg

Bus Depot

PART 3

Hillbrow

Hillbrow Club – Summit club

225

Black Sash protest outside Union Buildings

PART IV

*Don't touch my soul
with dirty hands.*

Attributed to Edie Sedgwick[55]

PART 4

Chapter 28

Del Monico Mansions, 1960–62

*Nothing big ever happens,
good or bad,
unless the floor falls out first.*

Jeanette LeBlanc[56]

My mother carried her journey towards poverty elegantly. In her mind our circumstances were transitory; she appeared to take it in her stride. Her mind continued to imagine a rosy future with her husband. Her couturier outfits and day frocks had survived many a good season, yet she looked a picture of style and glamour. Her beautiful diamonds, gold bangles, mother of pearl watch, dress rings and expensive accessories were being discretely sold off to use for rent, alcohol, cigarettes, taxis, cosmetics, manicures, hairdos and entertainment. Food, school uniforms, school books, bus fare, clothing or any similar items for me were never considered to be necessities. When I requested any item for school, her reply never faltered.

"Ask your father," she would say to me dismissively. It became her standard response. What she had in her purse was spent on herself. After all, it was important that *she* keep up appearances.

Although my parents' lives seemed to be sliding down the financial ladder, the Sixties in Johannesburg was a prosperous decade, despite the impact of apartheid. It was a decade of economic expansion with a huge boom in Johannesburg. Living in a luxury high-rise block of flats became very fashionable. It was an exciting era of new builds. The city was confident that there was sufficient stability in the gold market and a demand for minerals worldwide.

Hospital Hill sat between Braamfontein, Hillbrow and central Johannesburg. It housed a high percentage of medical and government buildings. The area ran from the bottom of Smit Street up to the Old Fort, over the hill, to the edge of Parktown. The area was neither city nor suburb and at night it was known to be dangerous. The wrong side of the tracks, one might say. It was a far cry from where my life began. In fact, it was a shock.

The area cultivated a way of life to which I never adjusted. It was a rude awakening to a level of life that was base, harsh and stifling. It was a time of constant adjustments: attending a posh high school, coming home to 'that place' and then in complete contrast spending gentle, conservative, weekends with my aunt and grandmother. I didn't know *who* I was supposed to be, *how* to behave, or *how to adjust* to the vastly different lifestyles. I was constantly adjusting my mood and emotions. It was a lot to deal with.

The entrance to Del Monico Mansions, a few minutes' walk from Johannesburg General Hospital, had a shabby 1940s façade kept scrupulously clean by the well-built black flat boys. Yet nothing could hide the lifeless dilapidation of the four-storey block. The white marble entrance lay between a small sour-smelling Liquor Store and a kiosk-sized pharmacy. The façade of this block had no appeal in modern bustling Johannesburg. It was situated opposite Park Railway Station and was a short walk to Joubert Park and the city bus service.

I remember the day we went to view the accommodation. My mother arranged a meeting with the caretaker, Mrs. van Rensburg, which became more like an interrogation. As we walked into the neat, front-facing flat to meet the caretaker, my mother grabbed my hand tightly—in fear rather than affection. From the moment we entered her flat, Mrs. van Rensburg barked questions at my mother. She was loud, threatening and direct. My mother shrank back as questions kept coming:

"How many of you are there?"

"Is this your daughter?"

"Can you afford the rent?!"

"Do you work?"

When my mother timidly replied, "No", the caretaker shrieked back at her, "*Well, dammit, how can I trust you for the rent?*"

"Where is your husband? We can't just take women off the streets here!"

And so she went on, by which time I wanted to make a dash for it.

Eventually she ushered us out onto the landing and down a flight to the first floor. My mother must have seen the look of horror on my face as we entered the dark room she was about to rent and quickly remarked, "Well, we can make do for a short while. It will be fine. The curtains will fit perfectly, and a lamp will go nicely over here and…"

She never finished her sentence, allowing the subject to fall flat. In spite of everything we had endured, my mother would still not accept that we were in dire straits. The real truth was *my father had left my mother struggling and almost penniless!*

The accommodation on offer was a dark, dingy bedsit, a small, square, claustrophobic room. My mother took it without hesitation. The room had a two-door built-in wardrobe and a wash basin in the left corner across which my mother hung a red and gold regency-stripe curtain, creating a little cubicle. A matching curtain was draped over her wooden trunk that became her 'throne', doubling as a telephone table. There was a square, wooden dining table and two chairs in the centre of the room, which took up most of the space, leaving only a narrow area to move around the room.

Under the wide north-facing window were two small single beds. The mattresses were so old and tired that the sagging springs creaked and groaned with every move. The 2-plate Hot Plate stood on a four-legged metal frame; a long narrow 1940s style oak sideboard was pushed against a wall. Close behind the front door stood one small armchair, allowing the front door to open only partially. Eventually the sideboard functioned as a general store cupboard. We used it to store crockery, cutlery and general supplies. It had a drop-leaf desk front that we used as a work surface and writing desk. The bathrooms and toilets, much to my *absolute horror*, were in each corner of the landing. They were communal, shared with twelve other tenants.

The outlook from the window was shocking. We both took a long time to adjust to it. The room faced the back of the next-door building. It was a two-storey block with a back entrance that led to a narrow lane used by black male workers. The lane led to a rickety, metal fire-escape ladder, which we looked onto from our window. At eye level we saw three small gloomy rooms: a washroom, a room for socialising and cooking, and a third room for the flat boys to sleep in. On the top level, there was a flat, concrete rooftop where black workers sat around during their lunch break or when they had time off. The rooftop was also used to hang out washing. These young tribal men had a powerful presence. They had physiques and physical strength that was both impressive and daunting.

The six-foot tall and almost as broad Afrikaans-speaking caretaker was also daunting. Her loud voice echoed along the corridors whenever she inspected the building. She was afraid of no man, black or white. Mrs. van Rensburg was rough, tough and cold-hearted. Her parents were originally Dutch or German settlers, and she enjoyed ruling her staff with a rod of iron. When she bellowed "*Magtig! Maak weer Skoon!*" ("Good grief! Clean this again!") her team of black flat boys polished harder and harder, usually on hands and knees. The old building, though decidedly dull and dark, gleamed.

After witnessing two cold-blooded murders, the grim situation filled me with terror. My mother, too, had traumatic memories of her own mother's murder. For both of us, these circumstances were *a living hell*. What possessed my mother to rent such accommodation? I never understood. I was twelve going on thirty and wiser than my years. I knew that Del Monico Mansions was *not* where we belonged, nor where I intended to stay. I was distressed and unnerved for months. Then, slowly, I began to visualise a future different from my mother's; thoughts of leaving home kept me sane. I felt frequently that, if anything more were added to my load in life just then, it would tip me over the edge, but deep inside me there was a strength, a resilience. I never accepted or admitted to being placed in such dire circumstances. It was something I learnt to endure.

My mother did her utmost to decorate the tired, dilapidated room. She draped heavily gathered voile curtains across the window, leaving only a small area in the centre for natural light to enter. She filled the windowsill with green plants. The men next door were respectful, averting their eyes and keeping their heads bowed. It was far from ideal and disturbed us every day. Those first weeks, going to sleep at night in a tiny room, knowing that a few feet across from our window was a powerful raw male presence and possible danger, I was terrified.

The drab bedsit became another of our 'temporary' homes. Not one of the tenants we met believed that it could be otherwise. We looked totally out of place amongst people predominantly on low incomes and less educated. Many had previously lived in semi-rural areas or farming communities and were there to work in the 'City of Gold'. They dreamed of forging a successful career and experiencing an exciting life. Over time, a feeling of hopelessness settled over them in their small, tired, accommodations. Many occupants on the lower floor were young men who came to Johannesburg to work as clerks for the South African Railways (known by locals as 'Park Station').

Within the block of rooms, I discovered that there were a few very interesting tenants. I had become a keen observer of people by then and found the tenants particularly fascinating. There were 'foreigners' of various backgrounds and ages. There were many who preferred to remain anonymous, rarely leaving their small rooms, living reclusive lives miles away from the dark disturbing days in Europe during World War II. These were people much like Doris and Nick and Irma and her husband whom we met while living in Parktown; people who had escaped, running as far away as possible from the trauma of war and bad memories to find safety and live quietly. Often, they became lost in their memories of what they had endured or the family they had lost but were unable to speak of it.

Sonia, a Russian Jewess lived on the top floor. Our neighbour Gerda was German and was frostily ignored by the Jews who lived in the building. Yet they all carried trauma and painful secrets. We called Gerda 'Frau-Sister' at her suggestion. Then there was Chaim, at the end of the passage and many others whom we often saw but did not get to know. There were also many young, handsome, gay men living quiet lives, confined to their own four walls.

Frau-Sister had been a Medical Advisor and Lecturer before the war. Or so she claimed, rather vaguely. Her reasons for being in South Africa were dubious. We could never fathom exactly who she was or what she was doing in Johannesburg. Frau-Sister offered little information about her life in Germany. She was untrusting, sceptical and preferred not to speak about Germany. She became highly distressed if asked any direct questions about her life. Frau-Sister wore severely cut tweed suits, whatever the weather. Her English was hesitant, her manner frantic as if in constant fear. She walked at a hurried pace like someone being followed. Her occasional smile was cautious.

Out of the blue, my mother would decide to cook Hassenpfeffer (rabbit stew) for Frau-Sister. How she obtained the rabbits I never knew. She would cook them all day on low heat, then at about 5 p.m. Frau-Sister came over to eat. With eyes gleaming she would begin running around and around the table with excitement, shouting *"Hassenpfeffer! Ach du meine Güte, das ist wunderbar! Hassenpfeffer!"* She would eventually settle, sit at the table and, with cutlery in hand, wait to be served, and eat hungrily.

While the stew cooked on the tiny 2-plate stove, my stomach growled. The wonderful aroma of rabbit stew, juniper berries, bay leaves, garlic and thyme wafted around our humble abode. I salivated knowing there would not be a plate of rabbit stew offered to me.

As my mother and Frau-Sister enjoyed the stew, I would eat crisps and sweets bought with my pocket money. If I asked persistently for food, my mother would give me a shilling; "buy a pie from Louis the Greek," whose drab café was around the corner. On other occasions my mother took a small plate of food up to the mysterious Sonia who never left her room.

Sonia would occasionally send a note, delivered to me by a flat boy. I would be invited to pay her a visit. Her room was neat, austere and sparsely furnished. She had no personal items or belongings in her spartan room. Sonia was usually overdressed in several layers of elegant clothing, yet she remained freezing cold. She dressed in dark colours, her long black hair, white at the temples, worn in a severe chignon; dark red matte lipstick was carefully applied to her lips.

We sat together for hours over small cups of sweet black tea, as she spoke to me philosophically about life. She also taught me Yiddish phrases. *"Oi Vey"* became a favourite expression of mine, which was strange for a child.

To me, as an open-minded teenager, Sonia was mysterious, wise and intriguing. Although there was a huge age difference, we respected and understood each other. I learnt from Sonia more than I am able to express. We spoke of deep feelings, acknowledging sadness, heartache and life's harsh experiences. She spoke of other countries, intellect, refinement, cultural issues and human suffering. How different we were, yet we found common ground and understanding, whilst preserving dignity and our individual cultures. I sometimes get a sense of Sonia in myself now, in my golden years.

PART 4

Then there was Chaim Levitt. He lived at the end of the passage around the corner from our room, adjacent to the communal bathrooms. Chaim was a very reserved man in his forties, neatly dressed in cheap suits, polite but deadly serious. He walked slightly stooped, as if carrying the world on his shoulders. Chaim had a stale musty aura around him, with sadness etched into his softly lined face. He had no living family except for one brother. I often wondered, as I got older, if his parents had died during the war in Europe. Chaim worked for his older brother as a clerk at his insurance company in central Johannesburg. Except for going to work and Friday evenings when Chaim joined his brother, wife, and children for a Shabbat dinner, he never went out.

Chaim had no telephone in his room, no radio and rarely struck up a conversation with neighbours. He kept himself separate from everyone, yet he would stop occasionally and share a few words with me. Once he entered his cheerless room, he lived in silence. It had an airless feel to it, the odour damp and musty, his furnishings drab, time-worn and sad.

I liked Chaim. He was a decent man; it shone through him, but I recognised deep sadness buried at the back of his eyes. The few words we regularly shared were always pleasant. I worried about Chaim. He seemed so very alone. Where had he come from? Where would life take him?

Aileen Katz worked in the pharmacy at the entrance of the building. With very limited space they managed to stock everything one could possibly need. Supplies were stacked to the ceiling, often with boxes teetering on the edge of a shelf, ready to tumble. Aileen ran up and down a sturdy wooden ladder, grabbing armfuls of stock for deliveries, orders, or customers in the shop. She was happy-go-lucky, helpful and kind to everyone. She needed her job and worked hard to be the best shop assistant.

Her real love was cosmetics and beauty products: perfumes, lotions, creams and make-up. Aileen tried anything new, and often wore it all at once. Her huge almond-shaped eyes were plastered in her favourite shade of shimmering green eyeshadow with thick black liner on her generous lids, then lashings of mascara, reapplied and reapplied. Her face and throat were covered in layers of foundation and finished with a dusting of matte powder. Finally, her full lips were smeared in bright orange lipstick, slowly and repeatedly applied. Aileen would step back, pout and scrutinise her face in the mirror. Her makeup was overdone, it looked cheap and tacky, yet her desire was to create a fashionable glamorous look.

Aileen Katz was in her mid-thirties and lived at home with strict elderly parents who had fled persecution from a small town somewhere in Europe. Her family information was obscure and fuzzy. She preferred to keep her family history brief. Like many others at that time, she remained silent about their past. She spoke only once of her parents being victimised and excluded. Aileen had never married but longed for a handsome man to arrive and sweep her off her feet. She spoke of weddings and marriage constantly.

Happy-go-lucky Aileen was in awe of my mother, her poise, her timeless glamour and her confidence in spite of our circumstances. My mother added sophistication, glamour and lightheartedness to the lives of many tenants living in Del Monico Mansions. They were unaware that she, too, hid her own trauma and family secrets.

Aileen began popping by after work, using any reason for doing so, gifting my mother with handfuls of samples: creams, lotions, lipsticks or vials of perfume. Aileen would sit staring at my mother unashamedly with sincere admiration.

A year later, Aileen began an affair with a married man. She was elated to have the attention she had always dreamed of. During those months she was in high spirits, her makeup more lovingly applied and her outfits modelled for my mother's approval. Every Tuesday evening after work Aileen would dash upstairs to use our humble home as a change room before meeting her handsome man. She spread her belongings across the beds: clothes, accessories, perfumes, creams and cosmetic jars everywhere.

I would sit on the corner of my bed, my hand supporting my chin, watching her, mesmerised. She applied layers of make-up to her face, her large protruding nose becoming more obvious with each coating of matte powder. It took an hour before she was ready. As quickly as she had arrived, she swept out of the door and down the staircase, leaving an array of items strewn all around the room. My mother carefully packed up Aileen's belongings and tidied it all away for her return the following week.

Her secret liaison went on for several months. Then one day, when I returned from school, Aileen was there in floods of tears, her nose and eyes reddened from hours of crying.

"It was *so* unexpected," she wept, "*so unfair and without any warning.*" "He says he *doesn't love me*," she yelped, blowing her large nose into a hanky. Tears flowed harder and harder, "*Why, oh why?*" she shrieked loudly.

My mother sat patiently, consoling her, listening to her loud sniffling and wailing. Aileen's mystery man tossed her aside without blinking. We never knew who he was, or how she had met him, but she had accepted love at any price, and he had left her without hesitation. For weeks after, Aileen had swollen red eyes, the joy drained from her face, her listless manner a tell-tale sign that her heart had not yet healed.

One evening, months later, she burst into our room with uncontrollable glee.

"I am having cosmetic surgery. *I am getting my nose fixed*. Then I will be sure to find a husband."

Aileen never married, even with her pretty new nose. At thirteen I was learning about disappointment, heartache and unrequited love. Her sorrow was palpable and made my heart weep. *All she wanted was to be loved*. I understood that.

During the years that I lived at Del Monico, a small group of gay men, all in their twenties, took care of me on a daily basis. Especially Louis Blanché, Lenis Esterhuizen and Louis Eybers. They included me in their coffee evenings, took me on outings, regularly styled and cut my hair and made sure that I was fashionable. They taught me about young fashion and how to dress. They cared deeply about my safety, 'mothered' me, and treated me like their little sister.

We had hilarious fun together. We laughed, danced, sang, told jokes, talked fashion, read fashion and movie magazines and enjoyed girly fun. Their conversations could be filled with naughty innuendos that were very funny, and we were often hysterical with laughter. Many people thought spending time with these young men was unhealthy for me, but I found them a breath of fresh air. It was an eye opener for me to another way of life. They taught me to be open minded.

"Never judge a book by its cover, Deary…"

I had no idea that, back then, being homosexual was against the law. These handsome gay men who had their own challenges to face each day helped me more than they realised. It was obvious that they enjoyed my mother's company, too. She was glamorous, sociable and accepted them openly, which they appreciated, but they did not approve of her careless attitude towards me and her nonexistent parenting skills.

Lenis was the outspoken one and would reprimand my mother in a loud, camp, voice "Yes, Gwenny! Where is her lunch? Come on, come on! Where is it?" then burst into very shrill laughter, but he made his point.

Occasionally Lenis would stand poised at the door, take one look at my mother's guests, roll his eyes and exclaim, "Oh, Gwenny, you are slumming it tonight, Doll. I mean...*really*!" He would turn on his heels and walk away. She got the message.

Having moved close to the centre of Johannesburg, my mother would insist I go with her to visit her friends Margo and Yango at the Diamond Horseshoe Nightclub where my parents had sometimes danced. Even though she was very aware that it was dangerous for an unaccompanied white woman to be out, we would walk into the centre of town late at night. I would be dragged along, I believe, because it made *her feel safer* than being alone on the streets of Johannesburg. She knew full well how dangerous it was for both of us. Yet, she took the risk.

The nightclub was hidden at the back of a luxury used-car lot. The flashing lights and red and white striped awning led members up the stairs to the main entrance. I spent many nights at the Diamond Horseshoe while my mother drank and danced the night away. I would be taken to the adjoining private flat, where Margo and Yango often slept over, to spend the night with their daughter Felicity, whom I had not seen in several years.

My mother would be the first up to dance and stayed until the wee hours of the morning, enjoying life to the full. She sparkled in society. She drank too much, danced all night, but always reverted to a melancholy state the following morning.

Completely forgotten, Felicity and I would sprawl lazily on her bed and talk until eventually we fell asleep, to be woken at dawn by bleary eyed adults. I would be dragged down the stairs into the crisp early morning air. It would be partially light, with streaks of gold and pink across the sky. We were driven home by taxi, my mother looking red-eyed and bone weary. Not a word was spoken.

A few years later my mother continued to frequent the club; but with less money available there was certainly no money for taxis to take us home. In the hours before dawn I would suddenly be shaken awake from a deep sleep. While half asleep, my mother would bundle me down the nightclub stairs, grab for my hand, which she did not normally do, and squeeze it tightly. I could feel her fear; it was palpable. She dragged me along as she walked swiftly through the centre of Johannesburg, over Noord Street bridge (a well-known danger zone), towards Hospital Hill and, finally, to our bed-sit in Del Monico Mansions.

The Diamond Horseshoe evenings with Margo, Yango and the nightclub gang, like many other scandalous evenings with friends, eventually came to an end. Couples who had been firm friends with my parents disappeared from my mother's life. I do believe some of her friends were concerned about her capricious behaviour and the gossip it may cause. She was no longer considered to be part of their exclusive social set.

My mother always made sure there was a half loaf of white bread in the cupboard for her morning toast and tea. She could have made a sandwich for me to take to school, but it *never occurred to her*. Buying the cheaper brown loaf was out of the question. The brown healthy nutty loaf was known as 'servant's loaf'. The white loaf, the flour bleached to a pristine white was the bread eaten by white people and, in my mother's case, with crusts neatly cut off and the sandwich cut into dainty quarters.

I was in the habit of buying sweets, crisps and in the summertime ice-cream after school. I shopped at the local café using my meagre pocket money, received from Aunt Alex or my father. Occasionally I received ten shillings from my father by post, which I used carefully. I had no idea that my choices were unhealthy, but *I did know* that I was hungry. My craving for sugar was possibly a deep underlying issue of feeling unloved, with little sweetness in my life. I have recognised along the way that, when upset or experiencing painful issues of the heart, I instantly have a desire for something sweet. Of course, I ended up with many cavities in my teeth from the sugary foods I consumed.

A sullen, seething anger was building inside me towards my mother that would eventually impact my health. At that point I was unable to recognise that my mother was scared, lonely and unstable. Her choice of friends and acquaintances had become reckless; her behaviour often ill-considered and impetuous. She was no longer in control of herself. Our life together seemed to be on a downward spiral.

1960: Southern Rhodesia (Zimbabwe) gets television.
The government of S.A suppresses liberal ideas.
Televisions in South Africa blocked until 1976.

PART 4

Chapter 29

A School Friendship

Who am I?

*I am pieces of all the places I have been
and the people I have loved.*

Brooke Hampton[57]

My days at Barnato Park finally began. I was studious, serious, and committed. I had made it! I wanted to be well educated, to learn, to grow, to achieve. I was first to volunteer to assist in the Science and Biology laboratory, before and after classes. If I was not there, I could be found sitting on the floor in the Library reading authors such as Emile Zola. I was much younger than the other girls and began the year as a conscientious scholar. With no effort, my grades for Mathematics and Algebra were usually in the 90% region. I had a natural ability to work with equations, figures and numbers, much like my father who refused to use a calculator throughout his life, no matter how complex the calculation.

That first year I kept myself to myself, travelling to school alone. The bus would be filled with giggling schoolgirls, but I made very few friends, remaining reserved and shy. With the home life I was experiencing I felt removed and indifferent to the girls at school. I listened, worked hard, paid careful attention, went home and studied.

After moving to Del Monico Mansions, which was further from the school but close to the city, life at home had become unsettling. I would often find complete strangers in our bed-sit on my return from school, people whom I knew were unacceptable friends for my mother. I felt troubled. These people would appear startled when I arrived home in my well-known school uniform. I also gave off an air of being 'snooty' which challenged them.

On the first day of the next school year, a blonde, skinny girl with an insecure smile joined our class. She sat at the only available desk, which was in front of mine. It was the front desk, on the left side of the class, against the wall. Her name was Irene. We were friends before first break and after a few weeks, we became inseparable. Once it was discovered that we lived close to one another, we began meeting each morning and travelling to school together.

Irene and I always walked briskly through Joubert Park to get the school bus. The bus took us up Twist Street, along Kotze Street, into Abel Road, finally into Tudhope, stopping right outside the school. Walking through Joubert Park on the way to get the bus, neither of us spoke. We hooked arms and hurried, especially in the winter months, with heads down against the icy wind.

No matter what the weather, we rarely noticed life around us. The people sitting on benches reading a newspaper, families strolling through the park, the pretty fish pond, fountains, trees, beds of colourful flowers and manicured lawns. We both understood what we may have encountered only hours before. We gritted our teeth and walked. Irene and I understood each other; no words were needed.

During the winter months both of us would be freezing cold. Johannesburg is bitterly cold in winter, and neither of us had the luxury of heating at home. Irene had no school blazer, and I had no regulation pullover, which meant that neither of us was ever warm. We shivered at the bus stop, Irene's thin legs buckling from cold as we huddled together praying for the bus to arrive. The journey took about twenty minutes but when we arrived at the school gate neither of us were ready for the day ahead.

Irene and I were both studious students and avid readers, yet circumstances had us behaving as if we were quite the opposite. As the year progressed, we began to feel the strain of our home life; neither of us prepared for tests or exams, nor did we do homework assignments. To cover up her embarrassment Irene would 'play up' in class. I do believe that the stress of our combined parental issues led

Irene and me to behave in ways that were totally out of character. We were often unable to focus on school work, yet we were bright, smart, and quick witted. We managed to do well at exam time, despite the challenges at home, which had all the elements of a soap opera. It was a miracle that we remained sane, but we were tenacious, we survived.

After a turbulent weekend, having faced several threads of drama from the adults around us, with some or other calamity to face, Irene and I would stay away from school on the Monday with her younger sister Desiree, affectionately known as Des. The three of us would play truant once or twice a year. Perhaps it was more often than I recall. We did this when we were tired, overwhelmed or behind on school work.

There were times when we stayed away for a fortnight. We dressed for school, said goodbye and walked down the long hotel corridor to one of the communal bathrooms. We hid until the Garretts left for work, then settled ourselves for a day to catch up on sleep or lazed about recovering until we got bored. Then the fun began. Often, we became hysterical with laughter, which was perhaps our way of releasing inner turmoil and distress. We created astonishing mini-musical productions, usually performed and directed by Des. We would also do a dressing-up routine.

There were many nights when the Garretts were asleep and we were wide awake. Des would begin bouncing on her bed; Irene and I soon joined in on our shared bed and before long we were in hysterics, well aware that it was rather childish. We would dress quickly, run along the dark corridor and out into the dark, shadowy street. It was usually close to midnight when we dashed into El Dorado, a late-night café a few minutes away. We gobbled down hotdogs and drank green milkshakes, giggling mischievously, talking loudly and relishing our secret midnight feast in peace. We were usually the only late-night customers.

We happily spent long days together, having uncomplicated fun in the confines of their small hotel room. We felt safe together. For me, deprived of attention or affection, the close connection with my two special friends, who were like sisters to me, was vitally important to me. It also offered me stability of a kind. The three of us needed down time and created our own imaginary 'normal' childhood, unhindered by adults with their self-serving attitudes and dramas. *We needed those days away from school* to revive our inner strength and vitality in order to continue in our respective dysfunctional environments. Those sneaky nights out gave us a huge sense of freedom, yet we were completely naive to the danger in which we placed ourselves.

After approximately ten days we usually felt ready to return to school. We wrote carefully worded letters for the class teachers, and off we went back to school, feeling more able to cope. My mother had no idea where I was during those days and never asked when I returned. For her, one day drifted into the next; she was emotionally numbed and absorbed by her own predicament.

During our third year we all began to feel the impact of our home lives. Irene, especially, found school days a challenge. Her nervous system was on edge; it became impossible for her to sit still through a single lesson. Eventually we were moved to the front of the class for all our lessons. Irene would insist on turning her back on the teacher, she faced me and talked incessantly in quiet tones throughout the lesson. We were both unable to deal with the strict structure of our school day and the disruptions at home. For reasons unknown, Irene's behaviour was allowed to continue without intervention from teachers. Naturally, we thought we were hilarious!

As one of the few in our class who eventually had a steady boyfriend, many eager questions were asked about kissing. An excited group of girls would form a queue at break time, wanting to know how to French kiss. I demonstrated, giving step by step instructions on how to be a good kisser. I was popular for a few weeks, but the more senior girls frowned on our activity. That amusing faze soon ended, but I did gain the reputation of being 'the best kisser' for years after. From that experience, I later became open minded about which gender I kissed.

Food continued to be a big issue for me. My mother appeared to be oblivious to my need to be fed and cared for. She had her own routine and ate little, but as a growing teenager I needed food! If I complained about the lack of meals, she would say, "Here! Take a shilling and go and get yourself a pie." This was not an enticing offer. 'Louis the Greek' was the owner of a small dingy café on King George Street close to Joubert Park. He baked a few meat pies each day, which were the strangest looking pies I had ever seen. The bright yellow pastry was hard and thin; the mince inside, though generous, was tough. Baking was not his forte, but on a hungry day I would buy one, cross over into Joubert Park and sit on a bench under a huge Oak tree, eating the grim pie hungrily. Needless to say, it would be forty years after living in such conditions before I considered eating any sort of pastry or pie again.

Most days I would share food at Longford Hotel with Irene and Des. Throughout the Del Monico years, Gertie, owner of Longford Hotel, who had been a friend of my parents for years, went out of her way to charge their parents for any food I ate at the hotel. She was truly mean-spirited. I uncovered that the Garretts had been billed each month for meals that I may or may not have eaten. When I was told this recently by my dear friend Des, I was shocked and angry. As a hungry schoolgirl, encouraged to join the girls for a meal, I was naive and oblivious that their parents would be charged. To this day, I am deeply grateful to Gay and Larry for their generosity of spirit and kindness.

Each school day at break time, I would wander slowly past the tuck shop and stare longingly at the tray of delicious soft white bread rolls filled with grated cheese and succulent sliced tomato. Irene and I never had enough money to buy one. Neither of us ever bought from the tuck shop, nor did we have a packed lunch. The other students queued to buy food, but never us. It was tough! Some days more than others. We walked away from the temptation and strolled around the school grounds. To this day, cheese and tomato is my favourite sandwich filling.

I would take small amounts of cash from my mother's purse when I could, a few shillings to buy either sweets, ice-cream or crisps from the only small shop on our street. If I was lucky, I would eat something with Irene and Des at Longford Hotel. Slowly I began to gain weight, yet I felt as if I was always hungry, scrounging for food during the week. During the weekend I ate well. My grandmother prepared tasty meals and treats for me which I enjoyed sharing with her and my aunt. A year later, when I began a Saturday job at the local hairdressers, I was able to buy sandwiches and decent food for myself.

Irene and I were unknowingly losing our ability to focus, and our school work began to suffer. We had become slack and demotivated. Life had become unpredictable and there was no balance. I became withdrawn and moody. Irene was often overwrought and nervy, but we pretended, even to each other, that life was great. We both had strong survival skills and an infectious sense of fun. We laughed at life often, which is perhaps what kept us going.

> ...*For the love of a friend who will see us through*
> *Whatever the hazardous things we do;*
> *Yet we will greet the future with this refrain...*
> *"Vincemus! Vincemus! We'll win yet again!"*[58]

PART 4

Chapter 30

Longford Hotel

Pull up a chair.
Take a taste.
Come join us.
Life is so endlessly delicious.

Ruth Reichl[59]

Longford Hotel was a large sprawling building that needed some care, repair and a lick of paint. It stood on the corner of Wolmarans and Wanderers Streets. The structure was solidly built but looked tired and unloved. There were additional rooms in an annexe behind the main hotel, spreading up to the next street with a short-cut to those rooms via the back entrance. The official entrance to the annexe was on Smit Street, across from Johannesburg General Hospital, known locally as 'Jo'burg Gen'.

Gertie had turned a third-rate residential hotel into a thriving business. The hotel was invariably fully occupied. She managed it alone, along with a large, all-male, black staff. Gertie was shrewd, with a steely coldness and a sharp tongue. Her voice could be heard bellowing orders to her staff as she shrieked commands that echoed along the dimly lit passageways. Gertie, unlike her sisters Molly and Edith, who had been good friends of my mother, cared little for her appearance. She dressed in drab frumpy frocks, her hair untidy, her nails grubby and her sallow complexion dull and lifeless. A slight smell of stale body odour lingered around her. Gertie looked as if she needed a long soak and a good scrub. Not even a smear of lipstick touched her thin tight lips. Yet, she showered her younger daughter, Mandy, with every possible fashion and beauty accessory.

The hotel rooms were small and sparsely furnished. Old-fashioned dark oak furniture added a touch of gloom to each room. The basic 'Table d'hote' menu was poor, many plates were returned to the kitchen untouched, with large quantities of bread and butter eaten, in place of the unpalatable courses and frugal portions.

The Garretts and their daughters lived at Longford for several years while Larry was employed by South African Airways. The offices were close by at Rotunda, next to Park Station. The girls occupied a small twin room in the annexe, their parents had a double room, with balcony, across the passage. The girls' room was dark, whatever the season. The rose-pink, candlewick bedcovers were worn and thin—they had seen better days. The blankets were coarse and rough. Overall the room had a cluttered, confined feel to it. The fact that the family were in separate rooms meant that they rarely spent time together.

The Garretts had moved from Durban to Johannesburg and were finding it difficult to adjust to a big bustling city. Irene did not fit in well at school, nor did she make many friends; I don't think that Des had any friends at the junior school. I had been through several challenging years and felt like a misfit myself. We bonded immediately and stuck together until I left home.

Soon the three of us were spending every afternoon in their hotel room, and eventually I slept over several nights of the week. We developed a cosy, reliable friendship and formed a tight-knit trio. Irene, Des and I made our own fun. We giggled and laughed often, but we also shared sadness, confusion and distress. The three of us went everywhere together. We supported each other during those troubled years, living in the dysfunctional world our parents created around us.

The bed-sit where I lived with my mother was exceptionally small and usually filled to capacity with mother's guests. It was far more appealing to spend time at Longford Hotel with the girls. I regularly ran up Wanderers Street late at night to get a night's sleep, sharing skinny Irene's single bed. There were never any questions asked of each other. It was our life.

Gertie and her husband Harry had been long-standing friends of my parents and knew that my mother and I were living in most unsuitable accommodation close by, yet Gertie never offered to accommodate us at the hotel, nor did she offer us a meal. I seemed to be persona non grata to Gertie. She knew I was friends with the Garrett girls and her daughter, Mandy. Yet, she chose to treat me unkindly, but would contact my mother when she needed a favour, usually advice for large social functions or help with special recipes.

I mentioned earlier in my story that I was shocked and disappointed when I discovered (in my adult years) that Gertie had charged the Garretts every time I stepped into the Longford Hotel dining room. Perhaps I have forgotten how often I *did* eat a meal there; but, to the best of my knowledge, I was often there sitting with the girls as they quickly wolfed down their food. I would have a few mouthfuls off their plates, a slice of bread and butter or a shared pudding. Gertie never took the trouble to discover the truth. It would have cost her nothing to feed one child.

I had met Gertie's daughters, Debbie and Mandy, many years earlier. Mandy, the younger daughter, and I had been thrown together whenever our parents were socialising. When I was about seven years old, we attended weekend parties at their lovely home, situated a few minutes' drive from Sandton. After my father left for Rhodesia, I continued going there with my mother.

Mandy and her parents were usually at the Hotel until late, returning home when Gertie's sisters—Tiny, Edith and Molly with invited guests—would be leaving after a day of tennis. Occasionally they arrived home early enough to join in. Mandy would immediately command attention from the adults and take control of the children. She would show off her shoes and dresses in every colour, style or brand and then decide on the entertainment for the children, and we all followed along unhappily.

Once we were all at high school, Mandy was brought back to the hotel by car from the private school she attended. She remained there until her mother closed the office at 8.30 p.m. Once she had greeted her mother, she set about transforming herself from a schoolgirl into a sex-kitten. With thick expertly applied make-up, false eyelashes, bright pink lipstick, teased up hair and hair extensions, she completed her sex-kitten look with a figure-hugging dress worn over a tight corset for exaggerated curves. She was a tall, well-built teenager, but by the time she was done she looked years older. *She looked stunning!* Her clever transformation fooled men into believing she was *no child!*

Mandy was audacious and reckless with people's feelings. She lured and ensnared men and boys alike. They found her tantalising. She discarded them with indifference, often as quickly as she had enticed them to her. It was a game she loved to play and did so well into her adult years. Her need to control was unmistakable. She bossed people around and demanded whatever she wanted. As teenagers it was the three of us who were bossed about by Mandy. I do believe she was unaware of how unkind she was to hotel residents, staff and friends.

It was not unusual for Mandy to barge into the main lounge after dinner service, when all the elderly residents would be relaxing quietly over an after-dinner coffee, some with eyes closed, dosing in the peaceful ambiance. Mandy would storm into the lounge with inflated confidence, throw open the piano and begin to play loud jangling tunes with gay abandon, often slightly off key. She would laugh loudly at her own mischievousness. She would call us in, as we stood cowering in the doorway, to join her in song. Of course, we coyly entered and obeyed.

The peaceful lounge was soon in an uproar with the residents cringing at the deafening tunes and the raucous onslaught of three or more rowdy teenagers. Many of the residents would get up and leave, whilst the more resilient ones would grin and bear it. As each resident left the lounge, Mandy would take over the chairs or the comfy old settee, sprawling across the chairs, legs akimbo, talking loudly, thoroughly enjoying the mayhem she caused. During her teen years Mandy developed an unabashed disrespect for others, both young and old. She became boastful and blasé, but she got little attention from her busy parents and her spontaneous dramas were her way of getting attention. She enjoyed herself thoroughly, but was she ever happy? I wonder.

I saw less of Mandy as a young child, when circumstances changed, and we moved. When we finally moved to the Del Monico Mansions years later, I saw her prancing around Longford daily, but by then I had little time for her pretentious manner and bullying ways. I kept my distance, but Irene was quickly ensnared. I understand that their one-sided relationship continued after I left Johannesburg.

Years later, Longford was sold and demolished, along with all the memories it held. To this day, decades later, the plot of ground in a prime location, remains vacant and undeveloped.

PART 4

Chapter 31

Renee and Gay

*My life isn't good or bad.
It's an incredible series of emotional and mental extremes,
with beautiful thunderstorms and stunning sunrises.*

Jaeda DeWalt[60]

Renee

Renee struck up a conversation with my mother at the local Liquor Store as they waited to be served. Renee began chatting to my mother and, without an invitation, followed her into the building and continued talking rapidly about nothing in particular. Renee walked closely behind my mother all the way up the staircase, until they reached the front door. My mother invited her in for a drink. Renee called on my mother every day from then on. Her early morning visits became a regular feature in our lives for a while. Renee would arrive in an alcohol and medication-induced stupor, shrieking with laughter, usually at her own jokes and ditties that she sang in between conversations. Her favourite ditty was a short verse ridiculing herself: "Renee is a *frot tomatie*" (rotten tomato), which she loved to sing repeatedly, laughing heartily as she sang to her own tune, over and over again.

Renee could sit for hours in her own hazy world, amused by her own thoughts. She was in her early forties with lines of life deeply etched into her once exotic-looking face; she looked worn and beaten down by life itself. She had thick dark hair, with streaks of pure white falling softly around her face, worn short, in a pixie cut. Her huge almond shaped blue eyes were glazed, the red lipstick smeared on her full lips, was always slightly askew. She focused on keeping a steady hand as she gulped her first tipple of the day, often before 8 a.m. My mother sat in her dressing gown, elegantly sipping her morning tea, watching over Renee with an amused, yet disinterested, gaze. After calling regularly each day for several months, Renee simply disappeared.

Gay Garrett

Another early morning visitor who arrived on random occasions was Gay Garrett, my best friends' mother. Gay was a lovely woman and a kind and caring mother—when she was sober. She was a frequent binge drinker, a chronic alcoholic. Gay constantly tried to master her craving for alcohol, but every few weeks or months, she would weaken and begin drinking from early morning. Later in the day Gay would become aggressive, occasionally violent, when her cleverly hidden bottles were found and withheld.

During those frightful incidents Gay would arrive at Del Monico Mansions about six or seven o'clock in the morning, often before we were up and dressed. Her family naively trusted her word, believing that she had left early for work, possibly for stock-taking or another plausible reason that she conjured up. When not on one of her binges, Gay never visited my mother. They were not friends, but Gay felt safe enough or desperate enough to call on my mother whenever she urgently needed alcohol.

Gay was a very attractive woman with a slim figure and thick platinum-blonde hair. She made the most of her looks. Her makeup was expertly applied, her hair attractively set. To an outsider she appeared to be 'happy-go-lucky' but she had one major weakness: alcohol had a strong hold on her. She relapsed regularly, yet she *did* want to overcome her addiction because, when Gay drank, she changed. Once she drank over a certain quantity, Gay was aggressive and uncontrollable. She became frantic if alcohol was running low and frequently came crashing through the front door of our bed-sit in a frenzied state, eyes wild, needing more drink. Her demeanour frightened me when she became erratic and volatile. Thankfully, my mother never lost her composure.

When Gay burst in unexpectedly I would become rigid, my heart pounding, but my mother would take charge. She would sit Gay down, hand her a drink and talk quietly to her. Gay would swallow the drink in one shot, while I looked on with big eyes. My mother would sit next to her, dragging elegantly on a cigarette, watching Gay's every move. She would talk to her as if everything was quite normal and Gay would smile and slowly regain her composure. After chatting for a short while, Gay would start fidgeting restlessly and, after swallowing a few more glasses of wine, she would jump up abruptly, knocking the armchair over or sending other things flying. She looked wild, possessed, and frantic, as she rushed out of the door without a goodbye. My mother said nothing and carried on with her morning, but her visits *troubled me*.

When Gay was on a weekend binge, the girls would search for cleverly concealed bottles of alcohol and pour the contents down the sink. When unable to find her 'stash', Gay would go into an uncontrollable rage, setting off on a rampage to find more alcohol. She screamed, yelled and lashed out at anyone in her way. She often punched her husband Larry, smashed anything in her way, including panes of glass with her bare fists. Such was her desperation to find a drink. It was frightening and disturbing to watch. Gay's inner demons would not let her rest.

When there, I tried to comfort Des who hid in the communal toilets, crying uncontrollably whilst she retched and threw up. I calmed Irene who eventually helped her father to physically control Gay. The 'episodes' usually ended when Larry managed to contain her. Gay fought and thrashed around on the floor with Larry sitting on top of her to stop damage to hotel property or injuries to herself. Larry was calm and patient, perhaps too much so. His casual attitude did not help Gay with her inner demons. Finally, after several hours of putting up a fight, Gay would surrender out of sheer exhaustion and eventually pass out. The silence that followed felt strained, unnatural and, by then, we were all bone weary and emotionally drained.

The binges could go on for a full day or extend into several days and nights of tirades and sleeplessness. Occasionally Gay went running around the hotel frantically looking to anyone who had alcohol or out into the night in her night gown. The traumatic effect and deep humiliation that her daughters endured would climax when their mother arrived at the hotel dining-room drunk, reeling and aggressive. It had a lasting effect on *all of us*. Gay would barge through the heavy dining-room doors during a packed dinner service, stumbling into chairs and tables while screaming.

"*Where is it, where is it*, what have you done with it?"

We would yelp in unison, "*Oh, no!*"

Des cringed, her body shook, her neck and face instantly red with hives. We leapt up immediately and made a dash for it, cleverly weaving our way between tables to give their mother a wide berth. We hoped to stop the scene from escalating in full view of residents and staff. Of course, her drunken escapades were juicy gossip for everyone who lived at the hotel. Gay would storm after us, shouting and waving her fists. We ran back to the room and locked the door, knowing we had poured away her stash and what was about to take place. The fear and distress were intense.

In the summertime I would be invited to a Sunday picnic. The picnic was usually at Hartbeespoort Dam. We would set off early in the morning with Duncan, a good friend of the Garretts, the six of us squashed into his small car. The idea was idyllic: a beautiful scenic drive, the huge dam, rushing waters, the famous tunnel, mountain views and beautiful picnic spots close to the river.

Duncan and Larry liked the occasional social drink. With the intense heat of the day, an open wood fire burning down for a braaivleis, the men began with a few cans of cold lager. During a long leisurely lunch in the blazing heat, Gay began to take a few sips. Larry never stopped her, even though he was aware of the ramifications. That puzzled me. By late afternoon, when the three of us got back from exploring the vast rocky area, we would find the adults, crimson from the sun, deliriously happy and decidedly intoxicated.

The journey home was a blend of terror and fun. The three adults would stagger up the uneven, rocky path to the car park. I always felt anxious as I watched them stumble and falter on the path. Gay laughed mischievously each time she stumbled. She was happy after a day in the sunshine with Larry and Duncan. The two men were attentive, and Duncan openly flirtatious, which Larry did not seem to notice. The road towards home was dangerous. It was a long, black meandering road, with moments when I felt genuine terror as the car veered towards oncoming headlights. Duncan swerved over to the right, then sharply back to the left side of the unlit road that led back to Johannesburg. The hour-long drive seemed to take an eternity. Once on our way, Gay would start singing 'Run Rabbit Run'. As we careered home at high speed, I sang along to steady my nerves, on yet another uncertain shadowy night.

> *On the farm, every Friday*
> *On the farm, it's rabbit pie day.*
> *So, every Friday that ever comes along,*
> *I get up early and sing this little song*
> *Run rabbit—run rabbit—Run! Run! Run!*
> *Run rabbit—run rabbit—Run! Run! Run!*
> *Bang! Bang! Bang! Bang!*
> *Goes the farmer's gun.*
> *Run, rabbit, run, rabbit, run.*
> *Run rabbit—run rabbit—Run! Run! Run!*
> *Don't give the farmer his fun! Fun! Fun!*
> *He'll get by*
> *Without his rabbit pie*
> *So run rabbit—run rabbit—Run! Run! Run! Rabbit, Run Rabbit*

It was often my mother who managed to keep Gay Garrett calm, probably because she accepted that she was an alcoholic and fed her needs, but those were harrowing times. It was not until recently, when I began to write about it, that I recalled how distressing those experiences had been for me.

Irene and Desiree remain traumatised by memories of those events and are unable to speak of it to this day. Their parents were oblivious to the damage Gay's behaviour was doing to their daughters. For that reason, I never told my friends of Gay's early morning visits to our bed-sit in Del Monico Mansions.

PART 4

Chapter 32

Louis Blanché

*There are moments which mark your life,
Moments when you realise nothing will ever be the same.*

John Hobbes in "The Fallen"[61]

Louis Blanché was in his late twenties when I first set eyes on him. He minced gracefully along the passage with head held high, his right wrist held limply midair. He was walking from the lift, even though we lived on the first floor. I was fascinated. Louis was effeminate, his style clean cut and trendy, his voice giggly and girly.

After a few months I discovered that Louis lived three doors away on the same dingy floor of Del Monico Mansions. He smiled widely as he passed me on the corridor and said, "Hello, *Skattie*." ("Hello little treasure.")

I smiled back and we instantly liked one another. Louis thought of me as his younger sister whom he missed dreadfully. She lived with their parents on a farm in the province of the Orange Free State and rarely visited Johannesburg.

When Louis's father discovered that he was a homosexual, he was forced to leave home. That was the plight of many gay Afrikaans men. In his father's eyes, Louis was a disgrace to the family and their community, a misfit, an embarrassment. It had been a very painful time for Louis. Being born homosexual was frightening to him. It was also against the law, and his staunch, narrow-minded Afrikaans father remained ashamed and disgusted.

Louis had no choice but to disappear and set up home in an obscure area of Johannesburg. As a child he had been protected by his mother who knew from the time she found him playing with his sister's dolls.

Louis and his friends soon discovered that Johannesburg was *not* paved with gold; instead it felt formidable, frightening and unfriendly. He kept to himself, only venturing out to work and directly back home.

My mother struck up a conversation with Louis in the elevator one day. He soon began popping by to say 'hello' after work, but quickly became aware of the constant stream of people arriving for 'drinkies' with mother centre stage, telling stories about her past. Her small audience was enthralled and entertained as she elegantly embroidered the tales of her 'grand life' for their amusement. Ah…I remember the stories well.

Louis did not drink or smoke. He found it distasteful, so he soon stopped dropping by. Instead, he would tap on the door and invite me over for cocoa in the evenings or ask me over to have my hair washed and set.

I was in heaven! It was like having a safe haven close to home where it was quiet, demure and sane. We began to spend many happy evenings together; and, eventually, when I decided to leave school, we worked at the same hair salon. He was a calm balancing influence in my life and amused me when he became overly dramatic.

From the very first shampoo and set that Louis did for me in his pretty room, I was enthralled. He shared advise and knowledge about hairdressing which I never forgot. He opened up my creative side which had been completely dormant.

He taught me about hairdressing, creativity and style during the time we worked together. It was through his skills that, in later years, I achieved an excellent reputation as a hairdresser, salon owner and businesswoman. It was far removed from my original plan to attend university and become a surgeon, but what I learnt from Louis set me on a prosperous career path.

Louis Blanché was the kindest human being I have ever had the pleasure of knowing. He was quiet, well mannered, elegant and perfectly groomed. His gentle voice was slow paced and articulate; his manner reserved, with a twinkle in his eye and a ready smile. Louis's creativity and hairdressing skills were incomparable to any I have ever seen. I was dazzled by his unassuming creative brilliance!

I will always remember him with fondness, along with the group of 'gay boys' who encouraged me to have a sense of fun and helped to save my sanity. They gave me hope during a very discordant time in my life.

1960, March 21st: Sharpeville massacre.
1960, August 26th: State of Emergency declared.

PART 4

Chapter 33

'Lana Turner'—Party Time

The thrilling false gaiety of parties
Masks the deep sadness
Behind the false, grinning faces.

An extravagant Birthday Party was planned for 'Lana Turner', a transvestite who arrived rather unexpectedly into our lives through the gay men that lived in the building. Lana simply appeared at our door one evening, and we were taken by surprise. I sat wide-eyed and speechless before managing to compose myself. Lana was dramatic in looks and gestures, yet nonchalant and laid back with it. 'Her' towering 6'3" frame was draped in our doorway with intoxicating 'Primitif' perfume hanging in the air. The aroma was absurdly exotic, causing my nose to become uncomfortably twitchy. Lana Turner's fashion ideas were unique and unconventional, even for the 60s. Her bizarre self-styled outfits were draped, pleated, or pinned, in a particular arrangement around her tall frame, which often made me suck in my breath and gasp. The colourful ensembles were astonishing.

It took a few moments for me to adjust to Lana's entrance. I had no knowledge of transvestites or cross-dressers, neither had my mother, but she showed no surprise. Acting as a convivial hostess, she welcomed Lana into our cramped accommodation with nonchalant ease. Lana never sat down, preferring to remain draped across the threshold, leaning on the doorframe. Each arrival at our front door was unexpected and pure theatre!

"*Daaaahling....,*" 'Lana Turner' shrieked loudly. "I have discovered *the* most *divine* perfume. Oh, with a most exotic aroma! I've been experimenting with a few of my favourite perfumes. I've mixed Primitive and Hypnotic together and *voila!* I have created this *fabuloussss* aroma, and *I feel so erotic!* Don't you just *loooove it,* Gwenny?"

I shuddered, my sinus's assaulted, my breathing shallow, the inside of my mouth tasted like the remnants of Lana's overpowering blend. Once Lana left, the potent mix remained hanging in the doorway, like an invisible haze of the most toxic kind. My mother coughed politely, then wiped her eyes and nose. Lana announced that the birthday celebration was to be held at her glamorous third floor flat, in a building nearby. We were all invited, including my best friend Irene and younger sister Des.

By then my mother's life was unquestionably spiralling downwards, yet she still refused to recognise the signs. The old 'high society' crowd long since gone, the good-hearted Hillbrow friends were no longer in touch, not even Pam, who had been her 'new best friend' for ages. Her current 'Sundowner Brigade' were a less salubrious group; her stories were retold, embroidered, embellished and adjusted to her audience. She had a way with people and was always adored and admired. What I did, where I went, was never questioned. It began to feel more comfortable away from my mother and her daily escapades, including the re-telling of stories I had heard all too often.

I planned to attend the extravaganza of a birthday bash with my friends and my mother. It was a first and a last that I would attend with her. The Friday prior to the party, my mother announced that she had invited someone whom she very much wanted me to meet.

I was immediately on guard. *Really?* All of a sudden, she had my interests in mind and, without discussion, had invited someone especially to meet me? Warning bells rang in my head. She seemed so certain that I would like 'Ernie'! I looked at her with narrowed eyes, my mind racing, looking for reasons behind her determination to put Ernie and me together. Who *was* this person?

It came out eventually. She had met Ernie at Tara Hospital Outpatients, a psychiatric facility[62] she had been referred to by her medical team. She went there each morning for many months. "Yes, Ernie is a *lovely boy*, I am so excited for you to meet him," she said.

"Why is he in Tara Hospital?" I asked curiously.

"Oh, he tried to murder his father," she added casually, as she stared blankly towards the window.

I was dumbfounded! My jaw dropped and remained open for a few seconds before I composed myself. Nothing she said surprised me after that.

The 'goings on' at the party as the night progressed became too bizarre for a young mind and difficult to process. There were gay men mincing about, transvestites, others dressed in glamorous drag outfits including sequins and feather boas, locals in jeans, lesbians in suits, several of us who were of school and college age, and an odd assortment of neighbours. Irene, Desiree and I stuck together like glue, observing the theatrical drama unfold. It was a place where the three of us, still innocent and extremely naive, should never have been invited. Once the party really got going, my mother was the 'belle of the ball' once more.

There were couples gyrating sensually, whilst others preferred a more formal style of dance, sweeping across the spacious floor. The three of us were completely gobsmacked as we stood pressed against the wall sipping Coca-Colas. We clung to each other, giggling hysterically at everyone, dazzled and transfixed by what we saw and totally overwhelmed.

Lenis insisted on having a dance with each of us. We jived joyously around the floor, using the latest jive steps with Lenis's competent lead. It was such fun, but Lenis was enticed away by my mother and the group of gay men buzzing around her.

Ernie, who I was not looking forward to meeting, arrived late with his friend Pete, who was wearing trousers tucked into western-style cowboy boots, something one never saw in South Africa. It looked weird and had us giggling all the more. Pete was tall, lean, and mean looking. Ernie was blonde and cute, with a golden suntan. There was something strange about the way Ernie knitted his brow in concentration, his pale blue eyes squinting narrowly, giving him a feline look that was sly and menacing. For boys in their late teens their presence felt heavy, dulled by life, even in youth. Both of them were twitchy and on edge.

After greeting my mother warmly and meeting me, they shrunk into the dim background, looking out of place and out of their comfort zone. Later they took to the floor together, dancing to a wild rocking tune, their bodies gyrating to a different rhythm than the music playing. I stared at the two young men. They looked as if they had walked straight out of a second-rate Hollywood western.

The dark starry night soon became a pale golden dawn. The weird assortment of adults looked like caricatures in the dim lighting. Thick smoke hung over the room, while stale, perfumed sweat wafted around. The atmosphere felt sticky and sickly with bodies and faces waxen, oily, with thick dramatic makeup smeared down faces, eyes red and glazed. There were frequent comings and goings to the bathroom, my mother included. It bothered me. Was she behaving inappropriately? I worried. But my eyes had become tired as I watched and wondered. I was unhappy with what I was privy to, but too naive to know if it was drugs, sex or nothing at all. Yet, I felt troubled.

It all began to feel rather seedy, shabby and sordid. I shuddered. The three of us decided to leave. As we left the building, we noticed 'Albie', a well-built female following us, but we were streetwise; we gave each other a knowing look and began to run up the street towards the hotel, running as fast as we could. Albie was close behind, running with great speed. One of us shouted *'fish pond'*, and we spun and doubled back, running full steam back to the party. In the entrance of the building there stood a large ornate concrete fish pond. The butch woman, Albie, followed close on our heels. As we got into the building the three of us stopped dead in front of the fish pond and stood, looking like three little angels. Albie lurched drunkenly at us, making a grab for me; the three of us locked eyes, grabbed her jacket lapels, and flung her headfirst into the pond!

Then off we ran at high speed into the dark night, up the street towards Longford Hotel, laughing all the way. The three of us fell into the two small beds, breathless, bewildered, sweating and stupefied by the whole evening, giggling hysterically until we fell into exhausted sleep, dreaming of meeting Albie, perhaps on a dark, lonely night.

There were occasions when I stayed away from home for days, living with school friends rather than at home. My mother never asked. I don't think she cared enough to notice. Fortunately, somewhere deep inside myself, was good common sense. I could have got myself into dangerous situations with no parental guidance or control; but, somehow, I knew better and had a future planned in my mind. Looking back, I see how protected I was, all through my young life. There were always a few exceptional human beings in the background who supported, protected, educated and guided me.

It was years later before I acknowledged the outrageous array of friends my mother had acquired after my father left us.

My formal yet completely unconventional upbringing, with no roots or stability, made it difficult for me in my adult life to adapt or align with any particular group of people. I had grown to expect the unexpected, accustomed to what was shocking, unusual and at times bizarre. My thoughts, opinions and outlook were not that of the person I portrayed outwardly. For many years of my young adult life, my well-dressed, conventional appearance was deceptive. I was not traditional by any means.

1961, May 31st: South Africa no longer ruled by the British.

1961/1963: Mandela heads ANC's new military wing. Sabotage campaign is launched.

PART 4

Chapter 34

Mornings after the Nights Before

*Sometimes, it feels like there is no time to cry
No room to wail.*

Alison Nappi[63]

As I matured, I became more aware of our circumstances. My mother and I were living what most would view as a bizarre life. We were certainly living in a state of poverty according to society's standards, yet we were often surrounded by affluent Johannesburg people. None of them ever offered my mother help financially; if they did it was certainly not enough to cover our basic needs. *How could my father let us to live this way? How could he!*

My ambition to attend the University of Witwatersrand to study medicine never diminished, it was constantly on my mind. I convinced myself that I would get to university; but at the back of my mind I knew that it would be impossible because of the circumstances my mother had led us into. She had absolutely *no idea* what I wanted to do when I completed my schooling. It had never been discussed. My education had never been considered or taken seriously. There were days when I was filled with a smouldering anger towards my parents.

I became openly irritated and unyielding of my mother's lifestyle. Her visitors, arriving at any hour of the day or night, were a constant intrusion. My mother, the life and soul of any party, charmingly welcomed them. She had an 'open house' policy that stood firm no matter what I said. She did not know when to stop, or how to say "No!"

Soon I began to look more like an adult than a child and was taller than my mother. From an early age, my aunts and grandmother had encouraged me to be confident. I had developed a refined manner like my mother, and I was proud that I attended a prestigious school in spite of our dire circumstances. This caused several of my mother's new acquaintances to feel uncomfortable in my presence; I admit to being aloof and standoffish towards them. My mother kept her elegant appearance in well-worn couturier outfits and a ladylike manner, which left people puzzled to find us in such inappropriate surroundings.

I was a serious student. Well, initially I was… As the alarm clock rang at 6 a.m., I would open my eyes, get out of bed, quickly dress and prepare for school. The front door, which my mother never locked, would frequently burst open and Gay or Renee would stagger in breathlessly with "have you got a drink for me?"

My dear mother never judged and never said, "No." Whatever the hour, she greeted friends warmly. She quickly put on her flowing floral dressing gown, ran a comb through her hair and added a touch of lipstick. She poured them a drink and made herself a pot of tea. I was left in the awkward situation of attempting to get dressed for school without privacy.

Random people began to appear through the door, as if out of thin air. My mother served copious glasses of wine in fine crystal glasses to her guests, and she remained vivacious, a good listener with a lovely sense of humour. She was a thoroughly congenial hostess who played her well-practised role expertly even in our cramped accommodation. She was kind and gentle and never said the word "No" to anyone—except for me and my brother.

These small, impromptu social gatherings went on for hours, often well into the night. During these extended gatherings, I was expected to fend for myself, carry on with my school work and ignore the packed bed-sit. To my recollection none of her friends ever arrived with a gift of any kind: a bottle of wine, flowers, chocolates, fruit or food. Nor did they ever invite her out. On reflection, it was obvious that it had become well known that my mother would offer drinks and good company to whomever arrived. She was generous to a fault, putting social appearances before her children's needs. On the rare days when she was not entertaining, she would be in bed and asleep by 8.30 p.m. She seemed unable to spend time alone and needed to be a popular social butterfly.

There were mornings when I woke to find one or two people still there, looking worse for wear. I disliked having no privacy. I felt intruded upon and my mood was as cold as ice. I had a practised routine: gather up my school uniform, a towel, toiletries and go to one of the communal bathrooms to wash and dress. Without breakfast or a goodbye from my mother, off I went to get the school bus, returning from school in the late afternoon, exhausted from tennis or hockey, at which I was useless, *to find more people there!* Often when several of her friends arrived together, an intimate party developed and just kept going.

When I walked into the room, filled with 'hangers on' and thick with cigarette smoke, my temper raged. In my frustration I would goad my mother, "Is there any lunch for me?"

The response would be a smiling nonchalant "No."

There was never a crust or a crumb to be had in that place. Her guests, usually about four or five of them, sat crammed together in the small space, looking far less attractive by the afternoon. Conversation would come to a sudden halt, everyone aware that the party needed to come to an end. They would gaze at me sheepishly, bewildered by my sudden appearance in my school uniform, yet surprised by my mother's dismissive manner.

The slightly inebriated guests would rattle in their purses and pockets to find a few coins, which they handed to me.

"Here you are sweetie-pie, go and get yourself something to eat," and off I'd go. By the time I got back from the local café, the party had usually come to an abrupt end. I would throw the windows open and breathe a sigh of relief.

On other occasions, my mother's guests would be too intoxicated to realise that I had arrived home. The jolly conversation would continue with my mother, ever the perfect hostess, putting everyone at ease. I was invisible to them, perched on the end of my bed, as close to the window as possible, attempting to do homework. On many of those occasions it felt so suffocating that I would leave immediately, walking quickly up the street to join Irene and Des at the hotel.

I would wake on a summer morning, the small room hot from the morning sun beaming through the window. I usually got onto my knees and put my head and upper body out of the window for air.

On those hot dry summer mornings, I wanted to scream. It would be early, yet the air hung low and heavy in that room, smelling of stale perfume, alcohol and cigarettes.

I was angry and felt caged and confined by life. I would sit at the window looking out and breathing in deeply, aware of tension running through my body. From where I sat on my bed, I was too close to the slurred voices of my mother's friends. Their speech was laboured from tiredness and an all-night drinking session.

I must add that *my mother was never noticeably intoxicated,* nor did she ever look the worse for wear. She simply did not know how to say "No" to friends who over-stayed their welcome. It was a normal school day for me, so I needed to wipe the sleep out of my eyes, get out of bed in front of strangers, go to the communal bathroom, wash the stale odours from my shoulder length hair, dress quickly and leave to meet Irene at Joubert Park.

The other girls who attended Barnato Park lived in Yeoville, Bellevue, Houghton, Orchards, Melrose and Dunkeld, with very few from Hillbrow or Hospital Hill. After school we got a bus home from Tudhope Avenue. Many of the girls were collected by beautifully coiffed mothers with long painted nails, who arrived in gleaming motor cars. I stood tall, knowing that, in spite of limited means and the repugnant place called 'home', *I alone,* was paying the fees to attend high school. I was immensely proud of that. I excelled at maths—algebra and arithmetic—and had a keen interest in science and biology. I managed above-average grades, in spite of not having space or privacy to study at home. In the Science and Biology Laboratory I found profound stillness in the cool, quiet, environment. It was my introduction into a world to which I wanted to belong, but the calm I found there was short-lived.

My frustration at my home life kept growing and, moving into the third year of senior school, I stopped taking pride in my work. I became blasé and uncaring about school in general. Irene and I both took that attitude; one of reckless indifference. By mid-year I was not coping and began to lose sight of my hopes and dreams. It no longer seemed to matter. By then I believed that I did not matter to *anyone.* That belief became an ingrained pattern in me; I carried it with me and recreated it in almost every situation and relationship until one day, much later in my life, I woke up one morning and declared *"What about me?"* But, during those senior school years, I bounced between indifference, determination and resistance, while also dealing with being a teenager—the hormones and overwhelming emotions.

From an early age my brother and I were expected to meet and greet guests; it was done rather formally. We had to be clean, well dressed and were reminded to sit quietly, be polite when spoken to and not to fidget. As a young girl I attempted to keep to those rigid standards; I endured my mother's lifestyle and forced myself to be tolerant of her friends with as much dignity as I could muster. I observed and internalised the life that I saw around me. As a young adult I never appeared to others to be an outsider, yet the combination of influences during my childhood—at times overly formal and cosmopolitan, but slowly moving towards the bizarre and outlandish—led me to become exactly that: an outsider.

I am still unable to be in small spaces. I constantly dream of wide-open space in front of me and larger airy rooms. I have never found the perfect home. I constantly searched for more space, bigger windows, higher ceilings and wider views. It is not claustrophobia exactly, but the memory of being trapped in a life confined to a small, crowded space and living in what felt like an unfinished Operetta.

There were many more indelible happenings that took place at the Del Monico Mansions; the finer details of those events, I am unable to put into words.

PART 4

Chapter 35

Daryl Returns

*You know who you are.
The walls around you don't change that.*

Late one afternoon, after two years, my brother, Daryl, stepped casually through the door of our humble abode. His arrival was completely unexpected. It wiped the smile clean off my mother's face. Her perfectly painted red lips dropped, her eyes were wild, like a frightened child. I saw the fear in her blue eyes as she struggled to compose herself. Daryl stood casually in the doorway as if he had returned from a brief outing. He said "Hello," and sat down before being asked. My mother stared at him wide-eyed and startled. I knew that Daryl's return would change *everything!* I smiled mischievously as I looked on.

Daryl was over six-foot tall by then and athletically built. He was a young man rather than a teenage boy. My mother was noticeably unsettled by his unannounced arrival. The air felt prickly as his presence filled the small room. She had not seen her son since the day he left for school that forgotten summer morning. She asked no questions and offered no excuses for not searching for him or contacting him after Mrs. Russel had visited us. I sat watching her awkwardness; her mind must have been reeling. Once she composed herself, her attitude soon became nonchalant. There was no doubt in my mind that it was *a huge shock* for our mother, but for me the scene before me was fascinating. I wondered what was about to unfold.

Daryl was reserved, vague and non-committal; he seemed to be a million miles away. I sat staring at him, curious about the day he decided to disappear. *Had he planned to leave or was it a sudden decision? What was it about that particular day that decided him not to come home again?* He left in a school uniform and arrived back home in denim jeans and a crisp white shirt. He had a holdall full of good clothing and personal items that the Russels had provided for him. He never explained why he had returned so suddenly, or what his plans were. Nor did he offer up the reason why he had left the Russels, since by then he had been accepted as one of their family.

After his initial greeting to me, "Hello, Sis," he did not utter another word to me. He hardly acknowledged my presence. It was surreal.

There was no joyous welcome home for my brother, no fanfare, no family discussion or cosy dinner around the table. He had come from a sprawling family home in Kensington, filled with family, friends and laughter; I could not imagine how he must have felt; but, like my mother, he revealed *nothing*.

My mother dashed off to see Mrs. van Rensburg, the Caretaker, and had extraordinary luck. A room two doors away, had become vacant only days earlier. With little fuss, within twenty-four hours, my brother was living opposite us in another bed-sit. I don't know how my mother managed to arrange everything so quickly and quietly but, *in that instance,* she made things happen. A single bed, a chair, curtains and a record player, were the only items put into Daryl's room. In my mind, she should have made more of an effort. The bare wooden floor and sparse furnishings gave the room a cold impermanent look. It was as sparsely furnished as a monk's cell.

News travelled fast. For the very first time there were no visitors that evening. The first floor was silent. I could hear whispers in the corridor, everyone intrigued by my brother's arrival. I imagined gasps from the gay boys at the whiff of a family drama, eager to know what was going on. Mother's cosy drinking companions stayed away for weeks, a few of her male friends, on seeing my brother's tall stature and athletic build, never returned. Most of her friends were startled. They had *no idea* that she had a son.

Daryl showed no outward signs of awkwardness or ill feelings. He kept his distance and offered little about the years he had been gone. He put on Elvis records and retreated into his own world.

Days later Daryl declared to my mother that he had no intention of returning to school to complete his education. As usual, my mother gave no response and let it be. Life quietened down for a while. My mother took on a more demure role. She put down her wine glass and turned her attention to the little stove. Wearing a new floral apron, she cooked meals for my brother and washed and ironed his clothes. In some strange way, having a man around gave her life a purpose.

Within days of meeting Daryl, my friend Irene was popping in to visit him every afternoon to listen to his extensive selection of rock & roll music. He was a huge Elvis fan and had all the latest records. For the first few months we spent afternoons practising our jive steps in Daryl's room, while he sat looking on, a wry smile on his face. The music was loud, our feet banging heavily on the bare wooden floor, but that did not hinder us at all. Fortunately, the neighbours were out at work; but we were teenagers and never gave the noise a thought.

My mother never said a word. In fact, she was strangely silent for the first month that my brother was back home. For Daryl, living at Del Monico Mansions was a total bore. He was nowhere near a swimming pool, rugby field or his friends. He became irritated with my mother and disliked her friends. He felt disdain towards her and did not hide it. He harboured an intense dislike for her that remained with him throughout his life. My sensitive brother struggled to settle into a very limiting life. His own room was uninviting for a modern young man, and he was living in a building that he saw as decrepit with an assortment of eccentric, unconventional, and outlandish tenants. He had a very traditional outlook, whereas I had adapted to all types of scenarios and people.

I had no idea that my brother had contacted my father after approximately five years of silence between them. Without a word, my brother wrote explaining that he could not live with my mother under the present circumstances. He was not impressed with her lifestyle and the conditions he found us living in. At that stage I was beginning to feel that I had reached my limit, too.

Within three months of arriving back home, without a goodbye to my mother, my disillusioned unhappy brother left Johannesburg by train for Durban. The warmth of the sun, the sea, his love of swimming and surfing and the happy-go-lucky holiday atmosphere soon restored his spirits. He found a place that felt right, and he finally felt at home. Daryl never left Durban, not even to holiday elsewhere, until his passing in April 2018. May he find love and real joy, on 'the other side'.

I discovered years later that my brother's reason for leaving the Russels was a serious falling out with Ronald, their son and his best friend. It was never mentioned by either of the boys, nor did his friends or Ronald's family speak of it. The two young men never saw each other again.

I learnt more about my father from letters I received from my brother. After approximately four years my father was still unable to walk or work. At Durban's Addington Hospital he continued with various surgical procedures and treatment to his badly smashed leg.

A few days after my brother left, life reverted back to how it had been before his sudden appearance. People slowly crept back, the room soon filled with intoxicated voices, and the drinks flowed. Mother dear dropped her demure façade, flung the apron aside and once again was the life of the party, celebrating for several days. I groaned as I watched new episodes of the soap opera unfold, with my mother as the star of a brand-new series. Her stories, embellished by her mannerisms, became even more exaggerated. Apparently, she had decided it was time to throw caution to the wind and live each moment with vivacity. I crept in and out unnoticed.

PART 4

Chapter 36

Survival—My Health

*Everything that's ever hurt you helped you hide
From your glory, your magnificence,
From the enormous inner power
under which no illusions of smallness can survive.*

Alison Nappi[64]

The situation at home in the confined space, devoid of personal boundaries, without privacy and lack of proper nourishment, while attending a prestigious high school, began taking its toll on my health. There were no warning signs, but I was about to reach breaking point. One day, sitting close to the open window away from my mother's two guests, I developed sharp searing chest pains; pain so severe that I was eventually doubled over on the bed groaning. It was unbearable. My mother disengaged from her conversation, looked across at me and asked what was wrong. I told her. She replied, as I lay writhing on the bed, "well, if it is *that bad*, you had better get the bus to the Children's Hospital." She turned back to her conversation. I lay still for a while, resting between the stabbing pains.

In the late afternoon I found the strength to drag myself up to the General Hospital and take a mini-bus to the Children's Hospital. On arrival at the hospital entrance I must have looked extremely ill; I saw two nurses run towards me and they half carried me to an A&E consulting room. I was kept in overnight. My mother did not call the hospital when I did not return home. In the morning, after several tests including an ECG, blood work and x-rays, I was placed on a drip.

The following afternoon I quickly dressed after the final bedside visit from the doctor and his team. I was sent back to the Jo'burg Gen by mini-bus, with a supply of medication for my heart, duodenal ulcer and hay fever. All that to deal with alone, before I had reached my fourteenth birthday! The next day I lay self-consciously with my face towards the wall, wishing I could disappear. I prayed for quiet. My mother's friends had no qualms about continuing their fun. Surrounded by a small group of admirers, aware that I was seriously ill, my mother made no effort to quieten down. I remained in bed for several days, unable to get myself up and about. Not even my naive aunts had been to see how I was. They had no idea how or where we even lived! I felt abandoned and alone.

As I lay in my rickety narrow bed with a circle of adults sitting a few feet away on the edge of my mother's bed, I made a sudden decision. My life had to change! It was obvious that my mother would never reach any sensible understanding of where her reality was taking her. Nor was she capable of caring for me. I understood, even at my age, that a university education had to wait. I needed to leave school and find a job. I was almost fourteen, going on forty, and at that point *I was deeply unhappy.* If I continued as I was, I had a strong feeling that I would not survive. Yet, I had no intention of stopping life from moving forward. Warning bells were ringing, and I intended to find an escape route.

Finally, I went back to school, feeling weak and run-down. I had no desire to be at school any longer, nor did I care to remain at home. I felt that something deep inside me had broken. The cardiologist had given me a letter excusing me from all sports activities that year. I returned to the hospital each week until my health stabilised. It took a year for me to feel well again. The heart issue has continued throughout my life.

PART 4

Chapter 37

Two Angels Appear

Things are only impossible until they're not.

Captain Jean-Luc Picard, Startrek[65]

Mary Russel

Mary Russel arrived in perfect time and probably 'saved' me. I had begun to dread having to deal with another day of the life I was living. I often wondered where God was in all this. I was feeling let down but slowly beginning to feel in better health. The medication had kicked in and each day I felt stronger.

Mary Russel arrived out of the blue one cold winter's evening. I was alone and taken by surprise. Mary had heard from friends of Ronald's and my brother's school pals that I had been ill. She decided to check for herself. Mary was in her mid-twenties and married to Ronald's handsome older brother, Brian. She had married into a well-educated Kent family but she was a true Cockney. Mary had been married for five years and had two young daughters. Even so, she was adventurous, daring and rough around the edges. She was fashion-conscious and especially loved the new 60s fashions. She was cheeky, flirty, forthright and fun to be with. Mary had little time for my mother, but she was polite.

From then onwards Mary visited me on Friday evenings when my mother went dancing. She made the visits interesting and exciting, openly showing an interest in my welfare. I began to relax as we talked. We spoke about fashion, music, boys, school, and she gently broached the subject of self-care, fitness and my weight. I had put on weight since starting high school due to eating whatever I could buy with my meagre pocket money. I had become plump. She told me how pretty I was, and if I lost the 'puppy fat' I could wear fashionable dresses just like hers. By then I was wearing well-worn items from my mother's wardrobe. I had lost confidence and lacked self-esteem. Mary encouraged me to eat fruit instead of sweets and do gentle exercises, even though space was limited. I did exactly that.

I have no idea what Mary knew, or her opinion of my mother, but guessed that she did not approve of how my mother treated my brother and cared little for her attitude towards me. If she knew more than I did, she never mentioned it. With each visit Mary brought the latest teen magazines, which gave tips on makeup, diet, fitness and new crazes, as well as full-page pictures of pop singers and young movie stars. I was hooked on the glossy magazines and began to follow them to the letter. *Jackie* and *Teen Scene* were my favourites. Mary continued to visit, and I began to eat healthily and think differently about myself and life in general. I began to feel good about myself and for the very first time I was excited about a future. I was becoming a proper, trendy, teenager!

I began buying my own half loaf of bread, made myself toast before school, then stopped to buy apples on my way home. I even attempted to create a salad of sorts, with what I could find locally for my evening meal. To my surprise my mother began preparing me an evening meal. She set a place at the table and when I arrived home there it was. A large mixed salad. I was surprised and suspicious, but eventually guessed that someone, possibly Lenis, had spoken to her. Neither of us said a word about it. She continued to do this each day while I was on my health and happiness regime. Her friends would sit watching me devour my healthy meal. Then Aileen offered to keep a record of my weight loss.

I went down to the pharmacy each week to be weighed on proper scales, which every pharmacy had in those days. Each night, once everyone had left, no matter how late, I would do stretches and simple exercises that I read about in the teen magazines. Using the Oak dresser as my handrail, I worked at my fitness. It was awkward, but I was determined. Each new day uplifted and inspired me; within three months I had lost thirty pounds. I emerged from my cocoon as an attractive young woman with poise and newfound confidence. I felt amazing.

Mary gave me the original dress she had worn on the first night we spoke about my weight. It was a pale green and white floral in glazed cotton with a deep V-neck and full skirt. She also gifted me with a wide belt to wear with the dress and a yellow, 30-yard, stiff net petticoat to wear under the dress. It fitted like a dream. I felt like a million dollars! After seeing the dramatic change in me, Aunt Alex helped me cut and sew a few skirts and bought me two crisp, glazed cotton blouses. My mother's friend, Michael Levy, then Manager of OK Bazaars in Hillbrow, was amazed at my transformation and allowed me to choose two new dresses from the store. I was thrilled. I had not had anything new in six years. Lenis, who watched over me, was a ballroom dance champion and teacher. He gave me quick daily dance lessons every evening, in the passage. It was enormous fun!

My life was changing. Mary planted the seed and continued to encourage me. Soon after I was able to fit into Mary's dress, she had Ronald phone to invite me to a house party. I discovered that the teenage parties were a regular happening at the Russels' home. His parents were present, sitting quietly in the kitchen while the boisterous crowd took over the house. They loved having young people in their home, knowing we were safe.

That first Saturday night I saw how Ronald looked at me. It was the first time I had met him, even though he had been my brother's closest friend. I was captivated by his quiet confidence, good looks and tall physique.

Mary continued to feature in my life, although once I began dating Ronald, we saw less of each other, but she was always there for me.

Paddy Fischer

On her twenty-first birthday Paddy Fischer's stepfather, a well-known race-horse trainer, presented her with the keys to a fully fitted hairdressing salon on King George Street, close to the extensive

Jo'burg Gen Hospital. Paddy had completed her hairdressing training, and this was an unexpected gift for lovable, disorganised, Paddy.

Paddy Fischer was about seven years older than I was. She was no longer a girl, but neither was she ready to become an adult. She was stuck in-between. Paddy had long gangly legs and a natural inclination to stoop because she was constantly reminded that she was 'too tall for a girl'. Her clumsy gait and knock knees had her frequently tripping over her own big feet. Paddy was kind and gentle but very immature and scatty. She was naive but enthusiastic and friendly to everyone, whereas I was untrusting and cautious.

I could not imagine Paddy as a businesswoman, but she was a hardworking and exceptionally talented hairdresser. Her physical characteristics were blurred by her creative talent. Paddy was a one-in-a-million talent, which is how her parents saw her, forgetting her lack of experience or the expertise required to manage a successful business.

One afternoon, to get away from the 'carry on' at home, I went strolling around the neighbourhood. I sauntered up the street, passing a new block of shops and a recently opened hair salon, Chez Petite. Paddy was standing at the door and I stopped, peering inside to get a better view. We began to chat.

Paddy's stylish salon had only been open a few days, which made Paddy restless and bored. She invited me in for a free hairdo and a cup of coffee. I was delighted and even though I was still in my school uniform, I accepted her offer. Paddy and I sat talking about hairdressing, fashion and style for hours. We clicked instantly and eventually became good friends.

I was more mature and serious than Paddy, even though there was a big age difference. Our budding friendship was spontaneous and comfortable, and I soon began popping by to see her. Without thinking, I would tidy up Paddy's trail of chaos in the stylishly decorated shop. It was obvious that Paddy needed help. She was a creative stylist, but needed an assistant who could multi-task and focus on other matters for her. That eventually became my role.

Paddy quickly became known in the area and was constantly busy. She soon asked for my help and I gladly accepted. I agreed to work whenever possible, even though it meant I saw less of Irene and Des.

PART 4

I began working on a Friday afternoon until late and within weeks I was also there on Saturdays. I loved meeting the clients and earning money of my own. It was a godsend.

I especially enjoyed spending time with Paddy and being part of her new venture. I watched, listened, learnt and absorbed, while sweeping the floor, making tea, passing curlers, sorting towels and eventually shampooing clients and applying colour. I was quicker at cashing up, which also became my job as well as making entries into the daily taking book and banking the money.

I was soon talking non-stop to Paddy about Louis and his exceptional talent and knowledge about all things related to hairdressing. Paddy invited him to meet with her and within weeks Louis left his job in Yeoville, where he had worked for many years, and joined Paddy at Chez Petite.

During a brief conversation about my circumstances, Paddy offered to help in any way possible. She suggested I begin full time employment officially, as her apprentice. My plans for the future were still to attend university, but those thoughts were gradually fading, even though in preparation my studies included Latin, science, biology and maths. Paddy understood that I needed time to think. It was a step in a very different direction, but life with all the difficulties had become too challenging to delay having financial independence.

A week later I nervously knocked on the office door of the school's Head Mistress, Miss Langley. She listened intently to my desire to leave school before the end of term, but I was only fourteen. My shame and pride did not allow me to tell her the truth about my home life, even though it was that which urged me to make such a life-changing decision. Miss Langley advised me to stay on and finish my education. She added that I was far too young to take up employment, but I was adamant. She informed me that by law I was *not permitted to leave* and explained that a school-leaver needed to be sixteen years of age or have completed the Matric (final) exams.[66]

Miss Langley wrote to my mother, but my mother had never attended any school meetings or functions except to enrol me. She ignored the letter. A few weeks later, she received an official letter from the School Board, summoning her to attend an urgent meeting. That shook her. It was a very serious matter back in those days. She had ignored Miss Langley's letters and officials had become involved.

I attended that meeting, held in Braamfontein, with my mother the following week. The School Board were stern, much to her alarm. In that instance her charm and graciousness went unnoticed. At the long table before us sat a serious group of serious men who challenged my mother and my determination to forego my education. They were intimidating.

"Why have you not taken up this matter with the school Principal?" they asked.

"I had no idea," whimpered my mother.

"How can you *not know* of your child's idea of going to work at fourteen?" they shouted.

Questions were fired at my mother for which she had no answers. She knew nothing about my school life or any of my exam results. The board members were staggered and appalled.

When they finally addressed me, they were interested in *my story* and were patient and kind. My mother, of course, had no idea how I had done at school nor that I was planning to leave, all of which was discussed before her. She was surprised by what she heard and aghast at being the target. When they reprimanded her for lack of interest in my education and vague answers, she remained silent, timidly responding with few words. She was clearly shaken, yet never accepted any blame for my need to leave school at fourteen, out of sheer desperation.

The meeting concluded. I would be required to attend a week of assessments, which included aptitude tests and interviews with various consultants and child psychologists. We both sighed with relief when their questioning was over. It had been a long-drawn-out, ordeal. I waited for results, which eventually arrived by post. I was informed that I would be required to complete the school year and attend a year at a commercial college to give me a better foundation for a working life. And that was what happened next.

Johannesburg High School for Girls no longer exists. The 1912 Queen Anne style building has been demolished. Sadly, the school eventually lost its shining reputation, prestige, and high level of education. Today, Barnato Park High School for boys and girls reflects the new demographics of Hillbrow and Berea.
June 1989: Johannesburg High School for Girls, was condemned after 102 years. It officially closed on 31 December 1989.

PART 4

Chapter 38
First Love

In the midst of hell...you can still find heaven...

Danny Dummitt[67]

Within weeks Ronald and I were inseparable. We only had eyes for each other. Soon we were 'going steady' and I was in heaven! At every opportunity he would take two buses after school to visit me during the week. He was in his final year of school.

Ronald's weekday visits were awkward. There was no space for us to be together, to sit and talk but, somehow, he understood. No words were needed. We would stand or slouch around the passages and corridors to have privacy and alone time. We even ventured up onto the roof-top of the building. We kissed intensely and passionately before he left in the early evening and spent every weekend together. I would travel by bus to Kensington and once he had his driver's licence, he came into town to collect me. We had fun lolling around their family home all weekend with his friends, listening to the latest records. 'Runaway' by Del Shannon and 'The Wanderer' by Dion, were my favourites at the time. We were both very tactile and would hold hands or cuddle up as we planned the music for each party. We enjoyed innocent teenage fun. I was finally happy! Or as happy as I knew how to be.

It was the first time that love and attention was showered on me. I soaked it up. I was like a sponge and could not get enough of his tender, loving, nature. Looking back, I can see that I spent most of my childhood as an observer, patronising my mother and her assortment of eccentric friends. This created a complete indifference and distance from young people of my age who lived 'normal' lives. I could not relate. I lived amongst a diverse bunch of adults who would be viewed as peculiar, pretentious, queer, bizarre, eccentric, drunks, or just plain odd. There was a serious, secretive, cautious side to me, but that did not stop me from having special times with Ronald.

Ronald was not a typical South African teenager. Originally from Kent in England, he was well spoken, well-mannered and had a mature attitude. He had a bright mind and a happy disposition. He was tall and good looking with an athletic build, yet he appeared slightly lanky. His disheveled appearance was appealing. His golden-brown hair fell over his left eye, and his sparkling, long-lashed, hazel eyes framed his mischievous doe eyes. Ronald's elegant hands with long slim fingers, when entwined with mine, were reassuring yet intensely sensuous. His soft mouth was inviting; our kissing sessions went on for hours (definitely the best kisser ever).

I enjoyed his light-hearted attitude towards life. He was amusing, flirtatious, tactile and charming. There was a confidence and refinement not seen in South African boys of his age. His parents had moved to South Africa before he began senior school, which is where he met my brother. I felt safe and exhilarated when we were together and, once we were more serious, I never considered a future without him.

I was challenged every day with the situation at home and my mother's ways. There were times when I had no idea where I was headed, but Ronald kept me centred and filled with hope for a brighter future. Weekends were the highlight of my week and my salvation. It gave me time away from mother's world and an opportunity to experience life as a 'normal' teenager. I spent time with other young people, being carefree: dancing, laughing and living a young teenage life. Yet, in the back of my mind, I knew how peculiar my home life was from that of other teenagers.

Those weekends were nothing like my 'other' life. I saw myself as the 'odd one out', but did my best to blend in. *I wanted to be just like them*, but my life had been very adult, filled with an assortment of grownups, living in the fast lane, unrestrained, flamboyant and utterly shameless. The weekend house parties at Ronald's place allowed me to pretend I was just like the other girls: a young teenage girl, dating a super cool, handsome, guy.

During those weekends, life felt good; but the real truth was that, in the world of 'normal', I felt awkward and out of place. In my world, I was surrounded by bizarre characters and circumstances and far removed from the world of 'happy families', but Ronald was a joy, and I was in love! He drew me in with a sweetness I had never known before, and something deep and strong developed between us. I could feel it even when we were apart. Socially we had good fun, but by comparison to what I had seen and experienced in life, it was young and innocent.

Whatever he knew about my life from his friendship with my brother, he never mentioned my home life. We never even spoke of the years my brother had lived with them, or how that came about. I am sure there had been many discussions about my brother and I with his parents. The Russels had been generous and unconditional to my brother, yet Ronald and I never spoke of the day my brother left home, nor of his reappearance years later.

During those blissful romantic times, Ronald and I were very happy. We enjoyed every minute we spent together! He made me feel alive and as happy as I was able to be.

Chapter 39

College

*What makes you brave is your willingness
to live through your terrible life
and hold your head up high the next day.*

Alysha Gwen Speer, Sharden[68]

No help or guidance was ever offered, nor intervention, from teachers, until I decided that I needed to leave the school. In those years it was against the law to leave at such a young age, even though I had completed standard 8/Form 3 with good grades, considering my haphazard study efforts. But I was surprised at how quickly the School Board stepped in.

It was the first occasion during my schooling that my mother attended anything to do with my education, and it felt rather strange. In that instance she had no choice. The conclusion was that the School Board had waived any fees at a selected commercial college for a year. There I was to study English, typing, Pitman's shorthand, letter writing, filing, bookkeeping and Mercantile Law.

And so, my college life began. I found the subjects tedious, the daily travel tiring and, overall, I did not enjoy the year. I attended without paying fees and books were supplied, but I did not have a typewriter at home for homework practice, nor did I have the uniform, which caused me great embarrassment yet again. I felt ashamed and uncomfortable every single day. My saving grace was Paddy. All through that year I worked as many hours as I could at Chez Petite.

As my year at college continued, I felt lonely and alienated. I had coped with my life whilst in close contact with treasured friends and others who supported me, and I had a daily routine that was familiar.

PART 4

At college I felt lost and out of place. To add to my awkwardness was the fact that I did not have the required uniform: brown shoes and stockings, dark brown skirt, white shirts and dark green cardigan. I could not escape the daily humiliation and indignity. Each day at college was a challenge. I began to wonder why 'my lot in life' was so tough and wondered if I was on my way to becoming a sub-standard human of little value. Those early teenage years, with hormones and emotions flaring, made my days at college a nightmare!

It took all my courage to walk out of the front door each morning to get the bus, knowing I looked out of place amongst the other students. My white shoes, smothered in brown shoe polish, were more oxblood than dark brown; my cinnamon-coloured dress had seen better days. *I felt sick!* My embarrassment caused me to become intentionally unsociable.

The Commercial College in Kensington was two bus rides from home and the students were a few years older and more mature. Many of the girls were sophisticated and smartly turned out, with pretty hairdos and manicured nails, and then there was me. I stuck out like a sore thumb.

The bookkeeping lecturer I remember well. He was pompous, quick-tempered and enjoyed picking on one of us during lectures. There were days when his outbursts were distressing. If you were not paying attention, he would stand close beside you whilst sticking his pencil into your ear, demanding that you listen more carefully. In present time that would *not* be accepted or tolerated, and rightly so. His lectures were more like an endurance test. Needless to say, I acquired no bookkeeping skills and disliked it intensely.

I have fuzzy memories of that year, but it was definitely my *'annus horribilis'*. During that year I behaved in a very aloof manner. I wanted to hide! I was unable to blend in or relate to any of the students, but the secretarial course stood me in good stead in later years when I was managing my own businesses.

To this day, decades later, while I do not lack confidence, hidden in my unconscious mind is a tiny remnant of those college days. I rarely step out of my door without the weeniest bit of tension about facing the world at large, wondering if I look presentable enough. Unconsciously I go through a routine of returning to a mirror two or three times to check that I am properly attired and comfortable in myself, ready to step out of the door.

On the upside, that year forced me to make life-changing decisions about my future. I knew that I could no longer condone my mother's apathy and indifference towards me, and I needed to feed and clothe myself. I was offered a full-time job at Chez Petite and, with a deep sigh, I took it. On that day I relinquished the future I had imagined for myself. It was forever lost.

After my first full month of work, I received the official brown envelope filled with cash. I was thrilled and delighted. A huge weight dropped from my shoulders; I felt as if I had been saved and was finally free. Arriving home that day, my mother immediately put her hand out for my pay packet.

"Oh good, I'll take that," she said demandingly.

"You will be paying for your keep from now on," she smiled jubilantly with her hand outstretched. For a second, I was stunned. I had not expected that.

I staggered backwards, but quickly regained my composure. I took a deep breath and responded caustically.

"That is not going to happen! Not now, not ever!" I hissed at her through clenched teeth, my eyes burning with rage as I glared fixedly at her.

My mother gasped, and *in that moment, it hit her*: I was no longer the child she had taken for granted and ignored. She turned away with tears in her eyes. It was my first expression of independence; a turning point in my life. I had become a working girl overnight, an angry one at that. Perhaps she had never intended our lives to turn out that way, but she had done nothing to change the direction it had taken, nor had she protected my brother and me or made sure we were safe.

My mother never asked me for money again, but I did, of my own accord, spend money on her. Years of being ignored and neglected made me determined to take good care of myself. I had no intention of giving my mother money to supply her friends with alcohol, cigarettes and entertainment. It had been a long, hard, road, and I had become bitter towards her.

I was fourteen and had grown up too fast. My working life had begun. Finally, it was a time to do some much-needed shopping for myself! I was still living with my mother, seeing my friends and dating Ronald, which made me as happy as I knew how to be. In spite of all I had endured, I never lost my dignity or my sense of humour.

The day after I completed my year at the commercial college, I began a twenty-year career as a successful hairdresser. At nineteen I took a job at a Durban salon and built up a huge clientele. Eight months later I was offered a managerial position at a prestigious, upmarket city salon. There were ten staff members, all older than myself, and from that experience I gained a wealth of knowledge. With a strong foundation in business management, I purchased my first hairdressing salon at twenty-five. By the time I reached thirty I had bought and sold five thriving businesses for good profit, and that was just the beginning!

My boss of that first Durban business I managed became a very dear friend. Yvonne van den Berg ran a tight ship. She was gregarious and fun-loving, but business was business! She taught me many invaluable tools. I matured quickly, mastering the art and skill needed to manage all aspects of business with a firm, no-nonsense approach. I was still officially a teenager, but the life I had lived gave me the ability to stand alone and do the job efficiently. It was a far cry from a university degree and a medical career, but it was the right decision at that point in my life.

Years later, after spending five years in England, Europe and Scandinavia I reluctantly returned to South Africa wiser, worldly and with fine-tuned business skills. I had worked at a fast-paced London antique export business and then spent a year managing a division of a well-respected London employment agency, including a South African division, where we placed high-level South African secretaries in London companies.

At that time, it was illegal for South Africans to work in England. The arrangements were done 'under the table' by 'Tricky Dickie' from South Africa, and Babs Mercer, director of Mercer Employment Agency in Wardour Street, who was a very traditional English woman on the surface. I would screen and interview all of the applicants. Interesting times were had as the cash flowed in. Once back in South Africa, I soon became a successful entrepreneur, buying and selling small businesses in Durban, Johannesburg and Benoni. I could not imagine then the career changes I would decide upon later in my life.

Life at 5 Del Monico Mansions was not over; there were new hurdles to climb. With my mother's lifestyle unchanged, the challenges at home continued.

PART 4

Johannesburg – Joubert Park

Addington Hospital - Durban

PART 4

Johannesburg – General Hospital

Mandela – Pass Book Burning

PART 4

Whites only bench

Apartheid – Whites Only Restaurant

PART 4

Johannesburg Girls' High School

Me Front Row, 2nd Right – both photos

PART 4

Me 2nd Row, 2nd Left

Miss Langley   *JGHS School Building*

*School Building –
Joel House Boarders*

292

PART 4

Me – Moody Teenager

Me, centre

Me, left

PART 4

Barnarto Park High School Gates

PART V

*We are an ancient sort of resilient:
Made for the falling and the rising,
Made for rose coloured glasses,
and finding home in one another.*

Jeanette LeBlanc[69]

Chapter 40
Mother—Cancer

She fought most of her battles quietly and alone...

My mother's health issues began early in her life. I was two or three years of age and unaware that she had been in hospital for several weeks because I rarely saw her day to day. She had a cancerous tumour removed from her umbilicus. Cancer reoccurred approximately eight years later in her parotid gland on the left side of her face. And so began a long journey of treatments as the cancerous tumour grew.

With no fuss or fanfare, in fact hardly a mention, my mother went into hospital for tests. She was diagnosed with cancer of the parotid gland, which required immediate surgery. They removed a tumour and the submandibular salivary gland during a long delicate operation. After the surgery she was gravely ill. Once she was well enough, she had intensive radiation treatments, all of which caused her to behave in a highly strung and agitated manner.

At that time cancer was a dirty word, a shocking illness not to be discussed and rarely mentioned. My mother never told me she had cancer. She told no one of the diagnosis or details of the operation she was to undergo. It was never a subject for discussion, nor was I offered any information or support from doctors, surgeons, or nurses when I visited my mother alone. There was no aftercare offered to patients in those days, no counselling, support or advice. She was left in shock after the surgery to her face and totally unsupported during the radiation treatments. I was also in the dark, wondering if she was going to die. *What would become of me?* I naturally expected the worst.

During the weeks that she was in hospital I took care of myself, living alone in the bed-sit. There was no money left for food or bus fares, and she remained in hospital longer than expected. With so much to endure herself, my care never occurred to her. Of course, I can see that now, through adult eyes. I was puzzled at the time that neither Uncle Mac, my aunts, or my mother's friends, offered to help me. Not one friend visited her in hospital; perhaps she never even told them. I am not exactly sure how I dealt with being alone, but I did it. I scrounged for meals from Irene and Des at Longford Hotel, and I survived it, but felt alone and scared at night in that dark, shadowy building.

I felt obligated to visit my mother in the General Hospital in the evenings. I was frightened being out alone in the dark, and I jumped at every shadow, aware that it was not safe. My visits were brief, and I never stayed the full hour. There were long silent moments; we had nothing to say. I was painfully aware of how gravely ill she was. Pre-surgery, her make-up, with fire-engine red lipstick, was carefully applied; after the invasive surgery my mother was frail and weepy, her pretty face badly bruised and swollen. Her main concern was not her wellness, but her looks.

While healing at home in the weeks that followed, my mother never spoke of the surgery, even though the side of her face was stitched from behind the ear to the chin. Her salivary gland had been removed, leaving her with an unpleasantly dry mouth for the rest of her life. She constantly sipped water, even during the night, yet she never complained of pain or discomfort. Looking back, I realise how graciously she dealt with her illness. There was no medical after-support, and she had no family or husband to help her through such a difficult time. She showed few outward signs of what she was going through.

Today, as I write, I do not know how she coped alone. Sadly, she offered no information during the months that she was undergoing radiation treatments; she asked for no assistance, and I did not offer any. I had no idea if she was in pain or discomfort, nor did I have any idea how serious the surgery had been.

Her friends did not visit for several weeks, and I realised that she had told them something different, perhaps that she would be away, because none of them called to enquire about her health. I also had no idea if my father had been informed, or if she still wrote to him. I never knew if my parents were in contact, but in all the years that we were apart, my father wrote to me each week; it was never more than one or perhaps two lines, without any personal details or ever asking how I was. Occasionally he enclosed a ten shilling note (±£50 today), but he rarely mentioned my mother. His actions led me to believe that he no longer loved me and had forgotten about us and moved on with his life.

My mother gradually pulled her life back together, behaving in much the same way as she always had, but I noticed how fragile she had become. She had never been one for sleeping in, or lying in bed, and was usually dressed and made-up before 8 a.m. But, after the surgery, she slept more, taking long afternoon naps once her morning or lunchtime guests had left. A few months after her radiation treatments, my mother began attending Tara Psychiatric Hospital as an Outpatient. It was weeks before I became aware that she left each morning to get the Tara Hospital courtesy bus.

When I asked about it, she offered a vague reply. I remember her telling me she was weaving a basket, but she never mentioned it again, yet each morning she strolled up to the Johannesburg General Hospital, a pleasant ten minute walk, to get the bus to Tara Hospital. She continued this daily ritual for a year, and I overheard the snippets of conversation about Tara Hospital from Aileen at the pharmacy.

During that time my mother became noticeably thinner. She appeared fragile and nervy and developed the habit of swinging her crossed leg back and forth, going higher and higher. It was unsettling to watch. I never understood what made her nervous system so fragile from the time of that surgery, but I was acutely aware of the changes in her.

Going to Tara Hospital each day did affect Mother's busy social life. She took naps when she returned home in the afternoons, and eventually her body gave in, and she began to stay in bed well into the morning. It took her over a year to recover from that invasive surgery. Many years later she mentioned that her operation was the first of its kind in medical history. The details of the surgery appeared in an edition of the medical journal, *The Lancet*. As a young girl, I had no clue how she actually felt after such intricate surgery and intensive radiation, but once we got over that year, life slowly normalised and resumed as before.

My mother behaved as if the cancer and ill health had never happened, even though she had a long scar down the side of her pretty face. Once she recovered, she became reckless, developing a 'couldn't care less' attitude towards life, but rarely left home. Nights out, dancing until the wee hours stopped. She had friends over, but rarely ventured out of the bed-sit. I began to notice that her elegant manners and high standards were more relaxed, her behaviour by comparison less sophisticated, her appearance less meticulous, and she became influenced by a few unsavoury people. She was changing before my eyes, and it worried me.

Her close friends and exclusive social circle finally ostracised her. In her mind *my father ruined her life!* Perhaps he did. It was well hidden, but my mother definitely made herself sick with worry over money, her social position and living alone, which was never what she wanted. She had irrational fears, that gradually became more pronounced. She developed an extreme fear of heights, fear of thunder and lightening, fear of elevators, tall buildings, walking under ladders, railway bridges and the dark. My mother had hidden her fears cleverly from friends, but they were very real to her, and after the surgery they were very pronounced, often leaving her shaking and in tears.

During those years of separation and waiting, my mother had little access to any funds. With no financial independence as is the norm in present day, she became angry that my father had control of her inheritance. My mother inherited substantially after her mother's death and the funds were placed in my father's care. Women rarely had bank accounts in the late 1940s and 50s. It would seem that he spent her money recklessly. He bought the Del-Dar farmland knowing my mother disliked remote places. He bought five thoroughbred racehorses knowing that she disapproved of gambling, especially horse racing, and there were many more such expenditures.

My father presumably transferred funds, including my mother's inheritance, to Rhodesia, using a good portion for pleasure and new ventures, including building a mansion in Salisbury whilst we lived on the meagre monthly allowance. My mother never asked about money because it was definitely *not the done thing* back then! A good wife *did not* pry into the finances. I am sure she was secretly seething by the time we were forced to live in a place such as Del Monico Mansions. Yet, in spite of it all, consciously or unconsciously, my mother continued to wait for my father, expecting to graciously resume her role as wife and homemaker. She *needed* my father, a man, to arrange everything for her, to manage her, *to look after her* and to give her life purpose.

Deep inside, I knew that she had been humiliated by my father; his disloyalty and indifference was unbearable. Being deserted by him is what finally broke her.

Motherhood was never a natural state for her. The responsibility of two children, without nannies, maids and a cook, was not what she signed up for. She did not have the courage to start a new life, yet she was in the prime of her life! Her structured childhood and rigid ideas about wife and marriage never changed, even in the swinging sixties. Her *one desire* was to be with *her husband*, at his side, managing his home perfectly and playing the role of the perfect hostess. It was *she* who needed to be treasured and looked after, not us. Living on her own did not make her feel free, it unsettled and embarrassed her!

Many years later we reconnected by chance. Or was it fate? She then began to mention her mother's death, the actual murder, which she had never elaborated on before. Shreds of information would come out during the few conversations we had. These instances were so random that each time it took me by surprise. The brutal murder had affected her far more than I was able to understand. I knew that it had been traumatic and a terrible shock, but the memory of that day terrorised her so many years later. Her unexpected snippets of information were often out of context.

I discovered that there was something about my birth, two years after her mother's murder, that bothered her. Having been married for nine years and unable to have a child, they arranged to adopt my brother. She could not bond with him. By then she may have gone past the stage of wanting children, perhaps they both had. A year, *almost to the day*, after the murder of my grandmother Dorothy, I was conceived. Did my mother feel guilty about my arrival? She obviously could not forget that traumatic period of her life, but there I was, a constant reminder. I am aware now, how the deeply chilling event impacted my mother, in more ways than I could ever have imagined as a child.

During those fleeting moments when my mother mentioned the murder, I learnt that Herbert Campbell-Gilchrist, her stepfather, had strict autocratic ways and an explosive temper. She indicated that she had always been afraid of him and afraid to disobey him, and that she had been controlled by her parents, their class and their social standing. She mentioned, by chance, the arrangement made by her stepfather for her to marry an English Baron. Unknown to him or her mother, she had met and fallen deeply in love with my father—a love she carried in her heart, to her grave.

She spoke briefly about her mother Dorothy's character. Her mother was deeply affected by the death of her son Clarence from pneumonia when he was twenty one. Dorothy had been a true matriarch and a powerful Medium, which scared my mother. My grandmother would go into deep trances lasting hours, attempting to contact Clarence. I learnt, too, that my mother was a broken woman after Grandmother Dorothy's murder. She was unable to cope with the way in which her mother had died and lost her direction in life without her mother's firm guidance.

My parents had married quietly and left Johannesburg soon after.

"I'd rather that you married a Jew, but a Greek? Never!" Those were her mother's fiery words to her.

My grandmother's murder went on to affect my mother's entire life, especially once my father left her on her own. She became more fearful. The act of her being murdered left her terrified, and she had repeated thoughts of a similar death. She became frightened of black men. Her fears were irrational, but they overwhelmed her mind and affected her daily life in untamed South Africa.

Twenty years later cancer returned in the same area. I took charge then and was assertive when I approached the medical team for information and answers. Another intrusive surgery was scheduled to remove a section of bone from the side of her face. I had spoken at length with the surgeon, but he had not given full details of the extent of the surgery until the night before.

While visiting my mother in hospital and hearing more about the procedure from the nursing staff, I took it upon myself to telephone the surgeon at his home. This was most unusual, but I was very angry at his nonchalant attitude towards my mother's condition.

"We take a very radical approach to cancer at the Jo'burg Gen," he barked loudly.

A long, heated discussion ensued. He insisted that the surgery would go ahead as planned. It was as if a 'free patient' at the hospital had no say at all. I was furious at his hubristic attitude and I was concerned for my mother, then in her early sixties. The shock my mother experienced, seeing her face in the mirror two days after surgery, caused her to suffer a stroke. She had not understood...

Until her death, my mother never mentioned the 'C' word. I have often wondered if she accepted how ill she was and if she understood that it was cancer. I don't think she wanted to know. My fragile mother's final days were insufferable, yet she never uttered a word of complaint. At the very end of her life, the cancer swiftly reached her brain, the pain too unbearable to endure. I will never forget her wild eyes as she lay screaming in pain when the cancer finally entered her brain, hours before her death. Her face haunted me for years.

My father, the coward that he was with matters of the heart and responsibilities, tried to slip out of the hospital ward to save himself a torturous parting. He tried to leave quietly, hoping I would deal with my dying mother and the legal formalities. I saw him from the corner of my eye whilst my mother screamed, gripping my hand with all her might. I prised my fingers loose, turned away from her and ran after my father as he tried to escape the horror of her death.

I grabbed him by his jacket lapels and shook him firmly "She is still *your wife*! Don't you *dare* leave me alone here!"

He looked at me sheepishly, tears welling up in his big dark eyes. He pulled away roughly and walked swiftly out of the ward as I looked on.

Those final harrowing hours are crystal clear. It could have been yesterday, except it was almost forty years ago. I never understood him and his inability to face family issues. I was also haunted by the secret conversations amongst my father and his family and the vagueness about my mother's past: secrets, always secrets, with no answers.

PART 5

Chapter 41

My Father

He thinks himself rather an exceptional young man, thoroughly sophisticated, well adjusted to his environment, and somewhat more significant than any one else he knows

F. Scott Fitzgerald, The Beautiful and the Damned[70]

As a young man my father was far too handsome for his own good. He was a table-tennis champion, first league tennis player and a keen golfer with a good handicap. He had two weaknesses: gambling and pretty women. As he matured his good looks, along with polished charm, made him very self-assured. His confidence allowed his commanding presence to lead him into many intriguing situations. He expected the very best of everything, wherever he went and never accepted less.

He was a man with a well-proven record of being irresistible to women. He felt invincible even in old age and was totally fearless. Many saw him as an enigma. As he moved through life his self-assured charm oozed effortlessly, and women swooned no matter what their age. I had the opportunity of observing the effect he had on women firsthand when I reconnected with him. I would roll my eyes towards the heavens in astonishment. I discovered then that he had been an inveterate gambler and womaniser for most of his life.

My father adored beautiful women and was unable to resist them, but he never regarded women in any way equal to men. He had the arrogance (or ignorance) to believe that a woman over thirty-five had lost her appeal. She no longer had a youthful body or glowing good looks. He had no interest in more mature women. No matter how attractive or charming, he simply ignored them. He was resolute about it. We had heated discussions on the subject when I was older. I found his generalised opinions shallow and demeaning. He never saw it that way. We agreed to disagree.

Along with a sharp intellect, his quickness of mind never ceased to amaze me. He had an extraordinary ability to do calculations in his head within seconds. In business he depended on no one but himself and was said to be 'ahead of the game' when negotiations were underway or when finalising a deal. After taking early retirement he was still sought after. His personal friendships with 'the right people', as well as mining magnets, and his knowledge of the copper industry were renowned.

He began his interest in mining in the early 1950s, when Northern Rhodesia was the largest copper-producing area in the world. I have wondered if that had an influence on his decision to leave South Africa in 1954. Acting as an Agent with an ability to negotiate comfortably with gazillions of dollars, he created trading partnerships. I was told that he had a natural ease during such negotiations. I have also wondered if he and his brother, Robert, invested in any ventures together in Rhodesia or Nyasaland (now Malawi). If they did, it was never mentioned, not even to family. My father spoke often, in his old age, of Lake Malawi and visited there several times during his retirement. He knew that region very well.

In Rhodesia and South Africa certain senior officials and company CEO's offered briefcases of cash for his services. There were times when rival companies attempted to bribe him to withdraw from or mismanage certain negotiations. I remember how perplexed he became as he got older with no interest in being part of such arrangements. The sums of money offered were vast. I saw that with my own eyes. There were frequent late-night phone calls from all parts of the world. Of course I don't know the half, nor do I have exact details, other than what I saw or overheard, or learned during discussions with him when he was in his seventies; he gave little away.

Once my father retired, he travelled extensively throughout Africa, leaving at a moment's notice and reappearing months later. He travelled alone through Malawi and South West Africa (now Namibia) several times a year. Where he went or what he did, he never shared. He said little about those long car journeys. I have no idea if he left remnants of another life there: property or business interests. He enjoyed the African people and spoke several African languages. He also travelled to Greece once a year to island-hop and liked to explore more remote islands. He was often the only guest staying at hotels on various islands and spent hours talking to locals.

I began to understand that he disliked being tied down to anyone or any place for too long; he needed to go off alone to feel free and unrestrained. This perhaps influenced his behaviour as a family man. He had no desire to be part of the crowd, nor did he ever go to formal social events. He had an aristocratic gift of command and a powerful presence. With few words he would get the best table, best wine and best service wherever he went.

He never queued or waited longer than five minutes for anyone, even if he were meeting me. "Right! That's it. I'm off…" he would say as he turned on his heels and walked away. I found him *infuriating* at times, but he was his own man.

In his late seventies, with failing eyesight, my father became a prisoner in his spacious seven-roomed Johannesburg flat in the suburb of Killarney. He had become an eccentric loner, pursuing few hobbies, but he kept a daily record of every penny he had, making detailed entries of money spent or loaned. His daily incomings and outgoings were meticulously analysed and recorded. He wanted a constant update of how much money he had. He became miserly and fearful of not having sufficient, yet happily squandered unlimited amounts of money on his long-standing Personal Assistant, Jeanette. He was completely captivated by her. When he did not spend on her and her extended family, she helped herself. He was naive; blinded by her girlish charm, which she used with cunning and ingenuity. She kept well away from me, aware that I could see right through her.

In spite of this, I do believe that my parents loved each other deeply until their dying day. There was no other person that they loved more completely; yet false pride, hurt, time apart and distance caused them to live completely different lives, separated by default. They never considered divorce, and neither of them ever settled with another partner. Both were alone in their old age and neither of them were happy. There was sadness and regrets in both of my parents.

This did not keep him from enjoying his 'little' luxuries. Throughout his life my father made sure he had the best of everything. Once retired and living alone, his one pleasure remained fine dining and shopping for fresh ingredients to prepare. His shopping excursions became a daily occurrence, even through the years when my mother was struggling on a limited budget.

From my very early memories, he enjoyed living! I remember my father ordering fresh salmon from Canada or freshly caught Mussel Cracker from the Cape. The orders were sent to him overnight by airfreight. He would drive across Johannesburg for top grade beef, freshly picked baby spinach or virgin olive oil, which he bought by the case.

As a very young child, I remember the walk-in pantries. Along the passage close to the kitchen there were four pantries. One used for the china and cutlery, the next filled to the ceiling with tins, packets, sacks, spices, dried meats, delicacies, oils, condiments. Then a cool room for wines and finally a small pantry with buckets of glorious-smelling flowers for the floral arrangements around the house. The walk-in, commercial-sized fridge was a treasure trove of delicacies; filled with crates, baskets and boxes of the finest food and drinks, ready for any occasion. Not to mention the hidden cases of well-aged whisky and fine cigars he kept for his close friends. My parents were generous with what they had. All their friends and family left the house with something special from the pantry.

He provided for himself and indulged himself. His life was one of privilege, with little risk or discomfort to himself. Perhaps this encouraged him, when in his prime, to squander money as if there were no tomorrow.

My father constantly reminded me that, as his only daughter, when he died, I would be well provided for. He claimed to have made 'adequate provision' that would keep me financially comfortable for the rest of my life. Weeks after he had passed in the 1980s, when I had dealt with shock, grief and burial arrangements, I found his bank accounts empty, and his priceless stamp collection had mysteriously vanished from his home. All private documents including his will, bank bonds, Rolex watches and other items of value, were gone from his wardrobe safe. No one saw or heard anything. There was no forced entry.

At the end of his recklessly extravagant and enigmatic life on earth, I inherited *nothing at all* from my father. It was a case of yet another unsolvable Arliotis mystery but, in this case, I have my suspicions.

PART 5

Chapter 42

My Greek Grandparents

*In deep dreamy moments, I sensed my ancestors,
especially my grandmother Ekatarina,
around me and with me, wherever I went.
It felt as if she was in that earth beneath my feet:
her love, her grace, her gentleness, her beauty.*

Thoughts from Corfu

Everything about my grandparents and their early life was a shrouded mystery. Perhaps the family chose not to discuss it. Or were their offspring also in the dark? It has taken me most of my life to put the pieces of the puzzle together, yet so much of their life is still a hushed secret.

My Grandmother, Countess Ekaterina Theodosius-Arliotis, was born in Corfu. Her distant ancestors, Venetians, settled in Corfu many generations before she was born. In a period of history long gone, the Venetians enjoyed privileges on the island of Corfu. They had money to build grand houses, one of which still stands in Nikiforou Theotoki Street, opposite St. Vasileios church: a tall five-storey building with vaults on the first floor. It dominates one of the busiest streets of Corfu.

A few years before World War 1 began, my grandfather, born Constantine Arliotti, made the decision to leave Greece, his family and properties he owned on Corfu. He and my grandmother embarked on a long, treacherous, sea voyage to South Africa. However, old records indicate that my grandparents may have been living in London, England, before setting off for South Africa. They arrived to a wild, untamed land and eventually settled in Johannesburg. My father, the eldest, was born five months after war was declared. To this day, it is unclear why my grandfather made the decision to settle in South Africa.

There was definitely an air of mystery about his life, including the decision to leave all that was familiar to him. What I have been able to establish is that he was born in Dorset, England, not Greece. His father, also Constantine, married into a wealthy Greek farming family with extensive land in Lancashire and managed the farm with his father-in-law for a time. My grandfather had strong ties to England, Greece and South Africa and lived in the three countries during his life. At the time of his death on New Year's Eve in the mid-1930s, he was found in his office with the safe wide open, completely empty. In that safe he had kept large sums of cash, bonds, insurance certificates and all family and business documents.

My parents had been at a New Year's Eve dance nearby and, on hearing the unexpected news, rushed to my grandfather's restaurant[71] in central Johannesburg. They found him slumped at his desk, dead. Whatever was of interest in that safe, or of particular value, *someone knew about it*. Whoever it was wanted the documents, or else there was an urgency to conceal certain information. Did the Arliotis family themselves hide or destroy the contents of the safe? Nothing further was said about my grandfather's death or what transpired in the months that followed.

The women in the family were told nothing. More interesting was that my father and his brother changed their surname after their father's death. One day, years after my birth, my mother innocently mentioned the empty safe, but the family secrets died with my grandfather and my father. Throughout my childhood my grandfather was rarely spoken of, nor was their life as a family open for discussion. Their early life in Johannesburg was never referred to by any of the siblings. It remained a tight-lipped secret.

My grandmother was deeply religious and dedicated to Mother Mary, the Theotokos, and to the Greek Orthodox religion. She had a private altar or prayer space set up in her home, adorned with beautiful silver-framed icons of the Theotokos. She believed in prayer and she prayed frequently. Her faith and loving commitment to Holy Mary was deep; it was as if she was surrounded by an air of 'holyness'. Those reverent moments, lighting a candle and standing close to her at the altar in prayer, still remain with me, and it is a practice I follow. Her soft words of prayer, with loving gestures and heartfelt feelings, were humble and beautiful. Those times of prayer gave me quiet strength and a sense of being in a protective bubble of Holy Love. My grandmother had profound wisdom, compassion, and a heart filled with love, yet I sensed that she carried her own pain; a deep sadness wrapped in memories of a life before South Africa.

I learnt from her the sheer enjoyment of food preparation. Cooking, sharing food and happy family mealtimes, no matter how simple, were a daily happening. Then there was her skill and love of knitting, sewing, dressmaking, millinery, embroidery and fine crochet work. Granny could cut well-crafted patterns on brown paper from memory, which she used for coats, jackets, dresses and hats. She chose black or navy fabrics for her simple classic style. She dressed with understated elegance and created garments that gave her a timeless silhouette, perhaps of a life and a time gone by, unique to her. She used fine fabrics, the best her money could buy, including crepe de chine, lace, embossed satin, tafetta, velvet and wool.

She took great care, using beautiful, fine hand-stitching. Few could compete with her skill. Her nimble fingers worked magic with a needle and thread. Her hats, or headdresses, were adorned with beads, pearls, sequins, feathers, fur, handmade felt flowers and finished with soft face veiling that was no longer seen in the 1950s. The hat designs were carefully considered, never flamboyant, always tasteful.

My grandmother could easily have sat on her long, pure white hair that she wore swept up in an elegant chignon, softly hidden under one of her unusual hats. Of course, no one would guess that she hand-stitched every garment and hat she wore.

Granny represented an aristocratic lineage unknown to most South Africans, yet those who had the pleasure of meeting her came away knowing they had been in the presence of someone unique. She certainly had an air of a *Grande Dame,* often reminding me of a dignitary from the days of the Venetian Renaissance. She was admired and adored by many, but lived a quiet, dignified life, rarely venturing out amongst neighbours or locals. She remained deeply religious and reverent, keeping to a small Greek community who called on her regularly for afternoon tea.

Her sons became a disappointment to her and caused her deep sorrow in later life. Neither of them provided for her in a way that she expected and deserved. It was customary in Greek society for the men to make adequate provision for their mothers. Her son's financial gestures were inconsistent. In my grandmother's opinion, the cash allowance from George and Robert were unreliable. My dearest, remarkable, Grandmother lived to the grand age of *one hundred and thirteen!*

Aunt Alexandra and Aunt Helen made their own clothes, too, which included beautifully worked artistic knitwear. They could hand stitch with perfect stitches, or design and sew (on a Singer treadle sewing machine) beautiful frocks. They could knit or crochet with wools, fine thread, silks, or cotton, to the highest standard; so fine was their work it looked machine made. The quality of their work was excellent. I was always transfixed and amazed at what they created. No one guessed that what they wore, including the ball gowns Aunt Helen wore to Masonic Balls, were designed and created by these two reserved, unassuming sisters.

My aunts and grandmother lived in their own world, encapsulated in a safe bubble that was very unlike the world at large or the life I had been thrown into. I struggled to live in both worlds, but never mentioned my unhappiness or the neglect that my brother and I were subjected to.

When the weekends that I spent with Granny were drawing to a close, we would walk silently down to the bus stop where I would get the Sunday afternoon bus. She knew of my reluctance to leave. We hugged for a long time and kissed cheeks, then, with pain in my chest, I stepped onto the red double decker bus and waved goodbye. My grandmother stood calm and still until the bus picked up speed and she was out of view. The red bus raced back towards my other reality, the place I was unable to call 'home'.

My Grandfather—Searching for Answers

As mentioned earlier, my father's father—my Greek grandfather, born in Corfe Castle, Dorset, as Constantine Arliotti, died unexpectedly at his place of business one New Year's Eve in the late 1930s. My grandfather was an enigma. I have wondered if he was in the military or perhaps the Greek or British navy, as a young man. I was told that "he traveled extensively" but mystery still surrounds most of his life.

Although my grandfather died of a massive heart attack, the circumstances remain mysterious. Perhaps there were family secrets amongst the men that my father and his brother took to their graves. Had my father and Uncle Robert cleared the safe once it had been established that their father was dead, or did they know who had cleared out the safe? The circumstances were never discussed.

Years later, it remained a delicate, off-limits subject, even with my grandmother. My grandfather was never spoken about and, as a curious child, I found it all very strange. His death left my grandmother and his two daughters in a difficult position for a while, and the family business in jeopardy. Everything about my grandfather's death was hushed up, including what became of the properties he owned and his thriving business.

My grandfather was rarely called Mr. Arliotis, everyone called him 'Costas'. Soon after his death my father and his brother, began using the surname, Costas. Years went by and life continued, but for the Arliotis family, it was as if their past never existed. Growing up I became aware that we were not known as 'the Arliotis family' because my father used a different surname from my aunt and grandmother. I had no knowledge that legitimately my surname was Arliotis until many years later. The name change held some family secret, but it was not open for discussion, *not ever.*

When in his mid-sixties, my father, who had never before spoken about his childhood, mentioned to me that his father "took the belt to me" even as a young man. This surprised me. It was the very first mention made about his father as a parent and the strict regime with his grown-up boys. None of his siblings mentioned their childhood or school days, nor did my father indicate that he, or his brother, had worked at the family restaurant; yet my father was very knowledgeable about cuisine and had excellent culinary skills. He read and admired famous French chefs such as Escoffier, and his preferred style of cooking was French.

There is no evidence of my father, or his brother Robert, having embarked on a career as a young man, or ever having a job, until he married my mother and they moved to Port Elizabeth in the Cape. The brothers appeared to have lived as two privileged young gentlemen. They came and went as they wished, spending time at the racecourse, dog track, private clubs, dancing and getting up to mischief. I have often wondered if they had private tutoring or a governess, because no mention of school friends, or attending local schools, was ever spoken of by the siblings. It was as if their childhood in South Africa did not exist.

PART 5

Chapter 43

Au Revoir

It had all become so deliciously squalid...

It was the weekend, and I was going to a Saturday night jive party at the Russels' house. It was a hot balmy evening, but otherwise it was an ordinary Saturday night. My mother seemed to be staying in and there had been few visitors that day. She had been looking strained and unwell for the past few days and less in the mood for grooming herself prettily.

The party at the Russels' was great fun. I was feeling heady, exhilarated, happy and tired after taking a long while to kiss and cuddle with Ronald before I left. There were several stragglers hanging around and his mother Anne, for reasons I don't recall, offered to drive me home. Mrs. Russel was a pleasant woman but very possessive of her youngest son. I don't believe she was happy about us 'going steady' or the intensity of our relationship. She regularly told Ronald that we were far too young. Anne preferred leaving him at the party with the late-night stragglers and possible temptation. I sensed that. She was no fool, but neither was I.

Since beginning to work full time, I saw little of Ronald during the week and there were whispers that he had been seen once or twice with an attractive blonde, older than himself. I was unable to spend much time with my best friends Irene and Des either, who were at college and school. No longer considered a schoolgirl, but too young to be working, it was a time of huge adjustments that were often difficult for me. I missed the daily comfort of safe friendships and weekday afternoons with Ronald.

Life at home had taken on a different atmosphere. With me out of a school uniform, I looked older than my years and my mother's guests were suddenly aware that I was not a child. There were awkward moments when I arrived home in the evenings, with long uncomfortable silences. My mother's friends felt unsettled by my presence, and I remained cool and aloof towards them. I had become far less passive about my mother's constant visitors.

It was a long drive from Kensington to the bed-sit and well after midnight when Anne Russel pulled up outside the building. A sense of unease gripped me as I got out of the low-slung sports car. I stood for a moment in the deserted street, shivering. That uneasy feeling encouraged me to ask Mrs. Russel to wait before driving away. I walked quietly up the staircase and along the dimly lit corridor. It was eerily silent. As I reached the door, I noticed that it was partly open. I drew back for a split second, slightly apprehensive; after all it was Johannesburg. I had learnt from an early age to be cautious and aware of danger. I peered inside, but the lights were dim, making it difficult to see clearly. The room felt heavy and airless. I held my breath, walked in and adjusted my eyes. What I saw stunned me. I stopped dead, my body rigid and my mind reeling. My body locked down in shock at what I saw before me, and I could not move. My usually elegant mother was in a state of undress and looked dazed. The scenario in my young innocent mind was obscene and salacious. It was as if raw, naked life had exposed itself to me for the first time, and I had no idea how to manage that.

Panic erupted in my sensitive heart, followed quickly by shame and confusion. Intense pain had a strangle hold on my throat. Before me, on her single bed lay my mother, every imperfection exposed. She was intoxicated, possibly drugged, for she appeared slightly delirious, her body almost lifeless. Seconds elapsed and my mind was still racing. It was too much for me to take in.

I saw a powerfully built stranger, his body naked, sweat glistening on his back in the dim lighting, leaning lustfully over my mother. He gazed across at where I stood, pressed against the wall, with a deep dark scowl on his face. I glared back at him. What I saw were blank soulless eyes. He was shameless, with no intention of discontinuing what they had begun. She, unaware that I was even in the room and he, with just a hint of a smirk on his lips. He looked lecherous. It was as if he relished the idea of me watching as he violated and exposed her. The woman lying on that bed looked nothing like my mother, but someone I preferred not to recognise or name. I looked on, aghast, ashamed to be there but frozen to the spot. It was something I should never have been privy to. Before me was a lewd scene with a sinister air hanging over the room. I felt as if I had been lured into something dark, graphic and too vivid for my naive, innocent mind to process.

I never imagined that our life would come to this. My mother had never even flirted with anyone in my presence, or acted inappropriately, even at wild parties when copious amounts of alcohol were consumed. *I had never even seen her undressed!* She had always been rather reserved and old fashioned about her body and nakedness.

Something inside me snapped. It was the culmination of the Greek tragedy we had been living through. All that I had endured flashed through my mind in a nano-second. Feelings of shame, anger, hurt, heartache and fear surged up in me. My constant battle to survive through years of humiliation, deprivation, exasperation and fears, hit me all at once. It was enough. It had to end!

That scene damaged my view of her, forever. In those brief moments, my heart pounding, wild with panic, tears welling up in my eyes, I ran blindly along the corridor, stumbling down the flight of stairs to the waiting car.

Anne took one look at my ashen face and asked, "What's happening up there?"

She leapt out of the car and marched up the stairs, with me running behind trying to stop her. I did *not* want her to go in *there*.

Anne stood rigidly at the open door, took one look into the room and whatever she thought she never shared, but she recognised immediately that it was not a place for me to be. Her eyes narrowed; her thin lips, tight with rage, were pulled back across her teeth. I stood beside her shaking; the blood drained from my face

"You are not living here *for another second!*"

Ronald's mother and I sat in the car for a long while, neither of us spoke. We sat in total silence. I shook uncontrollably as years of tears rolled down my cheeks. There were no words to share; both of us were in shock. Nothing could soothe my nervous system, and I saw no window of calm or tolerance opening up in the near future. In those silent moments I realised how much our lives had changed and what was becoming of my mother. She had lost her way. It was as if her moral compass had spun out of control. For myself, I understood that it was enough. I needed to draw a line in the sand, and that night I did.

Anne Russel dropped me up the road at Longford Hotel. We both knew that I would be safe there. It was gone 2 a.m. when I knocked on the door. Des let me in and, without a word being said, I slipped quietly into bed next to Irene. The next morning, I dressed quietly, not wanting to stir the girls. I left silently, marching purposefully down the road back home. I had no plan in my head of what I was about to do or say when I got there. My mind was filled with silent rage that had been suppressed for years.

As I opened the door my mother looked startled to see me, her eyes wide with surprise, then she quickly averted her gaze. She and her male friend were sitting on the edge of her bed. My mother, her body hunched over, looked worse for wear and bleary-eyed, her clothes from the day before, crumpled and creased. Neither of them looked completely sober. I stared down at my mother and was immediately aware that she did not remember the previous night. She was dazed and despondent and looked ill.

For the first time in her life, my mother looked completely defeated and broken. My heart ached. *Why had everything gone so horribly wrong!* My once much-admired socialite mother and her two well-mannered children who, to the outside world, had looked so perfect. And here we are, at this this place of utter brokenness.

He, whoever he was, sat brazenly watching me through cold, lifeless eyes. I looked back with an icy glare, filled with contempt. I turned towards the wardrobe and took down the only suitcase we owned and began packing.

My mother protested. I saw grief and shock etched on her pale face, her voice slightly slurred from lack of sleep.

"What are you doing?" she asked.

"I am leaving today and *never* coming back," I replied in a strong, steady voice. "*You*, this life, all of it, has gone too far. I have had enough. Know that you and I—we end *today*!"

She looked completely astonished. I swung round to finish my packing. In that final hour as I packed, my mother sat silently. Not a word was spoken. As I packed hastily, I realised how intensely I had come to dislike her. I locked the case and walked out of the room without a goodbye or a backward glance. I walked slowly down the long passageway, realising as I went that this place had never been a real home for any of us, but it was where I had become a young woman. Looking back now I recognise that I had lived through the strangest and most bizarre years, often in circumstances that would touch even the tough and the brave. They were years of the most harrowing, frustrating and often degrading times, with many haunting experiences. Finally, I understood that I had to leave.

I stood for a moment at the entrance of Del Monico Mansions, took a deep breath and, lugging the old suitcase containing my life, walked away forever. I never looked back.

1962: Mandela arrested.
I leave home.
The Rivonia trial begins

PART 5

Chapter 44

The Final Curtain

*Walk until you lose yourself,
and then walk until you find yourself,
and then walk some more until you forgot why you left,
and remember where you were going.*

Jeanette LeBlanc[72]

After I left my mother's 'home' forever and was living with my Aunt Alex, which was within walking distance to where Ronald lived, I was surprised to find that we were seeing less of each other.

One Saturday afternoon Ronald called on me at my aunt's. He stood firm and said gently but unemotionally: "I've come to tell you that it's over."

I was stunned, my head reeling, my heart pounding!

"Why?"

My body froze on the doorstep where I stood. I was unable to move a muscle. I was taken completely by surprise, in shock. He had no explanation, no justification, not even a tender heartfelt goodbye.

That day my heart shattered into millions of tiny fragments. The ache was so deep that it felt too painful to share with anyone. My mind was in turmoil, my body sickened. I do believe that his mother, Anne, influenced his decision after being with me on that final night at Del Monico Mansions. But in the years that followed, I pondered his reason for breaking off our relationship so unexpectedly and could see other reasons.

During the 'going steady' period, I was unable to show Ronald emotionally, or physically, how much he meant to me. I had shut myself away so tightly long before we got together. With my emotions hidden and my feelings masked, it must have eventually had him curious to explore more happy-go-lucky girls.

I never thought about it much at the time, but I was unaware of how cleverly I had masked my feelings. I was not like girls of my age who were frivolous, giggly, flirtatious and silly. I was reserved, serious, secretive, observing their behaviour as I had done with people from a very young age. Love was unfamiliar. It made me hold my breath, afraid to breathe. I was tight, at times overly cautious, without realising until years later that I was unable to open up. *I did not know how*. Of course, I could not see that in myself then or understand my behaviour. My focus was on survival in the best way I knew how.

It took me many more years to understand that I had been emotionally numb for most of it. Years later I slowly began to uncover my masked feelings, layer by layer. I allowed myself time to heal, to feel, to see, to understand and simply be me.

Did Ronald understand me? Did my serious nature intrigue him, or could he feel me holding back? I would like to believe that it was out of respect that he kept us from moving into a more adult relationship. Or was it simply not the right time for either of us? I have often wondered.

Ronald walked out of my life with the same gentle ease that he had walked into it. He never looked back. It was the last time I ever saw him, except for once, many years later. My heart leapt into my throat as I caught a glimpse of him. I knew in a nano-second that my feelings for him had not dimmed. The flame was alive, even after all that time.

After that shock, my gay friends, who had been so protective of me, saw me through the breakup. Even though my heart was breaking, Lenis, who had taught me to dance, would collect me on a Saturday evening at my aunt's home, and off we would go to any house party I knew of, or had been invited to. We would take to the floor and dance the night away. His professional dance moves and agile footwork soon had the room jumping. The crowd would surround us, clapping and whistling. We jived for hours non-stop. It was thrilling fun, which took my mind off my broken heart. My scars were raw, some of those shattered pieces from that time in my life still remain.

Whilst I lay on my bed night after night, feeling as if my world had ended, the pain in my heart unbearable, my aunt Alexandra had secretly reconnected with a past love. After meeting regularly for several weeks, they made an impulsive decision and got married. My aunt was then in her mid-forties. The unexpected news added to my distress. I felt crushed. The family was taken by surprise. Aunt Helen was amused, her mother unimpressed, but Cousin Norman was astonished by his mother's sudden marriage. The news left me floundering and depressed. My aunt was my rock.

Within a few weeks my aunt had packed up and moved away. She left the house for Cousin Norman and Kay, his new wife, and myself. My head was muddled, and at that point I could not see a way forward. I felt as if I was slowly unravelling.

Several weeks, perhaps months later, I was still feeling broken and irreparable. The one person who made me feel safe in the world had disappeared from my life. In fact, we rarely saw my aunt once she moved in with her new husband, Phil. They kept away from family for a long while, and I don't recall seeing my aunt for many years from the time that she married. Perhaps it was the excitement of a new marriage or his influence, but it changed the family dynamic completely.

I had disappeared from Irene and Des's life on that Sunday morning without a word, even though in my heart they were such an important part of my daily existence. Irene and Des were like sisters to me. To this day I have never spoken of *the day* I left home. I had *run away* from a situation that I could no longer cope with and, in doing so, had left behind people who were precious to me. I did not understand then that something serious was happening to my mind and emotions. My heart ached for Ronald, for my aunt, for my friends, all of which left me fragile and overwrought. I was fifteen, I was frightened, and I was totally alone in the world.

With each passing day, life was too much to deal with alone. My raw emotions and broken heart, along with the life I had run from, led to constant nightmares. I began sleepwalking through the house at night and was close to breaking point. I wanted to go to sleep and never awaken to face the awfulness of life. My cousin was kind and caring but unable to grasp why I was so distraught. He was puzzled by the change in me yet took no action to help. I felt unable to reach out to my friend Irene and was completely overwhelmed by everything but was not ready to verbalise what I was feeling.

With maturity and hindsight, I realise that I should have moved into the hotel to be closer to the girls and my place of work, but away from my mother's bizarre lifestyle. Instead I moved miles away and, within weeks, felt desperately alone.

My mother had taken her life and mine almost to the edge. Once we were ensconced in a place such as Del Monico Mansions, she began to crumble, and I held on as best as I could. Very gradually she began to care less about herself. She allowed her dignity and the principles she had held high, through all the years of waiting for my father and living alone, to fade. Her decline eventually shattered her inner stability. She fell at perhaps the last hurdle, went down a slippery slope, where she landed headfirst.

On that fateful day when Jimmy spilled the beans and my mother discovered that my father had other women in his life, she realised that he had never loved her exclusively. That realisation shattered her heart. My father tumbled from the pedestal upon which she had lovingly placed him. Of course, I never understood it back then.

Her privileged upbringing, within a British class system, had instilled a strict code of her parents' generation where men were the providers. Her role was meant to be that of a perfect wife, always at her husband's side, whilst he took care of everything. This was entrenched in her psyche, and she lived according to those ideals to the bitter end. Any other way was beyond her comprehension.

All my parents' friends who remained in lofty places with money to burn could have bought buildings like Del Monico Mansions many times over. They had eventually ostracised her socially and left her struggling, as did my father's siblings. My fragile mother was eventually totally alone with her perfect table manners, designer clothing, diamonds, jewels, furs and elegant social skills, but little else.

Dealing with cancer (which eventually reached her brain) over a period of years, unsupported with no comfort or care, was surely unbearable. Yet, she never mentioned the 'C' word, nor did she complain. Her pride stopped her from making any attempt at dialogue with my father, which created difficulties beyond her wildest imaginings. Communication between them would have changed everything! Filled with false pride, swollen with humiliation and heartache, they both allowed time to slip away. During those years they faced insurmountable obstacles and challenges on their own, both of them lonely and alone.

My mother was a gentle soul, a fragile creature, who never voiced an opinion on anything and never spoke a bad word about anyone. She was unable to live life alone. She needed to be guided, moulded, arranged, and managed. It was the way of her generation and that class of a woman.

Little did I know or understand on the day I walked out of my mother's life that I was, perhaps, the last ray of hope for her. I had kept her holding on and reasonably stable, after which she totally let go, descending into deep darkness, along a path of misery and despair. She chose that path and walked it totally alone.

A few weeks later, much like my aunt, I made a sudden, impulsive decision that was to be life changing. Out of the blue, in the midst of all my fears and sadness, I received a letter from my brother who was enjoying life in Durban. I nervously wrote back to him explaining what had happened. He convinced me to contact my father immediately.

I wrote and told my father the bare bones of my tale of woe: how I had walked out on my mother to live with his sister who had suddenly remarried. I told him how alone I felt and that I wanted to get away from Johannesburg. My wish was to leave as soon as possible.

There was no one more surprised by my decision than my father. He replied immediately, welcoming me, even though he must have had reservations and feelings of trepidation.

I booked a train ticket and handed in a letter of resignation. With long weepy goodbyes on the station platform to precious friends: Irene, Desi, Louis, Lenis and Paddy, I left on the overnight train from Johannesburg's Park Station, destined for Durban. I was *running away* from what my heart could not endure. This modus operandi was to become a habit of mine, a safety mechanism, my very own safety net.

If I am to be truthful and honest, it took *years* to recover from the break-up with Ronald and my aunt's sudden marriage before I was able to put my life back together. Unconsciously, I blocked all memory of my life in Johannesburg, and disconnected from people I loved. I know now that I did so in order to cope mentally and emotionally.

Once in Durban, I took daily walks on long sandy stretches of beach, lazed in the sunshine and explored Durban's beachfront. For six months I slept early and rose late and spoke rarely. My father and brother left me to settle, in my own way. My father asked no questions. I don't think he could face hearing about my mother's decline or what I may have endured. He carried massive guilt.

The accommodation my father and brother shared was too cramped for three of us. At times it was awkward, but within a month my father had found a spacious flat. We moved to a large, airy flat a few minutes' walk from the beachfront. My father provided me with my own bright sunny room with large windows and plenty of storage space. It offered me privacy, sunlight and peace. His calm presence, with a no-fuss attitude, helped us all settle in together with ease. Each day we went about our lives, ending with a family dinner that my father prepared for us. Once my brother and I had made new friends, the table became more crowded. Everyone was welcome, in true Greek style.

It was an amazing feeling to experience stability and security for the first time in so many years. The normality of everyday life was refreshing. It was also a huge adjustment after living my own life with no guidance from my mother since my father's departure, doing as I pleased. My father had several ground-rules for me. After all, I was his young daughter.

Initially it felt quite bizarre; at times it amused me. Yet I felt far more stable than I *ever had*. He was also learning how to cope with the return of his abandoned teenage children, and how to live with them. We made daily compromises and adjustments. Although he was firm, the general vibe at home was amicable and relaxed.

Naturally, I blocked the feelings of rejection that I had carried for all those years that my father had been gone. He had left us 'high and dry' for seven years, and casually began another life. Would he have invited me back into his life of his own volition? *I did not want to think about it.*

My father showed himself to be a kind man with a huge heart, but he was slightly formal, private about his life and, at times, detached.

He was very definite when making decisions, slightly dogmatic in his opinions and rather strict with me. I would eventually come to know that he had an 'out-of-sight, out-of-mind' mentality. A secure home life was not mine for long. Father had other plans...

Slowly I placed the Johannesburg years in the dark recesses of my mind and sealed the door tightly.
I picked up all the pieces of my terrible life and placed them in boxes, to be discovered further along my path of life...

12th June 1964: ANC leader, Nelson Mandela, is sentenced to life in prison.

EPILOGUE

To live this life with every day as consecrated.
I will honour all of its processes as if I were viewing the present,
and therefore my future, with new eyes, ears and an open heart...

I step forward one foot in front of the other,
becoming distinctly aware that I am leaving another life behind,
along with as many or as much of what I remember as the past...
because it is the end.

Years after I left home, my mother suddenly reappeared. She had been invited to holiday in Durban by my brother and his new bride. It was at the insistence of Ester that the arrangement was made. Without knowing anything of our past, or having the real facts, she incorrectly thought it the right time for my brother to forgive and forget and for her to meet her mother-in-law. It was not a wise plan.

I saw little of my brother once he moved in with Ester; she made sure of that, and I had not forgiven him for leaving me living in the beachfront flat, alone and without any support. My father and brother had left me high and dry.

I found my mother's presence in Durban unsettling. It was a huge challenge! Initially, it changed everything for me. I was not happy! I felt the anger that I had buried rising in my belly. It bubbled and raged.

As the years went on, I felt a moral duty to care for my mother until her death; I made sure that she was provided for and comfortable. Neither my brother nor father supported her or contributed to the costs of her care. It was left to me. My mother was in her early sixties when she passed. Three people attended her funeral.

Today I feel only a remote relationship to Delyse, the girl who lived in Johannesburg for fifteen years of her life. Since those far away days, I spent many years running away from myself, or looking for myself, never finding a place where I belonged. I am still searching. I often wonder, *Is there such a thing as a 'deep sense of belonging'—to a place, a home, a community, to any person, or way of life? Or is 'belonging' something deeper, something hidden in each of us?*

For most of my adult life I have searched for answers to questions relating to the past. I have looked deep inside of myself, searching through all my memories. I have pursued insights, information, and clues, often with the help of family, friends, and contacts in other countries, as well as through study, reading, and online research. I have many unanswered questions, but I have a deeper awareness of where I come from and understand that I am still 'becoming'. I will continue to search for my place in this world and, as I do, I am developing a deeper ever-expanding faith in God/Goddess/All That Is. I understand that I have a way to go yet, with a much bigger picture to consider.

The beginning of that deep feeling of 'not belonging' cemented itself into my heart one warm Sunday morning.

I was seven years old. We were visiting Aunt Helen and Uncle Mac in Roosevelt Park where we often had Sunday lunch with my father's family. I came skipping into the kitchen from the garden to find my father sitting at the head of the long well-used wooden table, with his mother and sisters. Everyone was talking at once in their mother tongue. They were leaning over a large bowl of hot *Skordalia*[73]. There were freshly baked loaves of soft white bread and farm butter on the table beside the steaming aromatic bowl. They took turns spooning portions of hot soft potato and garlic dip onto warm bread, then wolfing it down, only to reach for another spoonful. Again, and again, dipping and eating with relish, savouring every mouthful, adding a squeeze of lemon or a sprinkle of salt as they ate. Talking in happy, lively voices, with mouths full, enjoying the sharing of food together.

More *Skordalia* was eaten, peals of laughter, mouths constantly refilling, their chatter animated, hands and arms waving in the air… and so it went on. I stopped, stood close to the table for several moments, but no one looked up or glanced my way. They were totally absorbed and connected while sharing the food of their childhood. The aroma coming from the table was mouthwatering.

I stood there staring longingly at the warm buttered bread, feeling invisible, unseen. Something within me froze. I shuddered, my little body ice cold. Before me sat a closed circle of people, known to me as 'family', but I felt excluded. I had been placed outside of that circle. They were tight, close-knit, linked together by an unshakeable bond. I looked on innocently and sensed that, on that particular day, I was being *squeezed further out*. My heart ached. I experienced a deep feeling of isolation, knowing that I was an outsider looking in. That feeling has never left me.

I was deeply affected by the instability and aloneness of my childhood. It has taken decades to acknowledge how much it affected my whole life, including relationships with anyone I allowed close to me. In my twenties and thirties, I began to have a compelling need to be on the move. I found myself continually moving from house to house, from one area or town to another, exactly as we had done when I was a child. I was unable to give life a chance, oblivious of what was right in front of me. I found it impossible to settle, constantly dissatisfied, looking ahead, planning something new before settling down into what I had just begun. I was forever restless, moving, searching, longing.

The idyllic life lived in South Africa, before and during those apartheid years, was certainly a life of 'white privilege', created and held in position by ruthless men, governments, mining magnates, international companies, politics, radical government policies, and a police force we *all* feared. Looking back, I wonder how my grandparents and parents expected it to remain a 'privilege for whites only' country. After all, *it was Africa* we were all living in.

As for finding my place in the world, a place of my heart's belonging, each day I continue to discover more about myself. Frequently old memories will flood my mind, and I stop a while to reminisce, to remember those times long gone. Occasionally, feelings of melancholy flood in; and, constantly, I grasp for a deeper meaning to life, as my self-acceptance continues to grow.

With the arrival of maturity comes wisdom that allows deeper levels of understanding. I pray for forgiveness and rest in the knowingness that all is well, and *I am finally safe*. There are multiple facets to my persona based on an extraordinary life lived, in spite of early immutable chapters.

I am grateful to the many wonderful women who stepped into my life to guide me, nurture me, teach me, and who often kept me safe, and to the many nannies who took care of me and became, for a time, a surrogate mother. Each one of those warm, earthy, African women *was* my mother for a time, grounding me into the rhythm of Africa. I still miss their songs, their dance and their ability to anchor us dreamy white folk here on earth. The many precious souls who have walked this path with me thus far, I have loved more deeply than I was ever able to express.

I often wonder if I am simply 'a question' wrapped in my own history, never certain of who I truly am: a dreamer or the dream? a pacifist, visionary or idealist? often acting as a 'change-maker' and motivator to others. Traditionalist or rebel? Christian or modern-day mystic? Straight or gay? City girl or recluse? What *I am* sure of is that I am definitely a non-conformist. I have allowed myself to step away from the crowd and *be that outsider* looking in. Some have used the word eccentric. I leave that for others to decide.

I know for certain that Africa is in my blood, Greece in my heart, England in my genes, and for now England is home, although I am constantly reminded by the English that I am from 'elsewhere'. I survived the past, followed by a few ghosts of that time, when I faced dark nights and long challenging days. Life continues to reveal old memories, but nowadays they are but fleeting moments.

I have come to believe that life is a miracle, and I have always been protected from harm. I am blessed to share this life with many remarkable people as I continue my search for the lost pieces of myself. There is so much more that I understand now and *that understanding* reaches back, deep into my past. I relived that past as I wrote this book, finally letting go, with frequent offers of forgiveness and love. I have expanded in too many ways to mention—maturing, healing and finally *growing up*.

Living in England has allowed me to finally live my life in quiet seclusion, which has given me the opportunity to deal with the many layers of inner work required to truly heal. Writing it all down has been a cathartic chapter in my life, and I feel deep gratitude and reverence for the path I have walked. My ability to be alone has helped me. *What a journey it has been!* What an honour to experience a life of such intense learning in every possible moment. I finally accept that I belong to myself and to God, and I *will* continue this journey of self-discovery until my final days. There is more to experience in this life of mine! There is a new tomorrow awaiting me.

Is the Johannesburg I once knew to become known as the city of squalor and squander? I wonder what will become of that once fine city; and what of that magnificent country? Surely those who longed for the right to sing songs of freedom and who *live now* should have developed a sense of pride to be living in a 'new South Africa' with respect, care and kindness to the history and their present surroundings. Instead, I hear frequent talk of violence, separation, destruction, neglect, greed and confusion.

There are small areas of Johannesburg where exaggerated elegance and nonchalance prevail in stark contrast to other aspects of life, which are that of serious crime, poverty and political uncertainty. Yet, I carry a burning ache to be there, to live out my final years in the country where I feel most 'at home'. But, alas, to do that is a risky business for an elderly white woman who is also in need of comfort, peace, and safety. Yet, my heart's desire is constant: to pack up and go back 'home'.

I am not a politician, an intellectual, writer, academic or scholar. I have written this book based purely on the vivid memories I carry of my childhood. Most of the content is through the eyes of a child and from a young person's perspective and how I remember living it.

As that period of my life's history comes to a close on these pages, I feel a deep sadness at what may become of a once well-manicured, booming city. That land is truly beautiful; and, for many white South Africans just like me who were born and raised there, South Africa will forever beat a drum in our hearts because it is our home too.

There are no more words to be shared, no argument, no proof of what I have been through. There is but a pristinely clear vision of a field of Divine Love where all words come to pass into nothingness.

I continue to watch South Africa's history unfold. I don't wish to predict its future… not today.

The past is a foreign country to me and I don't live there anymore.[74]

NOTES
About These Notes

Researching for this book took me back (often via Google Maps) to many of the places where I once lived, went to school, or frequented—those that are still standing, that is. I felt shock, dismay and disappointment doing the research, finding the suburbs, streets and buildings either surrounded by piles of litter, dilapidated, derelict, or torn down, with no interest in past history or of replacement.

I am told that many buildings in Hillbrow have been taken over by gangs of thugs, with most of Hillbrow, Yeoville and the Berea on the way to becoming slums, unless the residents and communities wise up and take better care of their neighbourhoods. Too many courageous, dedicated people died for that land!

Research required me to search for people and places from a very long time ago. Sadly, many of those people have since passed away, or I was unable to find them. The book content also required discovering the perfect epigraphs to set the tone for each chapter of my life. These often helped me gain a depth of feeling and understanding of my early life and how to approach the writing. I highly recommend these sources and am including citations to them.

Prologue

[1] **Jan** wrote this to me from Australia where she now lives. We both often long to be back in South Africa. We feel Africa in our bones, our hearts, our souls, calling to us. This quote has been attributed to others.

[2] **Jan Smuts** attended Cambridge University and was instrumental in forming the League of Nations in 1920, now known as the United Nations. He served as Prime Minster and served the British monarchy in the Union of South Africa from 1919–24 and 1939–48. He died in 1950.

[3] **Alan Paton's** famous book, *Cry, the Beloved Country*, was based on my grandmother's murder case. In *White Mercy* Robert Turrell writes:

"Paton was impressed by a murder that took place just before he began writing *Cry, The Beloved Country*. The racial murder in the novel is a lightly fictionalised account of real events. On November 29, 1945, Dorothy Campbell-Gilchrist was murdered in her home in Forest Town, Johannesburg."

On June 8, 1946, two days before the trial began. Paton left for an extended trip abroad and wrote his novel between September and December of that year. He read about the murder and the sensational preparatory examination in the *Rand Daily Mail* of Johannesburg. He even used newspaper reports almost verbatim in his text: "These were the headlines that men feared in these days. Householders feared them, and their wives feared them. All law-abiding black men feared them..."

From Robert Turrell, *White Mercy. A Study of the Death Penalty in South Africa*, Westport: Praeger: 2004, pp. 202–208.

[4] "Two of the nine jurors had not been persuaded by the evidence against Ndwakulu [one of the accused] and had recommended acquittal."

From Ivan Thomas Evans, *Cultures of Violence: Lynching and Racial Killing in South Africa and the American South*, Manchester: Manchester University Press, 2009, p. 227.

[5] **Apartheid**, Afrikaans for 'apartness', was a political and social system in South Africa during the era of white minority rule. Made possible through the Population Registration Act of 1950, the apartheid system in South Africa was abolished in 1994.

PART I:

[6] **Quoted with permission** from Alison Nappi, Author. She is a talented and creative writer.

[7] **Lord Byron** (1788–1824), *Don Juan* in Sixteen Cantos, Halifax: Milner and Sowerby, 1837. Canto the Fourteenth. Gutenberg Project [website] <https://www.gutenberg.org/files/21700/21700-h/21700-h.htm#2H_4_0015> accessed 11.27.2020.

[8] **Quoted with permission.** E. A. Bucchianeri, *Brushstrokes of a Gadfly* (Gadfly Series, Book 1. Batalha Publishers, 2011).

[9] **Corfu** was ruled by Venice for four centuries, until 1797. Furthermore, continuously increasing commerce in the Ionian Sea made Corfu a very important Venetian trading station. In consequence, an urban class (bourgeoisie) was created early on, which was occupied in various commercial activities and acquired both wealth and education. In particular, a great many bourgeois youth studied regularly at the University of Padova. Then the French came, and then the British in about 1816.

[10] In South Africa, a **potjie** (pronounced /poiki:/), directly translated "small pot" from Afrikaans, is a traditional round, cast iron, three-legged (tripod) pot. It is similar in appearance to a cauldron and is usually black. It is used to cook **potjiekos**, a meat and vegetable stew, over an open fire. Among the South African tribes these pots also became known as **phutu pots**. Phutu is explained in Note 43.

[11] **Jostein Gaarder**, *Sophie's World: A Novel about the History of Philosophy*, translated from Norwegian by Paulette Møller, New York: Farrar, Straus, Giroux, 2007.

[12] **A braaivleis**, 'roasted meat' in Afrikaans, is a social event at which food is cooked outdoors over an open fire in a braai. 'To braai' means 'to roast'. It is similar to a 'barbecue'.

[13] **A sosatie** (pl sosaties) is a traditional South African dish of cubed marinated lamb cooked on skewers. The term derives from sate ("skewered meat") and saus (spicy sauce). The traditional Cape Malay recipe is well-known.

[14] **Paraphrased by** Professor John M. Mackenzie in his review of *Into Africa: The Imperial Life of Margery Perham* by C. Brad Faught, London: I.B. Taurus, 2011, posted on <https://www.britishempire.

co.uk/library/intoafrica.htm>) courtesy of the Overseas Service Pensioners' Association (OSPA) and accessed 6 September 2020.

[15] **Anna Akhmatova** (1889–1966), Привольем пахнет дикий мед "Wild Honey Smells of Freedom." This translation is from Roberta Reader, "Anna Akhmatova: The Stalin Years", *New England Review*, vol. 18, No. 1 (Winter 1997), p. 114. The translator is unknown. Reader says this poem was written in Leningrad, 1934, but not published until much later.

[16] **A biltong**, 'buttock tongue' in Afrikaans, is another traditional South African meat snack. Commonly made with beef, but also with game and ostrich, the meat is highly spiced, cured, sliced into thick strips and then hung on hooks in the sun to air-dry.

[17] **A boerewors**, 'farmers sausage' in Afrikaans, is a traditional coarse, fatty, sausage well spiced with black pepper and coriander and cooked on a hot braai.

[18] **'Coloured'** was a term for mixed race people who lived predominantly in the Cape. They were classified 'coloured' and given few opportunities or rights. It was a negative term suggesting that a person did not belong or fit into the country.

[19] Sebastian is the main character in *The Edwardians* by Vita Sackville-West, London: Hogarth Press, 1930.

[20] **The Karoo** region is a flat, sparsely populated semi-desert. Karoo is a Khoi-khoi word meaning '*great thirstland*'. It has endless vistas of dry plains and rugged cliffs.

[21] **Malawi**: Nyasaland became independent from Britain and renamed Malawi from 1964.

[22] **Dave Lee,** "*Night People: Nothing Rhymes with Silver*" 12 Bar Blog, May 6, 2015, <12barblog.com/category/nothing-rhymes-with-silver/> accessed 9.5.2020, a review of his novel.

I have never heard of Dave Lee. His novel is a fictional account. The *Jazz Journal* reports "Dave Lee, pianist with the Johnny Dankworth Orchestra was born in London. He studied music and for some years led his own band at Ciro's Club, Johannesburg" between 1947 and 1954. <https://jazzjournal.co.uk/2019/08/28/jj-08-59-dave-lee-in-my-opinion/> accessed 5 September 2020.

[23] I heard this in passing a few years ago, and it has stayed with me.

[24] **A snug** is traditionally British. It is a small, cosy room designed to offer peace, relaxation, and privacy. Traditional pubs usually have a

snug, separated from the main section of the pub by frosted glass, where a quiet drink can be had.

[25] **The boerboel,** an Afrikaans farm dog, is a large breed from South Africa. Bred as working farm dogs and to guard the homestead, they are one of the most powerful dog breeds.

PART II

[26] **Often credited to** *The Great Gatsby*, the 1925 novel by F. Scott Fitzgerald, this line actually occurs only in the 2013 film co-written by Baz Luhrmann and Craig Pearce. YouTube [website] <https://www.youtube.com/watch?v=2fYsc_DPMCY> accessed 5 September.2020.

[27] **Mary W. Shelley,** *Frankenstein or The Modern Prometheus*, London: Henry Colburn and Richard Bentley, 1831, Chapter 23. Gutenberg Project [webstie] <www.gutenberg.org/ebooks/42324> accessed on 5 September 2020.

[28] **Clare Leighton,** quoted in the Preface to Vera Brittain's *Chronicle of Youth: Great War Diary 1913–1917*, Glasgow: Fontana, 1982.

[29] Quoted with permission from **Jeanette LeBlanc,** *You Are Not Too Much: Love Notes on Heartache, Redemption, Reclamation*, Jeanette LeBlanc, 2018.

[30] **Attributed to Frances Hodgson Burnett,** *A Little Princess*, however, it is probably from a film version. This quotation does not appear in the first edition (New York, 1917) available on <https://en.wikisource.org/wiki/A_Little_Princess> accessed on 5 September 2020.

[31] **Attributed to Oscar Wilde** and believed to be adapted from his popular play, "Lady Windemere's Fan", a comedy of manners satirising the manners and affectations of contemporary society, in which a character, Duchess of Berwick, says, "Crying is the refuge of plain women but the ruin of pretty ones." This play was first performed in 1892 and published the following year as *Lady Windemere's Fan: A Play about a Good Woman*, London: Methuen & Co., 1893, Act One.

PART III

[32] **Mary Oliver**, "The Summer Day", *House of Light*, Boston: Beacon Press, 1990.

[33] **Sir Ernest Oppenheimer** (1880–1957) was one of the richest and most successful businessmen in South Africa, who had control over the diamond and gold deposits. His son, Harry Oppenheimer (1908–2000) followed in his father's footsteps, often ranked as the wealthiest man in the world.

[34] **Boerekos**, 'farmers' food', is typical Afrikaans home cooking.

[35] **Boereboontjies**, 'farmers' beans', Afrikaans vegetable dish of crushed green beans and boiled potatoes.

[36] **Melktert**, 'milk tart' is sweet pastry filled with a creamy custard.

[37] **Keoksister**, a 'sugared doughnut', is fried plaited dough infused with syrup.

[38] **Baragwanath Hospital**: In 1948 the South African government purchased the hospital from the British Government and, in line with the segregation policies of the day, transferred the 'native section' of the Johannesburg General Hospital to Baragwanath. The hospital was entered into the *Guinness Book of Records* in 1997 as the largest hospital in the world and has become one of the country's most-prized national monuments and historical landmarks.

[39] **Pass laws**, a dominant feature of apartheid. No black person/African over age 16 could be on the streets without an identity document, called a Pass Book or '*Dompas*'. A 'Stop and Search' policy, described in Chapter 23, caused great unrest.

[40] Although many attribute this quote to **F. Scott Fitzgerald**, it may be anonymous. See <ask.metafilter.com/330717/Who-really-said-it> accessed on 5 September 2020

[41] **Listen to Spokes Mashiyane** playing the penny whistle on his album "*King Kwela*" posted on <youtu.be/adyM1Gx1lHU> accessed 5 August 2020.

[42] **Di Brown**, "Randlords and Brickfields: Discovering Historical Johannesburg", *The Roaming Giraffe* [website] <https://theroaminggiraffe.co.za/randlords-and-brickfields-discovering-historical-johannesburg/> accessed on 5 September 2020.

[43] **Pap**, Afrikaans for 'porridge', is made from maize meal; it is very similar to polenta but white in colour. Cooked for a long time, it becomes 'stiff' **stywe pap**, perfect for dipping into spicy tomato and onion gravy. There is also **phutu pap** [*phutu* or *putu* in Zulu means 'thick'.] Pap was commonly eaten on a daily basis by black staff and enjoyed at a braai by Afrikaans-speaking South Africans. In present day South Africa, 'Pap and Gravy' can be found on the menu as a side order at steak houses. It can be eaten at breakfast, watered down to create a thin porridge and served with sugar, milk and butter.

[44] **Rumi**, *The Spiritual Poems of Rumi*, translated by Nader Khalili, New York: Wellfleet Press, 2018, p.107.

[45] **Pastitsio** – A baked pasta and minced beef dish with béchamel sauce and a thick cheese topping.

[46] **Pastitsatha** – A Corfu dish of braised beef in a spiced, fragrant, tomato sauce, cooked slowly for several hours and served over thick tubular pasta from Corfu called 'Perciatellli' or spaghetti.

[47] **Baklava** – A rich, sweet dessert pastry made with layers of filo, filled with chopped nuts and sweetened with honey.

[48] **Rizogalo** – [ree-zoh-gah-loh] – A dense rice pudding flavoured with cinnamon and vanilla.

[49] **Galataboureka** – [ga-lah-tah-boo-reh-kah] – a deep crisp filo tart, with custard, semolina and honey.

[50] **Winifred Holtby** in a letter to Vera Brittain included in *The Clear Stream: A Life of Winifred Holtby* by Marion Shaw, Virago, 1999.

[51] **Quoted with permission** from Oriah Mountain Dreamer, excerpt from "Life Changes Us", a poem posted on her blog, *The Green Bough*, October 21, 2016, <https://oriahsinvitation.blogspot.com/> accessed on 5 September 2020.

[52] **Quoted with permission** from Deena Metzger, excerpt from "Leavings", *Sacred Fire*, Summer 1990, and <https://chrisurquhart.wordpress.com/tag/leavings/> accessed on 6 September 2020.

[53] The old **Blue Room** at Park Station was once a grand place, part of the 'whites-only' main train station which is now buried four metres underground.

The once dramatic station concourse was restricted to 'Whites Only' for six decades, whereafter the racial signs were removed.

[54] **Alan Paton**, *Cry, The Beloved Country*, Scribners, 1948.

PART IV

[55] **From a popular t-shirt** with a sketch of Edie Sedgwick on it. No source given.

[56] **Quoted with permission** from Jeanette LeBlanc, "The Groundlessness of New Beginnings," 18 May 2017, *Jeanette LeBlanc* [website] <https://medium.com/@jeanetteleblanc/the-groundlessness-of-new-beginnings-f63d8938a2d3> accessed on 6 September 2020.

[57] **Posted on Twitter** by Tina Baines. "Who am I?" she asks, then responds with Brooke Hampton's popular response in *The Minds Journal* <https://themindsjournal.com/i-am-pieces-of-all-the-places-i-have-been/> accessed on 6 September 2020.

[58] School song of Johannesburg High School for Girls, 'Barnato Park'.

[59] **Quoted in** "Appetites" by Kate Christensen's review of Ruth Reichl's novel, *Delicious!* In *New York Times* (1 June 2014). Christensen writes, "Its title strikes me as perfectly apt, coming as it does from the woman who wrote: "Pull up a chair. Take a taste. Come join us. Life is so endlessly delicious!"

[60] **Quoted with permission** from Jaeda DeWalt, Shades of the Soul, Jaede Publications, 2009.

[61] **John Hobbes**, a character played by Denzel Washington in the 1998 movie, *Fallen*, and posted on Twitter by Toni DeWet.

[62] **Tara Psychiatric Hospital** is a provincial specialist hospital in Johannesburg, Gauteng. The hospital provides inpatient and outpatient psychiatric services. Tara Psychiatric Hospital serves as a tertiary training facility of the Wits Medical School.

[63] **Quoted with permission** from Alison Nappi's Blog posts.

[64] **Quoted with permission** from Alison Nappi's Blog posts.

[65] **Captain Jon-Luc Picard**, "When the Bough Breaks", *Star Trek: The Next Generation* (TV Series, Season 1, Episode 16, 1988). Created by Gene Roddenberry, written by Hannah Louise Shearer.

[66] In South Africa, **matriculation** (or matric) is a term commonly used to refer to the final year of high school and the qualification received on graduating from high school. The first formal examination was conducted in South Africa under the University of the Cape of Good Hope in 1858.

[67] **Danny Dummitt** – Facebook blog, ca. 2015.

[68] **Alysha Gwen Speer**, *Sharden*, Lulu, 2009.

PART V

[69] **Quoted with permission** from Jeanette LeBlanc, *You Are Not Too Much: Love Notes on Heartache, Redemption*, Reclamation, Jeanette LeBlanc, 2018.

[70] **Excerpt** from F. Scott Fitzgerald, The Beautiful and the Damned, Scribner, 1922, p. 6.

[71] I was told that my grandfather owned and operated Lucculus Restaurant, a 400-seater, which seems an unusually high number of covers. I have written what I was told.

[72] **Quoted with permission** from Jeanette LeBlanc.

[73] Skordalia, or skordhalia/skorthalia (σκορδαλιά [skorðaˈʎa]. Is a thick puree (or sauce, dip, spread, etc.) in Greek cuisine made by combining a huge amount of crushed garlic with a bulky base—which may be a purée of potatoes, walnuts, almonds, or liquid-soaked stale bread—then beating in olive oil to make a smooth paste. Plenty of lemon juice is added.

[74] **Jonas Hellberg**, "The Past Is a Different Country, I Don't Live There Anymore," *Octave of The Holy Innocents*, a collaboration between Buckethead, Jonas Hellborg, and Michael Shrieve [studio album, released in 1992]. YouTube [website] 8 November 2014 <https://www.youtube.com/watch?v=4QlZOg2sDUE> accessed 11.29.20.

ACKNOWLEDGEMENTS

First and foremost, my grateful thanks go to my dear friend Michael Avery who encouraged and convinced me that I could write. His persistent reminders eventually got me thinking more seriously about writing my story. Without his unfailing support this book would never have been written.

Bearnairdine Beaumont was there from my first writing day, offering suggestions, advise as well as constructive criticism. 'Irene' and 'Desiree' my precious childhood friends, have with trepidation, allowed me to write about our teenage years.

A special thank you to Anne Lehmkuhl, my Researcher, for her amazing job in discovering many newspaper articles, plus the murder trial case notes.

Thanks to the many friends (you know who you are) who have advised me, encouraged me and kept me inspired to complete this project.

There are a few remarkable souls, who have since passed, that influenced me. I have never forgotten you. You shaped my life.

There are dear friends and family that I have mentioned in this book, who I have not been able to contact or trace before publishing. I have done my best to honour the truth as I remember it.

ABOUT THE AUTHOR

The author was born and raised in South Africa. For many years she lived between Johannesburg, Corfu, Dublin and Durban. She lives quietly in the South West of England.

COMING SOON

BOOK 2
FIRE IN MY HEART

Fire In My Heart

*deep down, under
the layers of
the world
I stand
and watch!*

Metha

On a chilly winter afternoon, Christine and Michele came to visit. I had not seen them since my return from Cape Town. When I left I had been on a high; vibrant, full of vitality, with decor and menu ideas, ready for my new challenge. Since my return to the Transvaal, depleted, sad, penniless and worn down by life. I was far more ill than I realised.

The instant Chris stepped into the room, tears began to roll down her soft, pink cheeks. I looked up at her from where I sat in the afternoon sun, streaming through the large front window, puzzled by her reaction. I had been ill for almost a year.

"You are going to die! I know you are! Look at you!"

She wept openly as she sat on the floor next to me and held my hand.

"I have to fix you, I have to fix you! Look at yourself...." she said sadly between sobs.

My limp body was sprawled on the carpet in the sun, my hair lank and unwashed, my pallor deathly white. The picture convinced Chris of my state of mind.

"I don't care anymore..." I replied wistfully.

We sat in complete silence for what seemed like hours. The sun went in and the clouds darkened, but still we sat holding hands like two small children.

Printed in Great Britain
by Amazon